Building Hegemonic
Order Russia's Way

Building Hegemonic Order Russia's Way

Order, Stability, and Predictability in the Post-Soviet Space

Michael O. Slobodchikoff

LEXINGTON BOOKS
Lanham • Boulder • New York • London

Published by Lexington Books
An imprint of The Rowman & Littlefield Publishing Group, Inc.
4501 Forbes Boulevard, Suite 200, Lanham, Maryland 20706
www.rowman.com

16 Carlisle Street, London W1D 3BT, United Kingdom

British Library Cataloguing in Publication Information Available

Library of Congress Cataloging-in-Publication Data Available

ISBN 978-0-7391-8576-6 (cloth : alk.paper)
ISBN 978-1-4985-0525-3 (pbk. : alk. paper)
ISBN 978-0-7391-8577-3 (electronic)

♾™ The paper used in this publication meets the minimum requirements of American National Standard for Information Sciences—Permanence of Paper for Printed Library Materials, ANSI/NISO Z39.48-1992.

Printed in the United States of America

DEDICATION

To the love of my life and my muse, who inspires me to work hard to earn the trust and faith that she has gifted me.

Contents

Acknowledgments

Writing any book is a vast undertaking, and is only possible with help from many different people. One of those people is the Editor of Politics, International Relations, and Legal Studies at Lexington Books, Justin Race. He and his team at Lexington Books have been very supportive, and have provided everything that I have needed to finish this project. I last met with Justin at the International Studies Association Annual Meeting in San Francisco, California. He and I met and discussed my ideas, and after several minutes, he helped me solidify the topic of this book.

The return of a geopolitical struggle between Russia and the West over Ukraine has kept me extremely busy. I would like to thank the British Broadcasting Corporation (especially Ciara Riordan). I was always treated very professionally, and they always took the time to understand the nuance of what was occurring between Russia, the EU, and the United States. While many other news services were after the sound bite and presenting very shallow news, the BBC was much more balanced in its approach to the crisis in Ukraine as it unfolded. Further, the questions that the BBC asked challenged me to better understand the power dynamics in the post-Soviet space, which in turn helped to improve the arguments in this book.

I am also very thankful to Russia Direct and its many editors (especially Ekaterina Zabrovskaya and Pavel Koshkin). Their interviews were always thought provoking, and Russia Direct provided a very important service of providing analysis of Russian-American relations during the ongoing crisis without any bias. My first exposure to Russia Direct was when I wrote an analytical article about Russia's Monroe Doctrine and Ukraine. From that time forward, we developed a very good working relationship. I hope that when I next travel to Moscow to research my next book, that we'll be able to collaborate even more closely.

Several colleagues have been very supportive in this endeavor. Dr. Aakriti Tandon was instrumental in discussing many of my ideas. She always urged me to examine new information, and was tremendously helpful with the network analysis used in this book.

My family has been vital to this project. They have always been very supportive. My wife, Tanya, suffered through many late nights as I was working, first analyzing the information and then through the writing process. As summer approached, she measured the progress of the book by missed beach days, and urged me to complete the project as soon as possible so that we could all go to the beach for a nice vacation. My son, Nicholas, kept me grounded by constantly showing me that there was much more to life than this just this project. I am very thankful to my wonderful family for not only being supportive, but for putting up with me through this process.

Introduction

On December 25, 1991, the world watched with baited breath as Soviet President Mikhail Gorbachev resigned from his position. Stating that his position no longer existed, Gorbachev handed over the nuclear launch codes to his bitter rival, Boris Yeltsin. Gorbachev's reforms, which he undertook to reform the Soviet Union, ended up hastening its destruction. At 7:32 PM, the Soviet flag was lowered for the last time at the Kremlin, to be replaced by the flag of the Russian Federation.

This remarkable end to what former US President Ronald Reagan had once called the "Evil Empire," was truly astounding. Very few people predicted the demise of the Soviet Union, and the West was quick to trumpet the defeat of communism by capitalism, and the United States prepared to accept its place as the only global hegemon of a new unipolar world.

As the global hegemon, the US could ensure that it set the rules, and that the rest of the world would follow. The United States heralded its version of liberal democracy as being the rules that the other countries in the world should follow, including the Russian Federation and all of the former Soviet states. The US sent advisors to many Eastern European countries as well as to Russia and the former Soviet Union urging shock therapy and an immediate conversion from the planned economies under communism to market economies.

There was not only euphoria in the United States and its allies that the Cold War was over and that there was only one global hegemon who's rules would dictate the interactions among all of the states in the world, but there was also willingness on the part of Russia and the former Soviet states to adapt to the new world order and to become allies with the United States. Eastern European states began quickly to clamor to become allied to the West through EU and NATO membership. Russia also was happy to join with the United

States and attempt to embrace the values of liberal democracy by converting its economy to a market economy and privatizing enterprise.

Remarkably, there seemed to be little overarching plan on how to bring Russia and the former Soviet states to become allies. While the United States tried to cooperate with Russia in certain ventures such as the International Space Station and nuclear weapons security, there was no grand plan to rebuild Russia's economy the way the Marshall Plan had rebuilt the German economy following World War II.

The United States and Western Europe focused on incorporating the countries of Eastern Europe into their sphere of influence. Meanwhile, they left Russia to fend for itself and create a new regional order in the post-Soviet space. Russia understood that as the successor state to the Soviet Union, it would be the most powerful country in the former Soviet space, and that as long as it was willing to accept the broad rules of global interaction imposed by the United States as the global hegemon, that it would be able to create its own regional order.

The collapse of the Cold War led to a crisis of identity for the North Atlantic Treaty Organization (NATO). What had been an organization that was formed to prevent an attack by the Soviet Union upon Europe all of a sudden found itself without a purpose. NATO needed a new identity and mission.

While both former US Presidents George H. W. Bush and Clinton promised Russian President Boris Yeltsin that NATO would not expand, the United States nevertheless decided to expand NATO, offering membership to most of the Eastern European states that had at one time been satellites to the Soviet Union. While the Russians vociferously opposed NATO expansion, NATO nevertheless completed the expansion, promising that it would not expand to the former Soviet Union. Russia insisted that there would be repercussions if NATO accepted any new member states that were former Soviet republics.[1]

Between 1991 and 2001, the United States considered Russia to be a vanquished power that had the status of a regional power but nothing more. Government assets were shifted to other priorities, and the United States paid little attention to Russia and its relations with the former Soviet states. By 2001, with the attack on the World Trade Center, what few assets that paid attention to Russia and the post-Soviet space were now converted to face the new terrorist threat. They weren't considered a threat to US interests, and were really considered too weak to be a threat to any state in the region.

It wasn't until 2008 and the war between Russia and Georgia that the United States realized that it should have paid attention to Russia and the post-Soviet space. Georgia had convinced the United States that Russia was a neighborhood bully and that Georgia needed to be protected by the US. Convinced that the US would support Georgia in a conflict with Russia,

Georgia launched an invasion of South Ossetia, which was a breakaway republic of Georgia that had declared its independence from Georgia. Russian peacekeeping troops were killed in the Georgian assault, and Russia invaded Georgia, taking the US by surprise.

While Russia did not take over Georgia, the ease with which it defeated the Georgian Army proved to many observers in the United States that Russia was again a powerful state that needed to be taken seriously. Further, many Americans began to argue that Georgia and some of the other former Soviet states should be protected from Russian aggression, and that NATO should expand to include those states as new member states.

NATO was not the only organization interested in expanding into Eastern Europe and the former Soviet Union. The European Union (EU) was also looking to expand into Eastern Europe over the same time frame, and began by first expanding into Eastern Europe and then discussing expanding further by furthering cooperation with former Soviet states such as Ukraine, Georgia and Moldova. Eventually, the EU promised that those states might be able to join the EU.

Russia saw the expansion of the EU and NATO as threats to its regional order. It had argued against the expansion of both of these organizations into its traditional sphere of influence, and drew a line in the sand at the expansion of these organizations into the post-Soviet space. It declared a Russian version of the Monroe Doctrine, and tried to prevent the expansion of both the EU and NATO into the post-Soviet space.

By 2014, the EU was actively trying to spread its influence into the post-Soviet space, most notably in Ukraine. Heralded as the return of geopolitics, tensions between the EU, the United States, and Russia heightened to levels that had not been seen since the end of the Cold War. The great power rivalry led to a civil war in Ukraine, with separatist groups fighting against the Ukrainian government in Kiev, and Russia taking control of Crimea.

Both the United States and the EU were surprised by Russia's reaction to their expansion of influence. First of all, they did not think that Russia had the power and the influence to challenge their intent to expand their influence into the post-Soviet space. Second, they thought that Russia would be angry about their plans for expansion, but expected Russia to merely complain instead of taking direct action to counter the perceived threat from the West. In short, the West severely underestimated Russian capabilities and intent, and did not understand the security architecture that Russia had built in the post-Soviet space following the collapse of the Soviet Union.

Scholars of international relations have long noted structural hierarchies of power dynamics in the relations between states. They argue that in a unipolar system, there is one global hegemon that determines the rules of interaction between all of the rest of the states in the global system. Further, scholars have noted that regional hegemons are responsible for creating regional orders, where they develop the rules for interaction among the states within their regions providing that they don't violate the global order established by the global hegemon.

The problem with many of these theories of global and regional orders and hierarchies is that while they know that there are rules and that there is a specific order established by the global and the regional hegemons, no study has closely examined how the order is established and how to identify and define the order. It is extremely important to examine how a regional order is established, as that can help to predict the behaviors and the interactions among states in any given region.

International relations are characterized by global anarchy, making interactions and cooperation between states very difficult to achieve. With no overarching government to resolve disputes and facilitate cooperation, states are required to provide for their own security and well-being. States must strive to achieve order, stability, and predictability to ensure their own security as well as to achieve their strategic goals. While some scholars argue that the global hegemon creates order and rules of interaction, there is little consensus among scholars as to how the security architecture establishing order and rules is established. I argue that cooperation can occur provided that states create networks of international treaties and laws. These networks of international treaties create a regional architecture that provides stability to a region, ensuring that states can pursue their own strategic interests knowing that there are predictable behaviors among states.

This book examines Russia's emergence after the collapse of the Soviet Union and its creation of a security architecture in the post-Soviet space. While many scholars argue that Russia is a coercive power in the region that forces states to act in only its own interests. I argue that although Russia is indeed a powerful actor that tries to achieve its own strategic interests, it is not able to merely force states to behave as it wants them to. Instead, Russia must use bilateral and multilateral cooperation to develop a security architecture that provides order, stability and predictable behavior for both Russia as the hegemon and the weaker powers in the region. By building this security architecture, Russia and the other states in the post-Soviet space are better able to achieve their strategic goals and provide for their own security. To achieve this, weaker states are able to press for certain concessions from Russia regarding how to structure bilateral relations as well as multilateral organizations. While Western politicians have argued that Russia has tried to reestablish the Soviet Union through coercive means, the reality is much more of a nuanced interaction among all of the states in the region, which ensures state sovereignty while allowing the weaker states to pursue their own interests. Using network analysis, I show how the regional structural architecture of cooperation was built and indicate how Russia is able to achieve order. I also show that there is a lack of order where states have refused to cooperate in building the structural architecture, which has led to conflict and territorial disputes.

The collapse of the Soviet Union and the subsequent rise of Russia as the regional hegemon provides a unique ability to identify how a regional hegemon creates a regional order and how it builds a regional security architecture. Further, by identifying this regional security architecture and regional order, it is possible to examine relations between the states in the region and to predict areas where conflict and reluctance to accept the regional security architecture can develop. Finally, by better understanding the regional security architecture, scholars can better understand the dynamics of geopolitics, and understand the regional dynamics of regional orders in the global system.

The purpose of this book is twofold. First of all, I add to the theoretical understanding of both global and regional orders and how they are created. Second, I examine how a regional architecture is created using both bilateral and multilateral treaties to create a regional security architecture which leads to order, stability, and predictability. The post-Soviet space provides the perfect case study in which to better understand these important dynamics of international relations. Russia has had to develop a very nuanced approach to relations in the post-Soviet space, combining both multilateral and bilateral approaches, which have helped to build trust and establish its regional order.

In Chapter 1, I examine the theories of global and regional order. I show that while scholars note that there are rules established, scholars have not been able to adequately identify the rules that establish the order.

In Chapter 2, I examine Russia's bilateral relations with the states in the post-Soviet space. I identify specific regions within the post-Soviet space, and examine the relationships that Russia has built with these states. I identify problematic relations as well as good relationships and examine the specifics of the bilateral relationships.

In Chapter 3, I examine the multilateral organizations in the post-Soviet space. I examine the development of multilateral organizations in the post-Soviet space, and analyze their effectiveness.

In Chapter 4, I show that traditional approaches to hegemonic relations with weaker states are inadequate. Specifically, I argue that it is inadequate to examine bilateral and multilateral treaties as separate institutional arrangements. Instead, bilateral and multilateral treaties are part of the same institution, and are used in tandem toward creating a regional order and security architecture.

In Chapter 5, I illustrate exactly how Russia combined multilateral and bilateral treaties to establish the regional order and develop its security architecture.

Finally, in Chapter 6, I bring the arguments together, showing how a regional order is created, how to identify the rules within a regional order, and offer predictions for the future of Russia's regional order and security architecture.

NOTE

1. In this case, the three Baltic states (Latvia, Lithuania, and Estonia) were allowed by Russia to join NATO. Despite the fact that they were former Soviet republics, they had always been closer in identity to Eastern European states than the other Soviet republics. Thus, Russia's objection was to any NATO expansion that would include new member states from the former Soviet Union not including the three Baltic states.

Chapter One

Establishing Regional Order

The study of order has been a central component of political science. The problem of how order is created and breaks down has long puzzled scholars of comparative politics. For example, Huntington (1968) argues that order is the most important factor for a state's survival. The type of government is not as important as internal order. He argues that institutions create order, and that rapid social change coupled with the inability for institutions to meet the new demands of society leads to a lack of order and stability. While order and stability seem to be synonymous for Huntington, it is important to note several important aspects of his understanding of the concept of order. First of all, order is not a static concept. It is rather an evolving concept that depends upon the interaction between society on the one hand and institutions and rules on the other. Order is therefore more of a concept which creates predictability for its citizens. The rules and institutions that provide order also provide predictability and the ability for citizens to effectively operate in the system to achieve their personal goals. I should be clear that not all personal goals are alike, but rather the order that the system provides shapes the goals that individuals can have within the political system. While different regimes establish different institutional arrangements within their borders, the goal of each regime is to establish and maintain order.

While there is little debate about the nature of the concept of order within states, the concept of international order is debated by international relations scholars. In fact, Ikenberry (2001, 22) argues that the problem of order is the central problem of international relations. More specifically, he states that the main questions in understanding the concept of order is how it is devised, how it breaks down, and how it is created. In this book, I will examine how order is created at the regional level. I argue that regional order is more nuanced than many scholars of international relations realize. Specifically, I argue that while

1

capabilities are important in determining which regional powers are able to establish order, the establishment of order requires more of a nuanced approach to diplomacy that allows the weaker states to benefit from the regional order. In this chapter, I will define the concept of international order, discuss how international order applies to regional power structures and regional order, and then examine regional order in the post-Soviet space.

CONCEPTUALIZING INTERNATIONAL ORDER

While the Treaty of Westphalia guaranteed states the right to internal sovereignty, it also established anarchy at the global level. Realist scholars have noted the anarchy of the international system (Fearon 1995; Grieco 1988; Morgenthau 1948; Walt 2002; Waltz 1979). They argue that the international system leads to competition between states since all states must fend for themselves. States must therefore try to outcompete each other in the international system, leading to the security dilemma.[1]

This understanding of systemic anarchy leads to a predominant belief in relative gains.[2] If states are overly concerned with relative gains, then cooperation becomes more difficult to achieve (Slobodchikoff 2013). Ultimately, realists believe that systemic anarchy is a pretty static concept, which drives competition between states.

In contrast to realists, hegemonic stability theorists argue that global anarchy exists, but that it is not a static concept. Instead, a hegemonic power establishes certain rules that the rest of the states must abide by. The states understand their roles within the global system, and the hegemon provides benefits to those states provided they operate within the rules established by the hegemon. Specifically, scholars such as Gilpin (1983), the power of a hegemonic state creates both global stability and operative rules of interactions that reflect the preferences of the hegemonic state. More specifically, a hegemonic state will institutionalize a system of rules and institutions that preserve and advance its goals and values.

Both realist and hegemonic theorists understand the concept of international order in fundamentally different ways due to their assumptions of the nature of the global systems. Therefore scholars who have studied the concept of order have noted that there are basically two different ways to conceptualize global order in international relations. Specifically, Acharya (2007) argued that one way in which to conceptualize order is to examine the relative power capabilities of all of the states and assess the distribution of power. This is a descriptive and static conceptualization of order, which does not take into account the effect of order upon other states.

Realist scholars adhere to this first conceptualization of global order. For example, Waltz (1979, 89–92) states that international order is basically synonymous with the structure of the international system. Other realist scholars view international order as being synonymous with stability, which can only be achieved when there is a balance of power in the international system (Walt 1985).

Acharya (2007) states that the second conceptualization of international order is an increase in the level of stability and predictability within the international system. This conceptualization of global order is an outcome-oriented approach that is concerned with more stability and predictability than with the power distribution of states within the international system. Hegemonic stability theorists conceptualize international order in this way. They are concerned with the goal of establishing an order instead of just reflecting the international power structure.

Hegemonic stability theorists argue that a concentration of power in a specific state will inherently create order. This is due to the fact that the hegemonic power has enough power to enforce its goals and rules. More specifically, hegemonic states actively strive to establish order to ensure that their goals and rules are achieved and followed by the international system. For example, Bull (2002, 8) argues that international order will sustain the primary goals of international society. In other words, if a hegemonic state is able to establish order, then it can create and sustain the primary goals of international society. Other scholars have noted that the institutionalization of a system of order is driven by the desire to organize the system to preserve goals and values of the hegemonic state (Stewart-Ingersoll and Frazier 2012).

Ultimately, international order must be understood as a hegemonic state's rules and norms that are accepted by weaker states within the international system. Weaker states must abide by these rules and norms to receive benefits from the global hegemon. In other words, international order is a hierarchical relationship where the hegemon specifically establishes government through rules, principles, and institutions which govern the interactions between states (See Figure 1.1). More specifically, Stewart-Ingersoll and Frazier (2012, 18) argue that international order is made up of the "governing arrangements among the units of a system, including their rules, principles and institutions, which are designed to make interactions predictable and to sustain the goals and values that are collectively salient." Thus, an international order includes both a purpose and an organized means through which it is achieved, and the salient interests will be asymmetrically representative of the most influential actors in the system. This is especially so when the hegemonic power can effectively use coercive powers to ensure compliance with the international order.

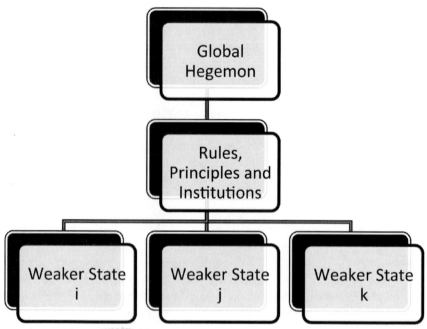

Figure 1.1.   International Order

It is important to note that according to Stewart-Ingersoll and Frazier (2012), one of the most important outcomes of international order is to make interactions predictable. While the hegemonic state is interested in sustaining its goals and values, one of the driving forces for the weaker states in accepting international order is increased predictability in their interactions with the hegemonic state. Ideally, according to Bull (2002, 16–18), international order should contribute to four main rules, specifically, maintaining the status quo of the system of states (especially in regards to internal sovereignty), protect the independence of states by recognizing territorial autonomy, try to promote the absence of war between states, and ensure that agreements between states in the global order are upheld. However, the specific rules that the hegemonic state institutes in creating international order depend on the goals and norms of the hegemonic power.

It should be noted that international order provided by a hegemon alleviates the problem of anarchy in international relations. Weaker states are not faced with the security dilemma, because as long as they play by the rules imposed by the hegemon, they can depend on predictability in interactions as well as the hegemon's protection of the independence and territorial autonomy.

INTERNATIONAL ORDER IN A BIPOLAR SYSTEM

The preceding discussion has focused on defining an international order where there is one global hegemon that is able to establish international order. For example, the United Kingdom was able to achieve global hegemonic status during the nineteenth century. Between 1815 and 1914, it established the order known as the Pax Britannica, where it set up a liberal trade empire. States had to abide by the rules set up by the British, and in return, the British helped to suppress piracy.

Pax Britannica lasted until the rapid industrialization period of the early twentieth century when Germany, Japan and the United States became able to challenge the United Kingdom's status as the global hegemon. Following World War II in 1945, two states emerged as being the most powerful in the system. The United States and the Soviet Union had differing ideological views, and quickly set up an international order in each of their spheres of influence which reflected that ideology. They established rules and institutions which created order over their respective spheres of influence, with most of Western Europe falling under the order that the United States established, while Eastern Europe fell under the order established by the Soviet Union (see Figure 1.2). Figure 1.2 shows the makeup of the international order during the Cold War period. Much of the Cold War period was both hegemons jockeying to try to expand their order over more of the system while limiting the other hegemon's ability to extend order over more of the international system. In the United States, the government developed a policy of containment to try and prevent the spread of communism around the world. Basically, the policy was established to prevent the Soviet Union from increasing the number of states that fell under its international order.

The preceding discussion has focused on the global system. Lemke (2002) argues that the global power hierarchy is often replicated at the regional level. More specifically, he states that regional hegemons create a hierarchical regional structure that falls under the global hierarchical structure. This regional hierarchical structure looks is very similar to the global hierarchical model. This is called the multiple hierarchy model. Therefore, we can adapt Lemke's (2002) model to determine how regional and international order are related (see Figure 1.3).

In the hypothetical example provided in Figure 1.3, there is one global hegemon and two regional hegemons. Each of the two regional hegemons must create its own regional order, and the weaker regional states must follow the regional order established by the regional hegemons. It should be noted that in this hypothetical example, the regional hegemons must enact

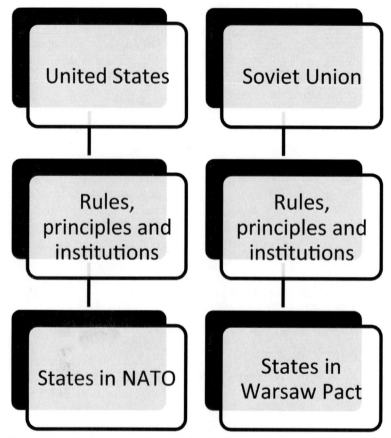

Figure 1.2.   Bipolar International Order During the Cold War

their regional orders so that it does not conflict with the global order established by the global hegemon.

During the Cold War, the bipolar global and regional hierarchies would
look similar to Figure 1.3, except there would be two global hegemons. The
regional hegemons in each sphere of influence would establish regional order
that would comply with the global order established by its global hegemon.

THE PROBLEM OF REACH

The preceding discussion is based on the assumption that the global hegemon
is able to project enough power to cover the entire system. However, some
scholars have argued that power projection can be measured geographically,

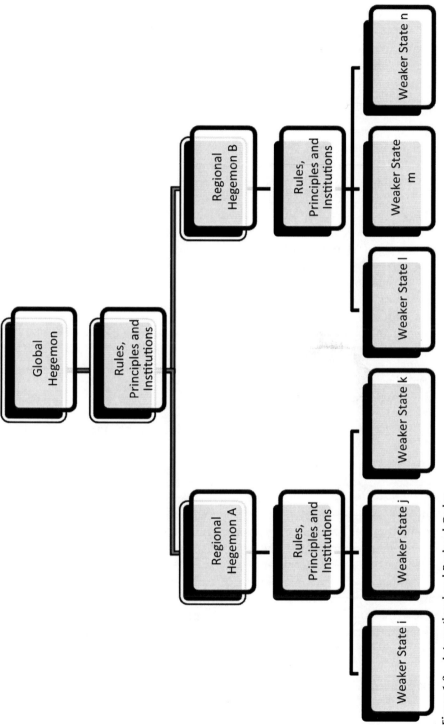

Figure 1.3. International and Regional Order

and that it is possible to determine where a hegemon is not able to project its power (Boulding 1962; Bueno de Mesquita 1981; Lemke 2002). Further, there are certain geographical zones that are referred to as power vacuums, where hierarchical relationships between states do not dominate (Rhamey Jr, Slobodchikoff, and Volgy [2014], 2013; Rhamey and Slobodchikoff 2010). In these geographical zones, there is no global order imposed by the global hegemon, but rather there is jockeying among regional powers to be able to establish a regional order.

In geographical spaces where there is a global power vacuum, regional powers will try to establish their own rules, principles, and institutions. These may or may not mirror the order established by the global hegemon, since the hegemon would not be able to enforce the global rules. Further, since the global hegemon would not have the reach to be able to establish rules and predictability, it is more likely that low-level conflict between regional states would occur. Regional powers would be more likely to enter into conflict over the right to develop the regional rules, principles and institutions and thus establish regional order.

Once regional order is established within a hierarchical global power vacuum, then the hierarchical structure of order will resemble Figure 3, minus the global order. There would just be a regional hierarchical structure of order, with weaker states within the region following the order established by the regional hegemon instead of the global order established by the global hegemon.

CREATING ORDER IN CHANGING SOCIETIES

Huntington (1968) discusses how political order changes and how stability is affected if societies go through changes that the state institutions cannot accommodate. Thus, he is concerned with the decay of state order. Scholars should not only be concerned with the decay of state order, but also the creation of order. In fact, the decay in state order can often lead to the establishment of regional order. Such is the case with the Soviet Union, its dissolution, and the creation of newly independent states.

Following the Russian Revolution in 1917, the Soviet Union began to consolidate its power. The Bolshevik party had seized power in 1917, but had to fight Poland, an Allied intervention of military forces from different countries, and a bloody civil war (Riasanovsky 2000). To consolidate power, Vladimir Lenin had signed the Brest-Litovsk treaty with Germany, which was disastrous for Russia. The treaty insisted that Ukraine, Poland, Finland, Lithuania, Estonia, and Latvia receive their independence, and that part of Transcaucasia would be ceded to Turkey. On the day that the treaty was signed, Russia lost 26 percent of its population, 27 percent of its land, 32 percent of its crops, 26 percent of its railway system, 33 percent of its manufacturing capacity, 73 percent of its iron industry, and 75 percent of its coal fields (Riasanovsky 2000). These tremendous losses of territory and economic capacity were in addition to having to pay Germany reparations. Lenin knew that he had to make enormous concessions to Germany to end Russia's participation in World War I if he had any chance of winning the Russian Civil War, consolidating his power, and creating the Soviet Union.

It was not until 1921 that the Soviet Union really began to establish its institutions. The government had to change from a revolutionary government to one that actually was responsible for building institutions and rules and creating domestic order. While the Russian Soviet Federated Socialist Republic (R.S.F.S.R.) was established in 1918 with the adoption of the first Soviet constitution, it wasn't until 1921, when the Soviets won the civil war, that true consolidation of power occurred.

In 1921, the Red Army invaded Georgia to overthrow the government and establish Bolshevik control. The invasion was largely led by Josef Stalin, who obtained Lenin's permission to supposedly support an uprising by the peasants and working class. In reality, capturing Georgia was a concerted effort on behalf of the Bolshevik government to gain back many of the territories that had been lost during the time of the Russian Revolution, and to restore the old Russian Empire under Soviet rule. The attack was successful, and Soviet troops captured Tbilisi, the capital of Georgia. However, fierce fighting ensued in Georgia, and the Soviet government was not able to consolidate its power over Georgia for a couple of years.

By December, 1922, the Union of Soviet Socialist Republics (USSR) came into being as a federation of Russia, the Ukraine, White Russia, and Transcaucasia (Riasanovsky 2000). The Soviet Union finally consolidated power in Georgia in 1924, and in the late 1920s, three Central Asian republics joined the Soviet Union and received "Union Republic" status. In contrast to the old Russian Empire, the new Soviet Union had lost Finland, Estonia, Latvia, Lithuania, and territories in Poland as well as the western Ukraine. The new Soviet Union was made up of fifteen new republics, with the Russian Soviet Federated Socialist Republic (R.S.F.S.R.) being the most important republic within the USSR.

Despite the fact that Lenin and the Bolsheviks had won the Russian Civil War, the state was in a crisis. Droughts had brought famine to the new country, and people were restless. People began to rise up against the new Communist government, and Lenin knew that he had to take drastic actions to maintain his control over the Soviet Union. He instituted a New Economic Policy, which allowed for a loosening of the socialist economic model, and allowed small businessmen to operate. The New Economic Policy was highly successful, and allowed the new Soviet government to further consolidate power during the early years following the end of the Russian Civil War.

Lenin remained in control of the Soviet Union for a short time following the creation of the New Economic Policy, as in 1922, his health began to falter. In May, 1922, he suffered a stroke which caused him to lose the ability to speak. He was able to return to his duties in August, 1922, but then suffered a debilitating stroke in December of the same year. After his second stroke, he withdrew from active politics. Finally, in March, 1923, Lenin suffered a third stroke, which left him bedridden until his death in January, 1924.

After his first stroke, Lenin dictated a testament to his wife, Nadezhda Krupskaya, which basically questioned the abilities of many of the leading Bolsheviks in power, including Josef Stalin. He worried that Stalin would not be effective enough as a leader, and did not have the necessary people skills to be an effective leader. Lenin cautioned that Stalin was too rough, and that he would cause a dangerous split in the Bolshevik party. Further, he urged that Stalin be removed from power. However, he was so weakened by his strokes, that he was not able to act on his testament, and he died before any action could be taken.

Lenin's death in 1924 did lead to a competition among the Bolsheviks to consolidate power over the country, with a great many factions developing. Stalin was able to overcome Lenin's testament, and proved to be very adept at joining factions and then turning on those factions to serve his own interests. He began to argue against the New Economic Policy, and instituted a period of rapid industrialization and collectivization. By 1930, Stalin had virtually silenced all dissenters in the Communist Party through a great purge, and had consolidated his power over the country.

Despite having consolidate his power, Stalin continued to look for enemies who opposed him, and instituted a reign of terror that would continue to consolidate his own power. He ordered the executions of many of the Communist Party leadership, and ensured that no one would be able to rival his power. Further, he centralized the power structures of the Soviet Union so that all of the republics would be reliant upon the leadership in Moscow for their own survival. Most of the agriculture and production from the republics had to first be sent to Moscow and then be redistributed to the rest of the country based upon need (Hewett 1988).

In establishing order in the USSR and creating the Soviet Empire, Stalin was often very strategic in his treatment of ethnic minorities in the Soviet republics. He would often first promise territory to one republic and then strategically change his mind and gift a territory to another republic. For example, in the early 1920s, Stalin promised the territory of Karabakh to the

Armenian republic. However, Stalin hoped to entice Turkey to turn Communist, and therefore gifted the territory of Karabakh to Azerbaijan, which was mostly Muslim. Many of these decisions by Stalin in the early formation of the USSR created severe ethnic conflict during the early years of the USSR. However, the Soviet Union was able to quell much of the ethnic resentment. This resentment never disappeared, and became an enormous problem following the collapse of the Soviet Union.

WORLD WAR II AND THE SOVIET UNION

The Soviet Union was extremely wary of the West in the years leading to World War II. This was exacerbated by the fact that Great Britain and France did not invite the Soviet Union to Munich in September 1938 where they tried to appease Germany by letting them annex the Sudetenland (Riasanovsky 2000). Although the Soviet Union had promised to protect Czechoslovakia from German aggression, it found itself in isolation from the West.

As Germany turned its sights on Poland, Great Britain and France tried to send a delegation to the Soviet Union to create an alliance against German aggression. However, they sent a weak delegation that was not able to overcome Soviet suspicion of Western intentions. Instead, on August 23, 1939, a German-Russian neutrality agreement was signed. Although the Nazis and Bolsheviks hated each other, both parties were looking for a temporary benefit. Germany was free to fight the Western powers, and the Soviet Union was looking to avoid war with Germany. Further, the agreement had a secret protocol which allowed the Soviet Union to seize territory in Eastern Europe in the hope of creating a buffer against German aggression (Riasanovsky 2000).

Taking advantage of the secret protocol, the Soviet Army occupied eastern Poland, reclaiming territory that had been ceded to end World War I. The Soviet Army signed mutual assistance pacts with Estonia, Latvia, and Lithuania, and were then incorporated into the Soviet Union. By the Summer of 1940, the Soviet Union took over the disputed region of Bessarabia. From this territory, the Soviet Union created the new Moldovan Soviet Socialist Republic. Finally, the Soviet Union signed a nonaggression treaty with Japan to ensure that Siberia would not be invaded. The nonaggression treaty was to last for a period of five years.

All of the effort to delay war was ultimately unsuccessful, and Germany invaded the Soviet Union aided by Finnish and Romanian troops on June 22, 1941. The invasion front stretched from the Baltic Sea all the way to the Black Sea. While the Soviet Union had expected war with Germany, it was unprepared for such a quick and massive invasion. The German Army was prepared to conduct a *Blitzkrieg* attack, planning on an attack that wouldn't last more than two or three months.

Initially, the Germans were able to push far into Soviet territory. While they encountered fierce resistance from the Soviets, the German troops were able to destroy entire units. The German Army quickly captured Minsk and Kiev, and pushed north toward Leningrad. They were able to lay siege to Leningrad, but could not capture the city. Leningrad blocked the Nazi troops from moving further north.

In the center of the front, the German troops tried to quickly reach and capture Moscow. However, the invasion got bogged down, and they were not able to reach Moscow by the end of the summer. Instead, the summer campaign was extended into fall, and despite the fact that the German Army got within twenty miles of Moscow and encircled it on three sides, the Germans were not able to capture Moscow (Riasanovsky 2000). Instead, the Russian winter wreaked havoc with the German Army since they were ill prepared for a long and extended campaign. The Soviet Army was able to counter attack the German Army and inflict tremendous losses.

The Soviet Army was able to open up its own offensive against German troops, and by 1943 had captured much of occupied Soviet territory. By 1944, Soviet troops were moving into Eastern Europe, and by autumn of 1944, the Soviet Union began its final assault of Germany. On May 9, 1945, fighting ceased and Germany had formally unconditionally surrendered to the Allies.

ESTABLISHMENT OF REGIONAL
ORDER FOLLOWING WORLD WAR II

Prior to the end of World War II, the Soviet Union actively engaged the Allies in determining the order of the post-World War II global structure. It participated fully in the planning and creation of the United Nations, it concluded agreements with Great Britain and France to achieve a permanent peace. As World War II was getting closer to being won by the Allies, the leaders of the United States, Great Britain and Soviet Union met to discuss the establishment of an international order once peace was achieved, specifically dividing Germany into zones of occupation and to bring top Nazi leaders to trial at Nuremburg. After that, cooperation began to break down between the Soviet Union and the Allies.

The Soviet Union had occupied much of Eastern Europe, and had installed governments that were sympathetic with their beliefs. Internally, the Soviet Union created new rules and institutions that solidified the Russian republic's dominance over the other republics. The Soviet government wanted a very centralized state with all of the decisions influencing the republics to be made in Moscow.

The economic system was developed to be integrated in such a way that the infrastructure of each republic would be tied to that of Russia (Hewett 1988). The republics developed economic specializations. For example, grapes were grown and wine was made in both Georgia and Moldova, while fruits were often grown in Kazakhstan and Kirgizia (Slobodchikoff 2013b). More fundamentally, raw materials often had to be shipped first to Moscow, and then redistributed to republics that would use them. For example, rockets were fired from Kazakhstan, but the raw materials needed to produce the rockets and the fuel and the parts were produced in other republics, sent to Moscow, and then sent on to Kazakhstan. Moscow became the center of the infrastructure, and all goods had to pass through Moscow before being sent on to their final destinations. This was necessary to ensure that all of the republics and regions of the Soviet Union would be reliant on the centralized state for their survival.

In Eastern Europe, the Soviet Union established rules that were to be followed by the Communist governments. The rules were similar to those established for the Soviet Union itself, except for the fact that not all goods had to go through Moscow. Instead, major issues and foreign policy decisions were often decided after consultations with Moscow. The Soviet Union wanted to ensure that the countries of Eastern Europe understood the rules, and were willing to use the Red Army to achieve the establishment of regional order.

One of the ways that the Soviet Union was able to establish order in the immediate post-war period was through treaties with countries in Eastern Europe. Between 1943 and 1948, Stalin initiated friendship and cooperation treaties with Eastern European satellite states that allowed the Soviet Union to help protect the satellite states from the West (specifically German aggression, while ensuring that the Soviet Union could be militarily involved in those states (Triska and Slusser 1962).

One of the most important aspects of the friendship and cooperation agreements were usually found in the first article, where the Soviet Union agreed to provide "mutual assistance to prevent Germany or any other state that joined Germany from preparing a new aggressive war" (Triska and Slusser 1962, 239). The interpretation of preparing for a new aggressive war was left open to interpretation, which allowed the Soviet Union the ability to station Soviet troops in Eastern Europe (Slobodchikoff 2013b). These treaties created military alliances with the Soviet Union, and required that the satellite states would have to mutually assist the Soviets with defending socialism and the Communist bloc (Korhonen 1973). By establishing military alliances first, the Soviet Union was able to establish regional order.

It is important to note that not all of the states in Eastern Europe equally followed the regional order established by the Soviet Union. The populace was not accepting of the new order, which was imposed in a top-down fashion. While most of the states in Eastern Europe were forced to comply with the new regional order, Yugoslavia did not like Stalin's regional order and refused to follow.

Ultimately, the rest of the states in the Soviet bloc joined the Warsaw Pact as a response to the North Atlantic Treaty Organization (NATO). By joining the Warsaw Pact, Eastern European states were signaling their intent to follow the new regional order imposed by the Soviet Union. While many of the states did not actually want to follow the regional order, the governments of these states recognized that they could not violate the regional order for fear of armed reprisal from the Soviet Union (Wolchik and Curry 2011).

Up until Stalin's death in 1953, the Soviet Union was very strict about prescribing the rules that had to be followed in the regional order. However, upon Stalin's death, the Soviet Union changed its approach to regional order from being prescriptive to proscriptive (Wolchik and Curry 2011). The Eastern European countries were allowed to accommodate their populace providing that the regional order was not directly threatened. There was much less of a guidance on how to follow the regional order, but rather any direct challenges to the regional order were met with quick military action. For example, when the populace in Hungary in 1956 and Czechoslavakia in 1968 demanded change, the Soviet Union was quick to send in Warsaw Pact troops to quell any rebellion and to install leaders that would be more amenable to following the regional order. This approach to regional order by the Soviet Union lasted until Mikhail Gorbachev came to power in 1985.

GORBACHEV AND THE DESTRUCTION OF REGIONAL ORDER

Following the stagnation in the Brezhnev era, it became clear to the Communist Party of the Soviet Union that they needed a younger leader with vision. Gorbachev seemed like he could conduct reforms without making drastic changes to the system. He had been adequately brought up through the Communist Party ranks through the system of patronage (Willerton 1992).

Gorbachev represented a hybrid of both new and old Communist ideology. He was a believer in Leninism and the rejected privatization and pluralism in Communist states. Yet he also was the only General Secretary of the Communist Party of the Soviet Union to have been born after the Russian Revolution and Civil War. This experience meant that he had a different view of the world than many of his predecessors. Chief among his different views was that he was categorically opposed to the use of nuclear weapons, and even famously offered President Ronald Reagan the option of jointly destroying all nuclear weapons instead of just reducing nuclear stockpiles.

Gorbachev recognized that the Soviet Union had fallen behind especially in the fields of science and technology. The military needed an extremely high percentage of gross domestic product to remain competitive with the West, and could not respond competitively to a new electronic age. The economic stagnation further affected morale among the general population (Riasanovsky 2000).

Early in Gorbachev's tenure, he had to be careful in his reforms, as he had to consolidate power. However, once he had consolidated his power, he launched a systematic effort to rebuild the Soviet economy, naming it *perestroika*, which literally means restructuring. The basic idea of perestroika was that the way to improve the economy was to fight corruption and try to increase productivity, and that only through improving the economy could the Communist planned economy survive.

It should be noted that Gorbachev's reforms were designed not to bring about the destruction of the Soviet planned economy, but rather to reform it. Therefore, there could be no talk of privatizing industry, or drastic reforms, but rather perestroika aimed to improve productivity by targeting workers. For example, Gorbachev instituted a war on alcohol, destroying many grapes and alcohol-producing capabilities. Further, he allowed economic enterprises to fire workers who were often absent or drunk on the job.

In addition to instituting domestic economic reforms, Gorbachev wanted more honest discussion and allow people to be able to voice their thoughts through providing more free speech. This new policy called *glasnost,* was designed to create a system of management that was more transparent and would thus limit corruption in the Communist Party and the government.[3] While glasnost had a big effect domestically, it had a profound effect internationally. Specifically, by instituting the new glasnost policy, the Soviet Union invited those states in the Soviet bloc to reevaluate the regional order and begin to challenge those rules.

By 1989, Gorbachev had repealed the Brezhnev Doctrine of allowing force to prevent Warsaw Pact member states from leaving the Communist bloc. Poland was one of the first countries to take advantage of the Soviet Union's relaxing the regional order, and massive demonstrations took place demanding change. Specifically, people called for the legalization of the Solidarity Political Party. By April of 1989, an agreement had been reached between the Communist Party of Poland and Solidarity to legalize the Solidarity party and to pave the way for free parliamentary elections. In those parliamentary elections, Solidarity defied all predictions and won in a landslide. The leader of the Communist Party resigned to allow the formation of a non-Communist coalition government, which was led by Solidarity.

Events in Poland had a tremendous effect on other states in Eastern Europe. Other Communist governments were worried that their control of government would in turn be challenged. Nikolai Ceausescu, the leader of Romania appealed to Moscow to send in troops to Poland to save Socialism. However, Gorbachev decided not to send troops and allow the events in Eastern Europe to continue to unfold without Soviet interference.

Following Poland's lead, Hungary soon followed. Hungary began dismantling the fence along the border between Hungary and Austria. This allowed many Hungarians to begin to flee Hungary. By September, 1989, an agreement was reached to change Hungary's constitution. The government would change to a parliamentary system with a weak executive. Hungary would change from a one-party state to a multiparty system.

In October, 1989, the most visible challenge to the regional order occurred when thousands of protesters took to the streets in Leipzig, East Germany. Despite orders given by the leadership of East Germany to shoot the protesters, the military refused to fire on the protesters. Buoyed by the success of the protests in Leipzig, other protests began occurring in East Germany, most notably in Berlin. On November 9, 1989, hundreds of thousands of people began to try to pass through border checkpoints between East and West Berlin. Border guards, who had not been briefed prior to these events, did not fire on the people, and just began allowing them to pass through the border. Those who passed through jubilantly began to celebrate their success as other protesters began removing sections of the Berlin Wall.

In an age of television news, protesters standing atop the Berlin Wall and dismantling it became a powerful symbol for the end of Communism in Eastern Europe. Within a few months of the events that had begun in Poland in 1989, all of Eastern Europe had revolted against their Communist governments, and had created new systems of government. For the first time since World War II, the regional order had drastically changed, and the Soviet Union no longer was able to establish regional order.

THE DESTRUCTION OF DOMESTIC ORDER

Following the collapse of regional order in Eastern Europe, many of the Soviet republics began voicing their discontent with the domestic order of the Soviet Union. Many of the republics wanted more autonomy in their own affairs. The Baltic republics (Lithuania, Latvia, and Estonia) wanted freedom from the Soviet Union, while other republics just wanted less influence from the Russian Republic. Ethnic tensions that had been dampened by Stalin again became problems. For example, Nagorno-Karabakh, which was an ethnically Armenian enclave located in the Azerbaijan Soviet Socialist Republic, passed a resolution calling for unification with the Armenian Soviet Socialist Republic.

To try to manage growing ethnic and political unrest, Gorbachev proposed a radical reformation to the Soviet Union. He proposed that the Soviet Union should become a confederation, where there would still be a central government and a president that would be responsible for conducting foreign and military policy, but that the republics would have much greater autonomy over their own internal affairs. This proposal became known as the New Union treaty, and would have taken the place of the 1922 Treaty on the Creation of the Union of Soviet Socialist Republics. While the New Union Treaty was well received by some of the republics, other republics such as the Baltic states (Lithuania, Latvia and Estonia) didn't want a redefined Soviet Union, but rather wanted freedom from the Soviet Union.

On March 17, 1991, a referendum on the treaty was held in the Soviet Union, and the New Union Treaty was approved by the public. Hailed as a victory by Mikhail Gorbachev as a way of reforming the Soviet Union, a special signing ceremony was to be held in Moscow on August 20, 1991. However, not everyone considered the adoption of the New Union Treaty to be a welcome change. While reformers in the West and in the Soviet Union were very happy with the changes, more conservative groups within the Communist Party of the Soviet Union were very concerned that the New Union Treaty would destroy the Soviet Union.

On August 19, 1991, tanks rolled through central Moscow, and a group of conservative collaborators took control of the government in a coup. President Gorbachev was arrested, and the leaders of the coup gained immediate control of the military and KGB. Those who had plotted the coup had been concerned that the New Union Treaty would lead to the destruction of the Soviet Union, and they felt that it was necessary to act to prevent this. Ironically, the coup hastened the end of the Soviet Union. As information about the coup spread, people began to take to the streets in protest against those who had taken over the government. Boris Yeltsin, who was President of the Russian Republic led the protests in Moscow, and demanded that those who led the coup give up and release Gorbachev.

The leaders of the coup sent troops to try quell the protest, but the Soviet Army refused to get directly involved and use violence to suppress the protest. Buoyed by the military's decision not to get involved, more and more protesters joined Yeltsin's protest. The coup quickly unraveled, and Gorbachev was freed. However, it was evident that the situation had changed. Gorbachev and the Soviet Union had lost its legitimacy. Yeltsin had captured the legitimacy, and a referendum was held on whether or not to disband the Soviet Union. Overwhelmingly, people voted to disband the Soviet Union. Each republic became a newly independent state.

In a very short time, not only had the regional order that had been established by the Soviet Union been dissolved, but so too had the domestic order. The order had to be totally rebuilt. Domestic order now had to give way to a new regional order, as former republics now could have some input in the establishment of the new regional order in the Soviet space. For citizens of the former Soviet republics, initial euphoria at gaining independence soon led to desperation as the economies of those states collapsed. However, despite the problems facing individuals in the new post-Sovietstates, the newly independent governments faced even greater difficulty in rebuilding their states and relationships following the collapse of the Soviet Union. Russia was by far the most powerful of the newly independent states, and was the regional hegemon. It was the main successor state to the Soviet Union, and thus had the power and ability to create a new regional order. All of the other newly independent states were much less powerful than Russia. Further, the hierarchical nature of the domestic order established by the Soviet Union showed the newly independent states that in addition to Russia's overwhelming power in the region, that it could not be trusted not to take advantage of its ability to create a new regional order that would benefit Russian interests at the expense of the newly independent states. They were worried that Russia would be willing to use force to protect its interests vis à vis the other newly independent states, or that they would even be willing to use force to recreate the Soviet Empire should the opportunity present itself.

The old domestic order established by the Soviet Union caused many problems as a new regional order was trying to be developed. This was especially the case in ethnic conflict and territory. Under the Soviet order, while ethnic territories technically belonged in the borders of a specific republic, they could do nothing to change the order. However, with the dissolution of the Soviet order, ethnic factions had the opportunity to challenge the new order before it was really established, and tried to either achieve their freedom or to become part of a neighboring state. Many of the rules and order pertaining to ethnic groups that had been established by Stalin now became extremely problematic for the newly independent states as they not only had to establish their new domestic economies, but also had to resolve new internal ethnic disputes. I now turn to a discussion of some of the ethnic and territorial conflicts that made the establishment of a new order difficult for the newly independent states.

ETHNIC CONFLICTS AND HINDERING THE
ESTABLISHMENT OF DOMESTIC ORDER

The Soviet government dealt with many of the ethnic groups by allowing them to have autonomous regions within the republics. For example, South Ossetia was granted an autonomous region status within the Georgian republic. With limits to free speech and demanding that Russian be spoken in schools, ethnic groups like the South Ossetians did not have the opportunity to voice their discontent with their treatment under Soviet order. However, with Gorbachev's glasnost policy, ethnic groups found a new voice to state their discontent. They saw opportunity in the fact that the Soviet Union had weakened, and with the dissolution of the Soviet Union, many ethnic groups declared their independence from the newly independent state.

One of the most well known examples of an ethnic group declaring their independence following the dissolution of the Soviet Union took place in Chechnya. The Chechen's had a long history of fighting against first the Russian Empire, and then trying to achieve their freedom from the Soviet Union. In 1944, Stalin deported many Chechens to Siberia and Central Asia as punishment for having helped the Nazis during World War II. It was not until 1957 that the Chechens were allowed to return to Chechnya.

As it became clear that the dissolution of the Soviet Union was imminent, Dzhokhar Dudayev, a Chechen militant leader, helped storm a meeting of Chechnya's Supreme Soviet, and declared Chechen independence from the Soviet Union. Initially, the Chechen-Ingush Autonomous Republic split into two parts, with the new republic of Ingushetia joining the Russian Federation, and Chechnya trying to secede from Russia. However, it was not until 1993 that Chechnya was able to fully declare its independence from Russia.

The Chechen act of seceding from the Russian Federation worried Russian policy makers (Jackson 2003; Malashenko 2002). They were worried that if the Chechens were successful in seceding, that many of the other ethnic groups in the Russian Federation would also choose to secede. Thus, a brutal war ensued from 1994–1996. Thousands of people were killed during the war. Despite the fact that a peace treaty was signed in 1997, Chechen militants continued to strive for independence from Russia. They were responsible for conducting terrorist attacks against Russia, and launched a military attack in 1999 in the neighboring Russian territory of Dagestan.

The Russian government responded by invading Chechnya a second time. Again, an extremely bloody war ensued, with very high casualties. Chechen separatists used terrorist tactics to try to win the war, and Russian troops brutally took control of the Chechen capital of Grozny. Russian troops finally took control of Grozny in February of 2000, having virtually destroyed the capital. The major fighting then went from the capital city of Grozny to the mountainous area around Grozny.

Ultimately, from the perspective of the ethnic Chechen separatists, the dissolution of the Soviet Union and thus the inability of Russia to establish and prescribe order over Chechnya gave them the opportunity to try to achieve their freedom from Russia. From the Russian perspective, if Chechnya was able to successfully challenge Russia's right to establish domestic order, then other ethnic groups would be able to challenge Russia's right to establish domestic order, and this would effectively challenge Russia's right to territorial integrity.

Russia was not the only former Soviet republic to have strained relations with ethnic groups that wanted to challenge the domestic order established by the newly independent states following the dissolution of the Soviet Union. Azerbaijan, Moldova, and Georgia faced similar ethnic conflicts. The main difference was that while the Chechen conflict was a question over domestic order, the other conflicts involved Russia's efforts to establish regional order. I will discuss each of these ethnic conflicts in turn.

ETHNIC CONFLICT AND THE ESTABLISHMENT OF REGIONAL ORDER IN THE POST-SOVIET SPACE

One of the major post-Soviet ethnic conflicts occurred between Armenia and Azerbaijan over an ethnic group in the region of Nagorno-Karabakh. Beginning in 1991, ethnic Armenians living in the Nagorno-Karabakh mountainous region of Azerbaijan began to secede from Azerbaijan. Their stated goal was not to create their own independent state, but rather to join Armenia.

By 1992, serious fighting broke out in Nagorno-Karabakh between Armenia and Azerbaijan. Despite attempts by international mediators such as the Organization for Security and Cooperation in Europe (OSCE), neither side could agree to any terms of mediation. Instead, by 1993, Armenia controlled territory bordering Nagorno-Karabakh itself. The conflict was so severe that it threatened to bring in other states in the immediate region, and threatened to destabilize the entire region. By 1994, Armenia had captured most of the Nagorno-Karabakh region, and approximately 9 percent of Azerbaijan (de Waal 2010).

By 1994, Russia was more able to reassume its role as regional hegemon. It was able to broker a ceasefire between Armenia and Azerbaijan. Azerbaijan's military was incapable of continuing the conflict, and Armenia's military was also taxed. Since the initial ceasefire, efforts have continued by the OSCE and other multilateral organizations to create a lasting peace in

Nagorno-Karabakh. However, a lasting peace has not been achieved. Instead, the conflict remains frozen, with neither side having an incentive to renew the conflict. However, more recently there is concern that due to Azerbaijan's wealth in natural resources and its ability to outspend Armenia militarily, that the conflict will again begin, with Azerbaijan's ability to retake the Nagorno-Karabakh region greatly enhanced (Barabanov 2008).

The Nagorno-Karabakh conflict was not the only ethnic conflict to occur in one of the newly independent states in the Caucasus. The Republic of Georgia also had two ethnic conflicts which destabilized the country and threatened regional stability and order. I now turn to a discussion of one of the main ethnic conflicts in Georgia, which led to a civil war and challenged the new regional order in the post-Soviet region.

The Conflict in South Ossetia

Prior to the dissolution of the Soviet Union, ethnic nationalism was on the rise in both Georgia and its autonomous region, South Ossetia. This was somewhat surprising considering that both the Georgians and South Ossetians had lived in relative peace during Soviet times. They even had high levels of interaction and intermarriage (Zverev 1996). However, by 1990, the Georgian Supreme Soviet banned regional political parties, which was taken by the South Ossetians as a move against their regional leadership. Further, the Georgian Supreme Soviet declared Georgian as the official language of Georgia, which only further alienated the South Ossetians. In response to these actions by the Georgians, the South Ossetians proclaimed their own state as a sovereign South Ossetian republic within the Soviet Union. The name of the new republic was to be the South Ossetian Democratic Republic. Further, the South Ossetians boycotted Georgian parliamentary elections, and held their own parliamentary elections instead.

By November, 1990, Zviad Gamsakhurdia was elected president of Georgia. He rode a wave of Georgian nationalism, and declared that the elections held in South Ossetia were invalid, and revoked South Ossetia's autonomous status. The South Ossetians further tried to secede from Georgia, and Gamsakhurdia sent Georgian troops into Tskhinvali, the capital of South Ossetia, in January 1991. Thus began the South Ossetian war.

Gamsakhurdia's policies became increasingly unpopular domestically, and he began to be viewed as a dictator. Further, his government was accused of human rights violations in the conflict with South Ossetia as well as within Georgian borders. Opposition to his rule developed quickly, and on December 22, 1991, a coup d'état occurred, with armed opposition forces taking control of many of the government buildings in Tbilisi. Heavy fighting lasted until January 6, 1992, when Gamsakhurdia escaped the country, eventually seeking political asylum in Chechnya.

Following the coup d'état, Eduard Shevarnadze, an old Soviet official who had served as the last Soviet Minister of Foreign Affairs, was appointed president of Georgia. Despite the fact that there was protest over the ousting of Gamsakhurdia as well as the fact that Shevarnadze was not elected president, Shevarnadze quickly consolidated power. One of his first major acts as president was to come to agreement with the South Ossetians and sign a Russian-brokered ceasefire, which ended the war in South Ossetia. The ceasefire included provisions that all military action would cease and that the South Ossetians would not have to face any sanctions from Georgia. In exchange, Georgia retained most of the territory of South Ossetia. However, the Russians created a peacekeeping force which was to be stationed in South Ossetia to ensure that the conflict would not renew. Further, the OSCE set up a mission in Georgia to monitor the peacekeeping efforts. Despite the fact that the peacekeeping troops reinforced a de facto independent South Ossetian state, the situation remained relatively peaceful for many years following the signing of the ceasefire agreement.

Similar to the Nagorno-Karabakh conflict, Russia was able to reassert its position as the regional hegemon in the South Ossetian conflict. It was able to broker a ceasefire when other organizations were not. It was able to work to create regional stability that was necessary to create regional order.

In addition to the Caucasus ethnic conflicts, there were ethnic conflicts that occurred in other former Soviet republics as well. I now turn to a discussion of the Transnistrian conflict in Moldova.

The Transnistrian Conflict

Similar to the situation in Georgia, Moldovan nationalism was growing at the end of the Soviet period. In 1989, Moldova passed a law which made Romanian the official state language, replacing Russian. Further, they replaced the Cyrillic alphabet with the Roman alphabet, which totally changed the language. These changes were a strong signal to both the Soviet Union as well as Moldovan citizens that there was not only a strong ethnic tie between Moldova and Romania, but also led to speculation that Moldova might seek to unify with Romania and turn its back on the Soviet Union. Indeed, these actions led to a cleavage along the boundary between east and west Moldova, with east Moldova being more sympathetic to the Soviet Union, and west Moldova being more sympathetic to Romania. The cleavage developed between what is now the Republic of Moldovia and Transnistria.

During the period 1989–1991, two significant events occurred. First, what began as a protest in 1989 by those living in Transnistria rapidly evolved into a revolt (1990), and a full separatist movement (1991). This revolt led to a civil war between Transnistria and the Republic of Moldova. Prior to 1991, the Soviet Union had been establishing bank accounts for the Transnistrians and also supplying them with weapons to help with their secessionist efforts (Kaufman and Bowers 1998; Kaufman 1996). In fact, during the revolt, the Transnistrians not only rebelled within their own territory, but also pushed into Moldova across the Dniester river and took control of Moldovan villages; an event dismissively called the "silent putsch" by Romanians (Chinn and Roper 1995). Second, in spring 1990, elections were held for the Moldovan parliament, with the pro-Romania Popular Front party defeating the Moldovan Communist Party. One of the Popular Front's main issues was for Moldova to become a part of Romania (Jackson 2003).

Before the beginning of the Transnistrian revolt, the Soviet 14th Army was stationed in Moldova, specifically in Transnistria. Many of the Soviet soldiers were allowed to settle there instead of being forced to return to the Soviet Union after their service ended. In fact, with many of the soldiers finding kinship with Transnistrians, there developed increasingly strong bonds with citizens living in Transnistria.

By 1991, Moldova's civil war had begun between the Moldovan central government and the ethnic Transnistrians. Although Russia's official policy was one of neutrality, the 14th Army provided weapons and logistical support to the Transnistrians. Many officers helped form and jointly served in both the Transnistrian Army and the Russian military.

Officially, Russia remained neutral, and pushed for a quick resolution to this crisis. President Yeltsin helped broker a ceasefire between Transnistria and Moldova, which succeeded in granting de facto independence to Transnistria (1992). In exchange for brokering the ceasefire in Moldova's civil war, Yeltsin agreed to remove the 14th Army from Moldova and use Russian peacekeeping troops to maintain the peace. However, the Russian Duma rejected this treaty. With the 14th Army still stationed in Transnistria, Transnistria had no incentive to settle its dispute with Moldova and was pleased to settle for the de facto independence that the Russian Army was willing to give them (Kaufman and Bowers 1998; Kolossov and O'Loughlin 1998; Lynch 2002).

In 1999, the Organization for Security and Cooperation in Europe (OSCE) was able to bring together all of the interested players to resolve the conflict. The first troops of the Russian 14th Army began to withdraw from Transnistria in 2000 (Hill 2002).

In 2003, Dmitry Kozak, a Russian politician who was very close to Russian President Vladimir Putin, proposed a permanent resolution to the conflict in Moldova. His proposal entailed giving representation to Transnistria in Moldova's parliament, which would have ensured that any major constitutional changes involving Moldova's constitution could be blocked by Transnistria. In exchange, Transnistria would remain in Moldova, and would not retain its de facto independence. The Russian Army would remain in Transnistria with a small force during a short transition period. However, Moldova refused to sign the Kozak memorandum. Instead, Moldova signaled its intent to try and have the EU fully resolve the conflict than have to rely on Russia for resolution (Melikova 2003; Tolkacheva 2006). Moldova's refusal to sign the Kozak memorandum immediately led to increased hostility between Moscow and Moldova (Tolkacheva 2006).

Ultimately, the Moldovans were unwilling to accept Russia's regional hegemonic status and ability to create a regional order. Instead, Moldova tried to turn to the European Union to establish a regional order. The problem is that Moldova was at the fringe of the European Union's reach. It could not effectively create a regional order in Moldova. Similarly, Romania could not provide stability and regional order for Moldova. Instead, Russia was the only regional power that was strong enough to establish a regional order.

In each of the cases of the ethnic conflict that I have examined in this chapter, Russia has been instrumental in negotiating ceasefires and providing peacekeeping troops. Each of these cases has threatened not only regional stability, but also regional order. The rise in ethnic nationalism that occurred at the end of Soviet power really illustrated that not only was the Soviet Union unable to provide regional order and continue to maintain the rules for interaction among the states in its region, but it was also unable to provide domestic order and could not continue to maintain the rules for interaction among the Soviet republics. Most of the republics became interested in seceding from the Soviet Union, and once that became a distinct possibility, many of those new states in turn faced secessionist national movements which threatened their new domestic order.

It was not until Russia was able to assume the role of successor state to the Soviet Union and establish its domestic order, that Russia was then able to reassert itself as the regional hegemon and thus begin to create a new regional order. In this chapter, I have focused mainly on examining and defining order globally, regionally, and domestically. I have defined the concept of order and shown that the Soviet Union created first domestic order followed by regional order, and finally was able to influence global order by challenging the United States' global hegemonic status and creating a bipolar global system. However, the Soviet Union could not maintain its global and regional orders. Instead, it slowly began to retreat as other states in Eastern Europe began to challenge its regional order. As its economy and power further declined, the Soviet Union did not only fail to provide regional order, but it also could no longer provide domestic order. For this reason, the Soviet Union imploded, creating fifteen newly independent states that had to establish their own domestic order.

Following the collapse of the Soviet Union, Russia was able to declare itself the successor state to the Soviet Union. It was able to restore domestic order, and begin to build a new regional order. The collapse of the Soviet Union and Russia's reemergence as the regional hegemon that had the ability to create a new regional order allows scholars the unique opportunity to examine exactly how order is created as well as examining the rules for interaction among states in the post-Soviet region. However, many of the newly independent states were much weaker than Russia in terms of both military and economic power. This power asymmetry between the newly independent states and Russia led the weaker states to be mistrustful of Russia's intentions in the region. Further, since the Soviet Union had often been heavy-handed in its dealings with the other republics, the weaker states further had little reason to trust Russia to provide regional order that would have any benefit to the weaker states.

In this book, I will show how regional order is constructed. By examining bilateral and multilateral treaties in the post-Soviet space, I can show how the rules for interaction are created and how regional order then follows. In Chapter 2, I will examine Russia's bilateral relationships with each of the former Soviet republics except the three Baltic states, as those states are considered to be in Europe's regional order, and not that of Russia. I will discuss the difficulty of creating a regional order and how Russia had to manage the problem of power asymmetry and mistrust in establishing its bilateral relations. I examine distinct regions in the post-Soviet space and how Russia was able to work bilaterally to create rules for interaction among the newly independent states.

In Chapter 3, I will examine the multilateral organizations that were developed by Russia in the former Soviet space, which further solidified rules for interaction among the newly independent states. All of these multilateral organizations were established to allow for varying degrees of economic integration among the former Soviet states while also achieving security and stability. Some of the multilateral treaties developed by these organizations are instrumental in developing the rules and order for the region.

In Chapter 4, I will illustrate how regional order is created through both bilateral and multilateral relationships. I create a treaty network combining the multilateral and bilateral treaties. This treaty network can show how strong a regional order is as well as identify certain lodestone treaties which are fundamental for establishing the rules for interaction in the post-Soviet space.

Finally, in Chapter 5, I will examine the post-Soviet space in light of regional order. By examining the combined bilateral and multilateral treaty networks in the post-Soviet space we can see which geographic areas have stability and are part of the regional order, and which geographic areas lack stability and are not a part of the regional order. There should be increased conflict within areas that are not a part of the regional order, as they do not follow the rules for interaction among the states in the region.

Ultimately, this book will show not only how a regional order is developed, but will illuminate the nuanced interactions among all of the states in the region to develop a regional order. While the regional hegemon is responsible for developing and creating the regional order, the weaker states also play an important role in establishing the regional order as they try to achieve their strategic goals through negotiations with the regional hegemon.

NOTES

1. The security dilemma refers to the fact that as one state increases security, other states in the international system must respond in kind, to ensure that they don't lose security in relation to that state which increased security. For more information on the security dilemma, see (Jervis 1978; Schweller 1996; Welt 2010).

2. Relative gains refers to a zero sum game between states. If one state makes gains in the global system, all other actors must therefore not be as powerful. For more information on relative gains, see (Grieco, Powell, and Snidal 1993; Snidal 1991).

3. The term *glasnost* comes from the Old Church Slavonic word "glas," which is translated as "voice."

Chapter Two

Bilateral Relations in the Post-Soviet Space

Following the collapse of the Soviet Union, all of the former Soviet republics became newly independent states. They had to forge new relationships with each other not only to ensure their survival, but also to split up the Soviet Empire. While the collapse of great empires has often led to wars between the former subjects, the collapse of the Soviet Union led to a relatively peaceful transition from a powerful Empire to fifteen newly independent states. As Russia had been the most powerful Soviet republic, Russia became the undisputed regional hegemon (Slobodchikoff 2013; Willerton, Goertz, and Slobodchikoff 2011; Willerton, Slobodchikoff, and Goertz 2012). Moreover, because of its history of first being the Russian empire and then its Soviet past, the states that comprised the former Soviet Union (FSU) did not trust Russia or its intentions. Further, one of Russia's first acts after the dissolution of the Soviet Union was to declare itself the successor state to the Soviet Union (Åslund and Kuchins 2009). In doing this, Russia sent a signal to all of the other states that it was the regional hegemon. The other states in the region signed bilateral treaties accepting Russia as the successor state to the Soviet Union, and allowed Russia to assume many of the debts incurred by the Soviet Union. The fact was that Russia possessed the necessary infrastructure and capability to assume that role, whereas the other states did not.

The FSU states mainly saw Russia as an aggressive regional hegemon who was not to be trusted to abide by their newly found sovereignty. Thus, all of the states of the FSU found themselves faced with a situation of Russian hegemonic dominance with a high level of mistrust of the regional hegemon. Therefore they had to choose whether or not they were willing to cooperate with Russia. Cooperation would allow those states in the FSU to achieve their own strategic goals, yet each state had to determine whether their mistrust of Russia outweighed the potential benefits of cooperation.

In other words, states had to determine whether Russia would threaten their security and territorial integrity to the point that the benefits of cooperation with Russia would not be prudent. Cooperation with in the post-Soviet space generally consisted of cooperation in trade or security (Garnett and Trenin 1999; Olcott, Aslund, and Garnett 1999; Slobodchikoff 2013; Willerton, Slobodchikoff, and Goertz 2012).

It should be noted that the post-Soviet region is not homogenous. There are various geographical areas in the Russian "near abroad" which should be examined individually. Specifically, I categorize the post-Soviet space into three distinct regions based on their geographical location (see Table 2.1). Specifically, the three distinct regions are the European FSU (Belarus, Moldova, and Ukraine), the Southern Caucasus (Armenia, Azerbaijan, and Georgia), and Central Asia (Kazakhstan, Kyrgyzstan, Tajikistan, Turkmenistan, and Uzbekistan). For the purpose of this book, I do not examine the Baltic states' relations with Russia, as they are no longer within the Russian sphere of influence in the post-Soviet space. In this chapter, I will first examine specific areas of bilateral cooperation, specifically security and economic cooperation, then I will introduce the methods of examining bilateral cooperation. Finally, I will examine Russia's bilateral relations with each of the states in the FSU based upon their geographical location within the post-Soviet space.

Table 2.1. Geographical Regions within the Post Soviet Space

European FSU	Belarus
	Moldova
	Ukraine
Southern Caucasus	Armenia
	Azerbaijan
	Georgia
Central Asia	Kazakhstan
	Kyrgyzstan
	Tajikistan
	Turkmenistan
	Uzbekistan

SECURITY COOPERATION IN THE POST-SOVIET SPACE

Following the collapse of the Soviet Union, security became one of the paramount strategic challenges of each of the fifteen newly independent states. The three Baltic states (Estonia, Latvia and Lithuania), were accepted quickly by the West. The West guaranteed their sovereignty and security interests, and they were quickly able to leave the post-Soviet space and join Western Europe. The West had always considered the Baltic states as not being legitimately part of the Soviet Union, even keeping their seats at the United Nations for the day when they would be able to rejoin the UN as independent states. After the collapse of the Soviet Union, the three Baltic States immediately joined the West, and had no interest in having good relations with Russia.

Contrary to the Baltic states, the other FSU states did not have the option of having their security guaranteed by the West. Instead, they had to ensure their own security. To achieve this, they had to rebuild their relationships with the other former republics. Indeed, while building up their relationships with the other former Soviet states, they had to decide how to build a relationship with the regional hegemon, Russia. While other FSU states were wary of Russia's intentions, the Russian Federation had a specific goal to its foreign policy. It wanted to rebuild the power structure and its influence with the former Soviet republics. One of Russia's main motivations in its foreign policy was its desire to reestablish its sphere of influence over the "near abroad," the former Soviet republics.

The newly independent Russia possessed a complex set of security concerns. One of the security concerns had to do with the borders of the new Russian Federation. During the Soviet period, borders between the republics did not need to be patrolled as vigorously as the external borders of the Soviet Union. While the borders were monitored, the military did not actively need to patrol the borders. Moreover, although Soviet military troops were stationed within the borders of Russia, many soldiers were stationed in outer republics closer to the external borders of the Soviet Union. With Russia declaring itself the successor state to the Soviet Union, technically all of the troops became Russian troops. However, they became Russian troops stationed in newly independent states.

The issue of military forces was further complicated by the fact that the newly independent states needed militaries of their own. There was no way to easily dismantle the Soviet military by just splitting the forces according to where the forces were stationed. To dismantle the military in that fashion would have placed Russia at a tremendous disadvantage relative to the former republics. Moreover, since the Soviet military was composed of soldiers from all of the former republics, citizens of one newly independent state might find themselves serving in a defunct state's army while stationed in a different sovereign territory.

In short, to address security concerns, Russia had to address the issue of the status of military forces with the other FSU states. Russia had to negotiate with each former Soviet republic to determine to whom the forces stationed in that state belonged and then determine whether or not those troops that

became part of the Russian Army would remain stationed in the newly independent state. With vital security interests in different areas coupled with
a lack of infrastructure to barrack a military of that size, it was in Russia's
interests to ensure that portions of its military could remain stationed in the
former Soviet republics. However, it was not necessarily in the interest of the
former Soviet republic to allow Russian troops to be stationed within its borders. The former Soviet republics could not ensure that Russia would adhere
to their territorial integrity and not directly influence the domestic politics
of the newly independent states through the presence of its military. In fact,
states like Moldova and Georgia were very concerned with Russian military
intervention within their territorial borders (Kolossov and O'Loughlin 1998;
Kolstø and Malgin 1998; Lynch 2002; Pardo Sierra 2011).

In addition to addressing the status of forces, the issue of nuclear weapons
was of paramount importance. During Soviet times, the nuclear arsenal was
well-protected, and upon the dissolution of the Soviet Union, there were concerns about not only the security of the nuclear weapons, but also to whom
those weapons belonged. This was an especially important concern for the
West, as they were concerned about rogue states gaining access to unpro-
tected nuclear weapons. Russia was not the only nuclear state at the time of
the Soviet collapse, as Ukraine, Kazakhstan, and Belarus also had nuclear
weapons within their borders. It was not in Russia's interest that many states
in its region would become nuclear powers, and thus wanted to ensure that
nuclear weapons remained Russian possessions.

In addition to immediate security concerns, Russia was also concerned
with its regional authority and to regain its great power status globally
(Olcott, Aslund, and Garnett 1999). As such, it needed a strong military presence in former Soviet republics. For example, of vital importance to Russian
strategic security was the access to naval bases on the Black Sea in Ukraine.
If Russia wanted to retain the Black Sea Fleet as well as the bases and not lose
control of a vital part of its naval forces including ships, weapons, and troops,
it had to find a way to cooperate with Ukraine and not lose access to those
vital security structures. To relinquish them would have been a tremendous
loss of strategic power. Although Russia did have naval ports in Arkhangelsk
and St. Petersburg in the North and Khabarovsk and Vladivostok on the
Pacific Ocean, the Black Sea Fleet was vital for maintaining interests in the
Mediterranean and Middle East.

For Russia to once again gain great power status, it had to be concerned
with its security infrastructure. For over twenty years, Soviet production had
been on the decline, and the collapse of the Soviet system virtually destroyed
state production. Factories were not functioning at capacity, and there was
a shortage of products available in the marketplace. In addition, one of the

biggest problems facing Russia regarding its security infrastructure was that the Soviet government had spread vital infrastructure among its republics (Hewett 1988). For example, steel that was necessary to produce rockets was produced in Magnetogorsk (central Siberia), rocket fuel was produced in Armenia, Ukraine, and Kazakhstan, and rockets were assembled and sent to outer space from the Baikonur Cosmodrome in Kazakhstan. This system of spreading vital infrastructure among the republics was extremely inefficient during the Soviet period, but became virtually unworkable once the republics gained their freedom.

Despite the collapse of the Soviet, Russia saw itself as a great power that could manage relations within its own region. While it had difficulties to face in rebuilding its military and economy, nevertheless, Russia was in a stronger position both in security and economically than all of the other former Soviet republics. Like the regional hierarchical structure proposed by Lemke and Werner (1996) and Lemke (2002), Russia sat at the top of the regional hierarchy.

As the state at the top of the regional hierarchy, Russia believed that it should try and manage regional conflicts that had flared after the collapse of the Soviet Union. There had been an increase in civil wars and interstate conflict following the collapse due to the regional instability and power vacuum that developed (Gayoso 2009; Jackson 2003; King 1999; Kolstø and Malgin 1998; Lynch 2002). Russia did not want to have conflict spread and therefore needed to ensure that it had a military presence in many of the FSU states through having military bases. Having military bases in FSU states ensured that Russia's security was ensured while also securing its power over the region. Most of Russia's military bases in other FSU states either were acquired by leasing it from the host state, or by other form of agreement.

Among the bases that Russia occupied in the FSU, Russia had air bases in Armenia, Kyrgyzstan, and Tajikistan, radar stations in Azerbaijan, Belarus, and Kazakhstan, ground bases in Tajikistan, Transnistria, Abkhazia, and South Ossetia, a Cosmodrome in Kazakhstan, and a naval base in Ukraine (Klein 2009). In short, Russia's security interests drove Russia to seek to station military troops in the "near abroad." Russia's push to occupy military bases in the FSU was not met with universal approval, especially by states that had internal conflicts and civil wars. Those states were wary of Russian efforts to "manage" the conflicts, where they saw Russia's intent as interfering in their domestic disputes (Slobodchikoff 2013b).

Even though security was extremely important to Russia and the other FSU states, economic interests were no less important to all of the newly independent states. I will now address the economic interests of Russia and those states in the "near abroad."

ECONOMIC COOPERATION IN THE POST-SOVIET SPACE

As the Soviet Union collapsed, scholars were quick to point out the fact that the economies of the former Soviet Union were absolutely devastated, and needed to be drastically changed to ensure the survival of the newly independent states. In fact, besides Russia, scholars believed that very few of the economies of the newly independent states would be able to prosper. The notable exception was Ukraine, which many scholars believed could become self-sufficient (Åslund and Olcott 1999). The reality was that so many of the economies of the newly independent states would have to rely upon Russia as a trade partner to prevent their economies from stagnating.

One of the most important drivers of the economic interests of the new FSU states was energy. Russian oil and natural reserves were plentiful, and it had the necessary infrastructure to export to those FSU states that did not have their own reserves such as Ukraine and Belarus. Russia also possessed the necessary pipelines and infrastructure to deliver oil and gas from other states that had vast reserves to those states that did not. Therefore, all of the FSU states were to varying degrees dependent on Russia in terms of energy. Energy exporters needed Russia to deliver their oil and gas to other markets, and energy importers needed Russia to help supply necessary energy. Russia's status in terms of energy made it extremely powerful in the region, and ensured that Russia would have more power than the other states in the region (Goldman 2010). It should be noted, however, that despite Russia's regional energy hegemony, it could not unilaterally dictate energy policy in the region. It needed the cooperation of the other FSU states to export oil and natural gas to those states that were reliant upon Russia. Specifically, Russia needed to negotiate specific agreements on the amount of oil and gas that would be imported, determine the price of the oil and gas, etc. Thus, energy importing states in the FSU (meaning that they did not have enough of their own reserves) had a strategic interest in building a cooperative bilateral relationship with Russia, and since Russia stood to benefit from exporting energy to those states that needed oil and natural gas, Russia too had a strategic interest in building a cooperative relationship with FSU states that imported energy. Further, states that exported energy had a strategic interest in building a cooperative relationship with Russia to facilitate access to other markets, and Russia had a strategic interest in building a cooperative relationship with energy exporters to ensure that they would have access to other sources of energy.

Traditionally, scholars have noted that it is much easier to build relationships by first cooperating in trade (Kydd 2000, 2001, 2005). However, in the case of the post-Soviet region, states did not have the luxury of slowly building trust through cooperation. Instead, they had to determine whether or not to cooperate, and if so, whether to cooperate in economics, security, or some combination of the two (Jones 2007; Keohane 2005; Lipson 1984). The decision to cooperate or not to cooperate lies solely with the weaker states in the region, as they must weigh the benefits of cooperation with their level of mistrust of the regional hegemon (Willerton, Goertz, and Slobodchikoff 2012). While Russia was able to create the regional order and the rules for interaction, nevertheless it was not strong enough to force all of the states to capitulate to all of its security and economic demands. Instead, it established rules for interaction among the FSU states based upon treaties and the rule of law. Russia had to rely upon treaty construction and treaty networks. In fact, no other state has initiated as many bilateral and multilateral treaties as Russia, and this treaty activism covers a wide range of issue areas (Willerton, Vashchilko, Powers, Beznosov, and Goertz 2006). These treaties formed the backbone of the order established in the post-Soviet space that allowed behaviors and interactions to become predictable, and allowed the states to develop cooperative relationships within the rules of the regional order established by Russia. I now turn to an examination of the treaties and the methodology used to examine the treaties in the post-Soviet space.

TREATIES IN THE POST-SOVIET SPACE

States will cooperate if it is in their own best interest, especially since states are rational actors. States must weigh the benefits to cooperation against their mistrust of the regional hegemon. Such is the case in the post-Soviet space, where there is a high level of mistrust of Russia. The weaker states must determine the level of cooperation with the regional hegemon based upon the level of mistrust. In other words, they must determine if their level of mistrust outweighs the potential benefits that cooperation could bring. It is also in Russia's best interest to cooperate with the weaker states as no state, even a hegemon, can maintain an international presence or reach without cooperation from other states. Former Finnish Foreign Minister Keijo Korhonen has observed, that "even the most powerful state in the world cannot protect all of its citizens without the help of other states; cooperation is a necessity for all states who wish to have an international presence'' (Korhonen 2010).

Following the collapse of the Soviet Union, Russia had to rely upon treaties to build its relationship with the FSU states. However, treaties and agreements need to be defined clearly as this study proceeds. In terms of international law, a treaty refers to any written agreement between states (Carter, Trimble, and Weiner 2007). According to the Vienna Convention on the Law of Treaties, a treaty is defined as any legally binding written agreement between states (Sinclair 1984). While states sign other agreements such as memoranda of understanding, unless it is a legally binding interstate agreement, I do not include it in my analysis.

Ultimately, legally binding treaties establish a set of rules for cooperation between states. They establish regional order and security by creating predictable outcomes for both strong and weak states. For weak states, treaties provide protection from stronger states, while still providing the opportunity to cooperate within the order established by the regional hegemon. For example, in 1948 the Soviet Union insisted on developing a friendship treaty with Finland. The Soviet Union was interested in using Finland for strategic purposes to station troops there as well as to create another satellite state that would serve as a buffer to protect the Soviet Union from a German attack through Finland. However, although the Finns realized that they had to engage the Soviets, they also realized that they could use the treaty to help create and modify the regional order, as well as create predictability in the behavior of the Soviet Union toward Finland. Thus, the Finns insisted on using specific language in the treaty with the Soviet Union to ensure that they would not become satellite states to the Soviet Union (Korhonen 2010). The Soviet Union, however, realized that it could not just station troops in Finland without an agreement, and it strove to develop an agreement that would allow Soviet troops to be stationed in Finland. Thus, despite the Soviet Union's hegemonic strength, treaties and cooperation were a necessary component of creating regional order. The Soviet Union also realized that adherence to treaties established a pattern of behavior through regional order on which other states within the region could rely. The 1948 Friendship and Cooperation Treaty between the Soviet Union and Finland helped establish the regional order. The two states compromised on the exact wording of the treaty, where the Soviets offered military assistance to the Finns should there be a threat to Finland from the West. Specifically, the Finns insisted upon wording that ensured that the Soviet Union would help the Finns only should the Finns not be able to defend themselves. Thus, although the Soviets wanted to station troops in Finland for their own strategic purposes, Finland was able to work within the rules established through the regional order to protect itself and prevent the Soviets from making Finland a satellite state. This way, Finland, as the weaker state, was able to insist on specific language which protected the Finns from Soviet aggression. The Soviet Union, as the hegemon, realized that a friendship treaty with Finland was necessary to ensure cooperation in the regional order in the future. Thus, the Soviet Union was willing to agree to certain specific language in the treaty while keeping in mind that the existence of the treaty was of paramount importance (Slobodchikoff 2013b).

The 1948 Friendship and Cooperation Treaty between the Soviet Union and Finland illustrates that certain treaties are fundamental to building a relationship between two states, which is fundamental to creating order. The Friendship and Cooperation Treaty also illustrates a problem with the way scholars examine treaties. Specifically, scholars examine individual treaties in isolation without examining the interaction of treaties or the relative importance of certain treaties. To be fair, it is fairly difficult to systematically identify treaty interactions and the relative importance of individual treaties. Network analysis of treaties is a way of solving the problem of how to examine treaties. I now turn to a discussion on treaty networks and the analysis of treaty networks in the post-Soviet space.

TREATY NETWORKS IN THE POST-SOVIET SPACE

Certain scholars have begun to use network analysis to examine treaties (Slobodchikoff 2013;Willerton, Goertz, and Slobodchikoff 2011; Willerton, Slobodchikoff, and Goertz 2012). For example, Slobodchikoff (2013b) uses network analysis to determine the quality of cooperation between Russia and the other states in the FSU. He discovers that the denser the treaty network between two states, the less likely there was to be violent conflict between those states. It should be noted that his findings did not support that there would not be conflict between the two states, merely that the conflict would rarely, if ever, become militarized interstate disputes (MIDs). Instead, states that had dense treaty networks were more likely to resolve their disagreements through diplomacy and negotiations rather than through the use of force.

It should be reiterated that treaties form the rules of the order established by the regional hegemon. In the case of bilateral relationships between the hegemon and weaker states, these treaties form the rules of interaction in the bilateral relationship. In turn, the combination of bilateral and multilateral treaties in turn forms the rules of interaction for all of the states in the region to create a regional order. Network analysis allows scholars the opportunity to not only identify how the treaties interact to create a regional order, but can also identify specific treaties which are the most important treaties, further referred to as lodestone treaties. The lodestone treaties are the most important treaties because they serve as the foundation for all of the other treaties within the relationship. Specifically, using degree centrality can determine which network nodes are the most important to a network precisely because the majority of the nodes are tied to the most central nodes (Everett and Borgatti 1999; Latora and Marchiori 2007; Opsahl, Agneessens, and Skvoretz 2010; Wasserman and Faust 1994). In the case of this analysis, individual treaties are the network nodes, and determining degree centrality can help identify the lodestone treaties.

While network analysis is the most appropriate method for evaluating the relationships between treaties as well as which treaties are most central to a relationship, it is necessary to first understand how treaties are tied to one another. To do so requires an understanding of the formulation and negotiation of treaties as well as how traditional scholars of international relations have approached the study of treaties.

Traditional scholars of international relations have argued that each individual treaty is its own institution (Koremenos 2005; Koremenos 2002; Koremenos, Lipson, and Snidal 2001; Koremenos 2009). For the purposes of studying treaties, each individual treaty should be examined on its own merits, without taking into account prior treaties or groups of treaties. Often studies of treaties involve treaty design of types of treaties and the goals of each state involved in the treaty creation. For example, Koremenos, Lipson, and Snidal (2001) focus on the rational design of treaties by arguing that each treaty is a rational institution constructed by rational agents. They argue that international actors design treaties to maximize their own preferences, and that treaties are therefore a reflection of their interests. Specifically, they examine the institutional design of treaties and identify specific characteristics such as membership, scope and flexibility. The authors argue that actors are goal-oriented, and as such will choose specific treaty characteristics that will maximize their ability to achieve their goals. This views each individual treaty as a means to achieving a specific goal, where there is little cumulation occuring over multiple treaties. Each treaty therefore achieves a small goal toward achieving specific foreign policy preferences of each state.

While examining the rational design of individual treaties and focusing on treaties as institutions is important, the problem with such an approach is that it assumes that individual treaties are negotiated in a vacuum, and are not constrained by prior treaties. In reality, each new treaty is a product of previous treaties in some manner, and often builds upon prior treaties. Further, treaties constrain states' behaviors. A state is thus constrained by all of the treaties that it has signed. Therefore it is logical to examine individual treaties as institutions, but also to understand that groups of treaties constitute an institution. A bilateral relationship between states is an institution in the same way that a bilateral treaty between states is an institution. I now examine the ways in which treaties can be grouped to form an institutional relationship between states.

GROUPS OF TREATIES AS INSTITUTIONS

Scholars have long noted that institutions are not created in a vacuum, and many have tried to determine the relational aspect of institutions. For example, Aggarwal (1998) argued that institutions built upon and constrained prior institutions. He referred to this phenomenon as nested institutions. Thus, institutions that built upon and constrained prior institutions were nested within the prior institution. The concept of nestedness was expanded to the study of treaties (Slobodchikoff 2013b; Willerton, Goertz, and Slobodchikoff 2012; Willerton, Slobodchikoff, and Goertz 2012). Specifically, treaties actively build upon and constrain prior treaties, meaning that treaties are nested within prior treaties. However, it is difficult to determine which specific treaties are nested in other treaties, and which treaties are merely stand-alone treaties. Slobodchikoff (2013b) argues that the treaties specify their own classification of nestedness. Specifically, treaties that explicitly refer to prior treaties within their text are nested within those referenced treaties.

Once treaty nestedness has been determined, it becomes possible to understand the relationship between these treaties. Thus, groups of treaties can become their own institutions based upon their nestedness in other treaties. Further, it then becomes possible to use network analysis to further understand the relationships between treaties and to determine which treaties are the most central to a specific relationship. To do this, each individual must be read and coded to determine whether it is nested in prior treaties, and then which prior treaties in which the given treaty is nested. Using nestedness to show how treaties are related to one another, it is then possible to then use network analysis to visualize the relationship between the treaties as well as determine the degree centrality and relative importance of certain treaties.

Treaty networks can also help illuminate the strength of a bilateral relationship and the likelihood that the relationship between two states would devolve into conflict. For example, Slobodchikoff (2013b) finds that the stronger the treaty network, the less likely there is to be bilateral conflict. Thus, by examining the relationship between treaties we can analyze the strength of the bilateral relations between states and their levels of cooperation. I now turn to an analysis of specific bilateral relationships within the regions in table 1.

BILATERAL RELATIONS ACCORDING TO REGIONS IN THE FORMER SOVIET SPACE

For the purposes of this analysis, I have broken the former Soviet space into three distinct geographical regions (Table 2.1).[1] Specifically, I will discuss the European region, the Southern Caucasus region, and the Central Asian region. Russia has unique strategic interests in each of these regions, and the states in each of these regions all have varying degrees of strategic interests in cooperating with Russia.

EUROPEAN FSU

Russia's interests in the European FSU are both cultural and strategic. The cultural interests stem from the time of Kievan Rus. Kievan Rus was the cradle of Slavic culture, and the principality was the historical origin of the current Russian state and culture. Thus, many Russians have felt a kinship with Ukraine and Belarus as being part of the same Slavic heritage.

Despite this shared cultural heritage, the European FSU is much more important to Russia's strategic interests. The states located in the European FSU are a gateway between territory influenced by the EU and territory that is influenced by Russia. With EU and NATO expansion having subsumed most of Eastern Europe, the European FSU is critical for Russia to act as a buffer zone and prevent either organization from spreading into territory influenced by Russia.

Great power conflict between the EU and Russia over influence makes the states in the European FSU of paramount importance to Russia. For the states in the European FSU, Russia is an extremely important actor especially because of its ability to supply necessary natural gas, which is vital for their heating needs. Despite a deep mistrust of Russian hegemonic interests, the European FSU needs Russian energy resources to survive (see Table 2.2). As Table 2.2 shows, the European FSU is extremely dependent on Russia for their energy needs. This is especially true for Moldova and Belarus. Each of the European FSU states requires cooperation from Russia to achieve their energy security, yet each state is extremely mistrustful of Russia and Russian intentions.

Despite the lack of trust among the European FSU states and Russia, the European FSU states actively engaged Russia through treaty building (see Table 2.3). In fact, as Table 2.3 shows, both Ukraine and Belarus actively

Table 2.2.   Average % of Energy Imported from Russia by European FSU States (1991–2005)

State	Avg Imported Energy (%)
Moldova	98
Belarus	87
Ukraine	46

Table 2.3.   Number of Bilateral Treaties Signed
(1991–2005)

Bilateral Relationship	Bilateral Treaties
Russia-Ukraine	217
Russia-Belarus*	198
Russia-Moldova	92

*Treaties are only bilateral treaties, not economic union treaties

engaged Russia, while Moldova reluctantly engaged the regional hegemon. I now turn to a discussion of the bilateral relations between each of the European FSU states and Russia.

Russian-Ukrainian Relations

Russia and Ukraine have always have always had complex and problematic relations. While Russians have often viewed Kiev as the cradle of Slavic civilization which should be naturally a part of Russia, Ukraine has viewed Russia as an overbearing and untrustworthy neighbor. They have remained skeptical of Russian intentions toward them, and severely lacked trust that Russia would not interfere in the domestic politics of Ukraine.

During Soviet times, the Russian and Ukrainian republics were often antagonistic to each other. Many Russians believed that Ukraine was inferior to Russia, and looked on Ukrainians condescendingly. Ukrainians thus experienced considerable political and cultural suppression throughout the Soviet era.

With the collapse of the Soviet Union, animosity and mistrust between Russia and Ukraine was very high. Ukraine was wary of Russian intentions toward its sovereignty, especially over issues involving the former Soviet Black Sea Fleet. To balance Russian regional hegemony, Ukraine tried to gain support from the West, but the West was strategically engaged with much of Eastern Europe, and was not able to fully engage Ukraine.

Ukraine's economy was largely dependent upon Russia's, especially for supplies of natural gas (see Table 2.2). Between 1991 and 2005, Ukraine imported an average of 46% of its energy needs from Russia. Further, Russia needed access to the Black Sea for its naval forces, and Ukraine possessed the Black Sea port of Sevastopol, which was vital to Russian security needs. The combination of the economic reliance upon Russia and Russian strategic security interests in Ukraine led some Western observers to predict that Ukraine would have difficulty maintaining its sovereignty, especially as Russian policy makers wanted to create a union between Russia and Ukraine (Balmaceda 1998; Bremmer 1994; Burant 1995; Mroz and Pavliuk 1996; Rumer 1994; Trenin 2007). Some scholars even questioned whether Russia wouldn't just invade Ukraine and force Ukraine to join Russia (Bremmer 1994; Rumer 1994). In short, following the collapse of the Soviet Union, the deep mistrust that characterized Russian-Ukrainian relations continued unabated.

Despite the mistrust between Russia and Ukraine, several pressing security and economic issues needed immediate attention and resolution. Specifically, Russia needed to address the partitioning of the Black Sea Fleet as well as its need for access to the port of Sevastopol. Russia did not have any other warm water ports for its naval forces, and the port of Sevastopol was of vital interest to them. Further, Russian military forces were stationed in Ukraine at the time of the collapse of the Soviet Union. Finally, nuclear weapons had been stationed in Ukraine, and Ukraine and Russia needed to ensure that requirements based on the START missile treaty were upheld given that Ukraine was now an independent state.

Ukraine's strategic interests were initially in ensuring its own sovereignty, partitioning the Soviet military forces to ensure that it could provide for its own security, and assuring a stable supply of energy imports. Even though their relationship was very mistrustful, and often confrontational, they were able to cooperate on many different issues (Slobodchikoff 2013; Slobodchikoff 2013b).

Between 1991 and 2005, Ukraine and Russia signed 217 bilateral treaties covering a myriad of issues areas dealing with security, economic issues such as trade, and integration. While they did sign a wide variety of different treaties, the majority of the treaties signed were those that dealt with economic issues (see Table 2.4).

Table 2.4. Russia-Ukraine Bilateral
Treaties by Issue Area (1991–2005)

Security	64
Economic	105
Integration	54
Total Bilateral Treaties	217*

*Some treaties address more than one issue area,
so are classified in more than one category.

An analysis of the treaty network between Ukraine and Russia shows that they deliberately built a treaty network in which treaties built upon prior treaties to create a cooperative relationship despite the lack of the resource of trust (see Figure 2.1). Specifically, there are two major parts to the treaty network. One of the parts encompasses most of the bilateral relationship, while the other part deals with matters of free trade between the two states (this part of the network is located at the bottom center of Figure 2.1).

It is important to note that the two most contentious issues between Ukraine and Russia are located within the main part of the treaty network.

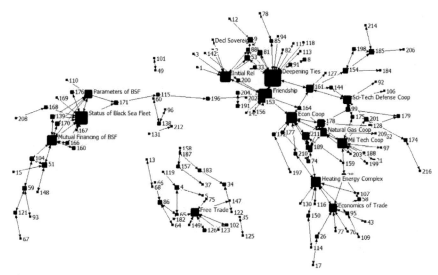

Figure 2.1.   Russia-Ukraine Treaty Network

Specifically, the main treaties addressing the Black Sea Fleet are located on the left side of the bilateral treaty network, and treaties dealing with natural gas and energy are located on the right side of the main treaty network. Located between each of these contentious issues are treaties such as the Friendship and Cooperation Treaty, which serve as lodestone treaties for the bilateral relationship.

The three main Black Sea Fleet treaties, specifically the Status of the Black Sea Fleet, the Mutual Financing of the Black Sea Fleet, and the Parameters of the Black Sea Fleet were all signed on May 28, 1997. Despite the fact that Ukraine and Russia had begun their relationship in 1991, their relationship didn't evolve enough to be able to adequately address the Black Sea Fleet until 1997. Further, the treaties on the Black Sea Fleet paved the way for the Friendship and Cooperation Treaty, which was signed on May 31, 1997. In other words, the relationship between Ukraine and Russia was contentious enough that they needed to build up enough cooperation in other areas before they were able to address the most important issues. With the resolution of the Black Sea Fleet Treaties and the Friendship and Cooperation Treaty, Ukraine and Russia were able to cooperate in other areas.

Despite the fact that Ukraine and Russia were able to finally achieve a cooperative relationship, they nevertheless continued a contentious relationship. The two states often had arguments over gas leading to the Ukrainian gas crisis of 2006. Despite the fact that the Ukrainian gas crisis occurred after the period of study in this book, nevertheless, the Ukrainian gas crisis showed the importance of the treaty network between the two states, which allowed the governments to resolve the conflicts peacefully.

The conflict between Ukraine and Russia over the Crimea is a much more fundamental issue that is extremely problematic in the analysis of the treaty network between the two states. Despite the fact that the conflict between the states occurred after the period examined in this book, I will nevertheless examine this case to show the importance of treaties to this relationship.

The Crisis over Crimea

Following the end of the Cold War, states that had been within the Soviet Union's sphere of influence quickly began reforms that would bring them within the sphere of influence of Western Europe and the United States. They quickly tried to join both the EU and NATO, and became part of the Western security architecture. Despite Russian objections, NATO expanded its security architecture into what had been part of the Soviet security architecture. Russia had no choice but to accept the result, but cautioned the West against interfering within the "near abroad," or the FSU (Slobodchikoff 2013a).

The FSU became a region that Russia determined was vital to its own interests, and made clear that it didn't want Western influence to interfere with its strategic regional interests. However, the EU wanted to further its own influence, and targeted four of the FSU states for developing association agreements. Specifically, the EU targeted Georgia, Moldova, Ukraine, and Armenia. The EU was successful in signing association agreements with Georgia and Moldova in 2013, but was unsuccessful with Armenia and Ukraine.

In the case of Ukraine, Russia was able to successfully convince Ukrainian President Yanukovych not to sign an association agreement with the EU. Russia promised Ukraine economic aid and increased cooperation through the Eurasian Customs Union. Ukraine's decision to not sign the association agreement sparked protests in Kiev, and eventually led to Yanukovych fleeing Ukraine, and a new interim government took power. The new government wanted closer ties with the EU, while distancing Ukraine from Russian influence.

The ascension of the new interim government in Ukraine led to massive protests in Eastern Ukraine. Even more important, however, was the fact that Russia was worried that the new interim government would not abide by Ukraine's obligations under the Black Sea Fleet treaties signed in 1997. Under the Black Sea Fleet treaties, Russia could protect the naval base in Sevastopol, and could do so by stationing troops within Crimea. Russia quickly moved in the troops allowed by treaty into Crimea, and isolated Ukrainian military forces to fortify their interests. The Crimean autonomous government requested Russian assistance, and scheduled a referendum for not only seceding from Ukraine, but for ascension into the Russian Federation.

On March 16, 2014, Crimea held the referendum, and overwhelmingly voted to join Russia. Over 95% of those who voted, voted in favor of joining Russia. Russia said that it would abide by the results of the referendum, while Western Europe refused to recognize the legitimacy and constitutionality of the referendum. Soon after the referendum, Russia officially annexed Crimea. These actions have made relations between the interim government of Ukraine and Russia extremely tense.

Ultimately, one of the arguments for Russia's military intervention in Ukraine was that they were worried that Ukraine would not abide by treaties that they had previously signed. While there are certainly other reasons for the conflict, the important role of treaties and treaty networks in this conflict should not be underestimated.

While Ukraine and Russia have often had a conflictual relationship since the collapse of the Soviet Union, Belarus and Russia have had a much more friendly relationship. I now turn to a discussion of the relationship between Belarus and Russia.

Russia-Belarus Relations

Following the collapse of the Soviet Union, Belarus became a buffer state between Russia and the West. While the Baltic states looked toward Europe and the West, Belarus had more difficulty in choosing its orientation. Once the Baltic states became members of the EU, Belarus became a border state between the EU to the west, and Russia to the east. While some in the West have seen Belarus as only cooperating with Russia and turning its back on Europe, others have argued that Belarus has had a pragmatic approach towards both the East and the West while not turning its back to either side (Allison, White, and Light 2005). In fact, Belarus signed a friendship and cooperation agreement with Poland in 1992, and joined the Central European Identity in 1994 (Burant 1995). It should be noted that Belarus first engaged Europe by signing the friendship and cooperation agreement with Poland in 1992, and then began to engage Russia by signing a friendship and cooperation agreement in 1995.

Despite engaging Europe, the Belarussian leadership knew that it had to engage Russia, and cautiously engaged Europe. Belorussian politicians even publicly acknowledged that although they wanted to engage Europe, they were were so dependent on Russia for their energy needs, that they did not want to hurt their relationship with Russia by engaging the EU (Burant 1995). The West was concerned with Belarus' reliance upon Russian oil and gas as well, and thought that Russia would use this to force Belarus to cede sovereignty to Russia (Allison, White, and Light 2005; Burant 1995; Cameron and Domański 2005; Dahl Martinsen 2002; Kanet, Miner, and Resler 1992; Oldberg 1997; Wallander 2007).

Although Belarussian President Alexander Lukashenko initially tried to manage relations with both East and West, his authoritarian policies began to frustrate the EU. The EU isolated Belarus, which only served to force Lukashenko to more actively engage Russia. Initially, Lukashenko's relationship with Russian President Boris Yeltsin was a cooperative one, however, the relations between Russian President Vladimir Putin and Lukashenko became strained. In fact, Putin became very cautious of engaging Lukashenko, and was not happy with the level of integration that had occurred between Belarus and Russia during the Yeltsin years (Burant 1995). Ultimately, both Russia and Belarus sought to engage one another and build a successful cooperative relationship. I now turn to a discussion of how Russia and Belarus built their successful relationship.

Russia-Belarus Treaty Networks

An analysis of the relationship between Belarus and Russia indeed shows that the two states were very actively engaged with one another (Table 2.5). Much like the relationship between Russia and Ukraine, Russia and Belarus mainly focused on economic issues, especially involving trade and natural resources.

Table 2.5.   Russia-Belarus Treaties by Issue Area (1991–2005)

Security	36
Economic	138
Integration	25
Total Bilateral Treaties	198*

*Some treaties address more than one issue area, so are classified in more than one category.

Analysis of the treaty network between Russia and Belarus shows how interconnected the relationship between Russia and Belarus became between 1991 and 2005 (Figure 2.2). Figure 2.2 shows that the most central treaties to the relationship are the Charter of the Bilateral Union, the Treaty on the Bilateral Union, and the Treaty on the New Bilateral Union. Specifically, they are the treaties that establish a bilateral union between Russia and Belarus and seek to integrate their economies and trade. For example, on the left hand side of Figure 2.2, the establishment of a monetary union between the two states figures prominently and is developed out of the Agreement on Trade and Economic Cooperation.

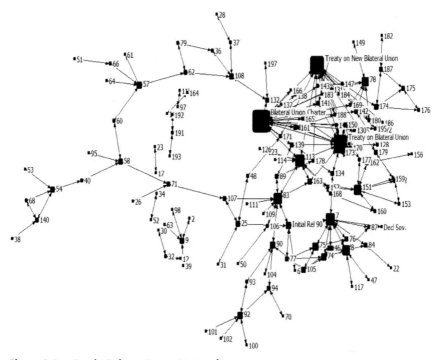

Figure 2.2.   Russia-Belarus Treaty Network

Figure 2.2 also shows the interconnectedness of the treaty network. Most of the economic treaties are located on the left of the Figure, while the security treaties are generally located on the bottom right of the Figure. While the treaties involve different issue areas and are located in different locations of the treaty network, nevertheless they are connected to each other through ties between the treaties, specifically through integrative treaties such as the Bilateral Union treaties.

Further examination of Figure 2.2 shows that the Belarus-Russia bilateral treaty network is fairly cohesive, meaning that there are few sub networks that are separated from the main treaty network. One notable exception is the network in the bottom left quadrant of Figure 2.2 that deals with the effects of the Chernobyl disaster and its after-effects. However, most of the networks are tied together into one main network. This shows a concerted effort by treaty negotiators to build a relationship over time and not just address specific issues in an ad hoc manner.

While Belarus and Russia have also had disagreements over natural resources, Belarus has been isolated from Europe by the European Union, and has had no other option but to develop a good relationship with Russia. It has especially pursued economic relations with Russia and has worked toward integration especially through trade. While Belarus, like Ukraine, is reliant upon Russian natural resources exports, it has developed a good enough relationship with Russia that it is unlikely that its supplies would be disrupted in any major disagreement between the two states.

Contrary to the enthusiastic approach to relationship building between Belarus and Russia, and the more cautious relationship building between Ukraine and Russia, Moldova was extremely wary of building any relationship with Russia. After the collapse of the Soviet Union, Moldova was very interested in turning to the West and leaving Russia's sphere of influence. I now turn to an examination of Russian-Moldovan relations.

Russian-Moldovan Relations

Like the relationship between Ukraine and Russia, the relationship between Russia and Moldova has always been problematic. Geographically, Moldova was a perfect buffer state between the East and the West. Western Moldova was constantly being fought over by both the Romanian Empire in the West, and the Russian Empire to the East. Western Moldova was often captured by one side or another, and thus changed hands between the two empires despite the fact that its culture and language more closely resembled Romanian than any Slavic language (King 1994, 1998, 1999). Being fought over by two empires caused the Moldovans to distrust empires and view them as expansionistic (Löwenhardt, Hill, and Light 2001). Following annexation by Russia in 1812, Moldova remained a part of the Russian Empire until 1918 when it again became a part of Romania.

As a result of the Molotov-Ribbentrop Pact, Moldova was assimilated by the Soviet Union in 1940 and remained a Soviet republic until the disintegration of the Soviet Union in 1991. It is important to note that modern day Transnistria was always a part of the Russian Empire and was not fought over as had been western Moldova. Thus, Transnistrians generally identified more with Russia than Romania.

Relations between Russia and Moldova reached new lows just before the breakup of the Soviet Union. Specifically, in 1989 Moldova declared Romanian its official state language (instead of Russian), and replaced Cyrllic letters with Roman letters. This law had the effect of signaling to both Moscow and Moldovan citizens that not only was there a strong ethnic tie between Moldova and Romania, but that Moldova was much closer to Romania than to the Russian republic. Indeed, there was a strong suggestion that Moldova might seek to unify with Romania. This issue and the general idea of becoming closer to Romania led to a cleavage along the boundary between east and west Moldova: between what is now the Republic of Moldova and Transnistria.

In 1989, a protest occurred in Transnistria. This protest against the government of Moldova evolved into a revolt by 1990, and by 1991, became a separatist movement. The separatist movement directly led to a civil war between Transnistria and the Republic of Moldova. The Soviet Union was said to have been conspiring against the Republic of Moldova by setting up bank accounts for the Transnistrians and also supplying them with weapons to help with their secessionist efforts (Kaufman and Bowers 1998; Kaufman 1996).

During the civil war, Transnistrians crossed the Dniester river and took control of Moldovan villages that were not in Transnistria. This event was called the "silent putsch" by Romanians (Chinn and Roper 1995). Further enflaming the separatist movement were elections that occurred in the spring of 1990, where the pro-Romania Popular Front party defeated the Moldovan Communist Party. One of the major issues that the Popular Front advocated for was for Moldova to become a part of Romania (Jackson 2003).

Relations between Moscow and Moldova significantly soured over both the revolt in Transnistria and the elections of 1990. By the time of the dissolution of the Soviet Union, neither state was very willing to form a cooperative relationship. Despite the fact that by 1992 Moldova no longer wanted to become a part of Romania and that Romanian nationalism in Moldova had transformed into Moldovan nationalism, there was a continuing deep mistrust of Russian intentions toward Moldova. However, Moldova was still economically dependent on Russia. Thus, when Russia threatened to stop trading with Moldova if it did not join the CIS Economic Union, Moldova had no choice but to reluctantly join the CIS Economic Union. While Moldova did join the CIS, it did so reluctantly, and publicly stated that it was doing so only to appease Russian interests. It made clear to Russia that Russia should not expect to have a cooperative relationship with Moldova, rather that they would cooperate only on economic interests that were vital to Moldova's survival.

An examination of Russian treaties with Moldova shows that Moldova engaged Russia in more economic treaties than either security or integration (see Table 2.6). In fact, as Table 2.6 shows, only approximately 20% of the treaties signed between Moldova and Russia addressed security needs, while over 40% of the treaties dealt with economic issues.

An analysis of the treaty network between Russia and Moldova shows that issues between the two states were addressed in an ad hoc manner (see

Table 2.6. Russia Moldova Treaties by Treaty Area (1991–2005)

Security	19
Economic	40
Integration	33
Total Bilateral Treaties	**92**

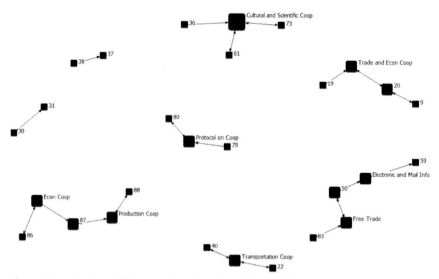

Figure 2.3.   Russia-Moldova Treaty Network (1991–2005)

Figure 2.3). Contrary to the treaty networks between Russia and Ukraine and Belarus, the treaty network between Russia and Moldova have no real connectivity in the treaty network. Each issue area might have a couple of treaties that are tied to a more central treaty, but there is no overarching architecture to the relationship. There is no coordination even among treaties dealing with the same issue area. For example, in Figure 2.3, the Trade and Economic Cooperation Treaty (upper right corner of the treaty network) is not tied to the Economic Cooperation Treaty (bottom left of the treaty network). This is more evidence in the ad hoc nature of cooperation between Russia and Moldova between 1991 and 2005.

Ultimately, the states in the European FSU approached cooperation with Russia in different fashion. While Belarus actively engaged Russia, Ukraine took a more cautious approach to cooperation, while Moldova disdainfully cooperated with Russia only on those issues which were vital to Moldova's interest. Slobodchikoff (2013b) argued that it was possible to measure the level of cooperation between bilateral states by dividing the number of treaty ties in a given relationship by the number of treaties. If the level of cooperation is greater than 1, then the relationship is a cooperative one. A score that is equal to 1 indicates a neutral relationship, while a score less than one indicates that the relationship is non-cooperative. The benefit of this measure is that it allows a direct comparison between relationships and allows scholars to determine which relationships are more cooperative and which are less comparative. Further, the relationship can be examined over time, which shows the dynamic nature of bilateral relationships. Table 2.7 compares each

Table 2.7.   Comparison of Levels of Cooperation between European
FSU and Russia (1991–2005)

Year	Ukraine	Belarus	Moldova
1991	0	0	0
1992	.62	.46	0
1993	.66	.61	.14
1994	.92	.81	.26
1995	1	1.17	.33
1996	1.04	1.33	.38
1997	1.15	1.36	.36
1998	1.18	1.56	.36
1999	1.24	1.66	.33
2000	1.36	1.75	.33
2001	1.39	1.82	.35
2002	1.42	1.80	.40
2003	1.47	1.83	.41
2004	1.53	1.80	.41
2005	1.53	1.80	.41
Average (1991–2005)	**1.10**	**1.32**	**.30**

of the European FSU states' relationship to Russia to compare levels of cooperation over time (see Table 2.7). As we can see by the results, both Ukraine and Belarus developed cooperative relationships with Russia, while Moldova always remained uncooperative. Both Ukraine and Belarus developed a cooperative relationship by 1995. Further, it is possible to ascertain that the relationship between Belarus and Russia was slightly more cooperative than the relationship between Ukraine and Russia. This is not a great surprise given the high levels of mistrust that the Ukrainians have for Russia.

Ultimately, the European FSU is extremely important to Russian interests in the region. Not only does it import the majority of its energy needs from Russia, but it also serves as a buffer region between Russia and Europe. Most of the natural gas pipelines that supply energy to Europe pass through the European FSU. Further, Western Europe has shown interest in expanding their influence into the European FSU. Thus, it is an extremely important region for Russian strategic interests. However, it should be noted that while the states in the European FSU must definitely take Russian interests into account, they can choose their level of cooperation. All of the states in the European FSU have distinct strategic interests that can be achieved through cooperation with Russia, yet each state must decide what level of cooperation with Russia they are comfortable with. While Belarus was very comfortable with a high level of cooperation with Russia, Ukraine was a little more wary. However, Ukraine still had a high level of cooperation with Russia, just not as high as Belarus did with Russia. Finally, Moldova was extremely hesitant to

cooperate with Russia on any level, and developed an uncooperative relationship with Russia. I now turn to an examination of other geographical regions
in the post-Soviet space and their degree of cooperation with Russia. I will
first examine the Southern Caucasus region.

SOUTHERN CAUCASUS REGION

The Southern Caucasus region of the FSU contains Armenia, Azerbaijan, and
Georgia. The post-Soviet history for each of these states is problematic, and
often violent. For example, Armenia and Azerbaijan fought a war over the
Nagorno-Karabakh region, which could still flare up at any time. Georgia,
on the other hand, fought a civil war, and has had problems with secessionist
movements in Abkhazia and South Ossetia.

Russia's interests in the region have been strategic both in terms of energy
and also geopolitical in nature. As Table 2.8 shows, Armenia imported an average 73% of its total energy consumed, Georgia imported an average of 62%
of its total energy consumed, while Azerbaijan exported an average of 40%
of its total energy consumed between 1991 and 2005. In the case of Armenia
and Georgia, they needed to import their energy from Russia, while Azerbaijan needed access to Russian gas pipelines to export its energy. Thus, all of
the states in the region needed Russia to achieve their strategic energy goals.

Table 2.8.   Southern Caucasus Region Average Energy Imports and Exports
(1991–2005)

State	Avg Imported Energy (%)	Avg Exported Energy (%)
Armenia	73	—
Azerbaijan	—	40
Georgia	62	—

Russia's interests in the region are much more than just energy. The Southern Caucasus is a very ethnically and religiously diverse region. For example,
approximately 90% of the population of Armenia is Armenian Orthodox
Christian, 75% of the population of Georgia is either Georgian or Russian
Orthodox Christian, and 93% of the population of Azerbaijan is Muslim.
Linguistically, the languages of the region are very different. The Armenian
language is an Indo-European language with influences from Greek and its
own unique alphabet. The Azeri language is a Turkish language, and the
Georgian language is classified as a Kartvelian language with its own unique
alphabet and number system. None of the languages are Slavic in origin.

From a geopolitical standpoint, the Southern Caucasus region is a buffer region between Russia to the north, and Iran and Afghanistan to the south. Further, the Southern Caucasus region is close to Chechnya and Dagestan in Russia, where Russia has been fighting secessionist movements and terrorist groups. Fighters have travelled from Iran and Afghanistan to Chechnya to help fight the Russians in the two Chechen wars. Thus, from a security standpoint, the South Caucasus region is vital to Russian interests. I now turn to a more focused discussion of the relations between Russia and each of the states in the Southern Caucasus region of the FSU.

RUSSIAN-ARMENIAN RELATIONS

Russia had long been a guarantor of Armenian sovereignty and security interests. Before the collapse of the Soviet Union, the Russian Socialist Republic and the Armenian Socialist Republic had a very good relationship. At the time of the collapse of the Soviet Union, while many of the states in the European FSU wanted to distance themselves from Russia's influence, Armenia wanted to create a positive relationship with Russia. Not only would a positive relationship with Russia strengthen its own security interests in the South Caucasus Region, but it would also enhance its standing against Azerbaijan in the conflict over Nagorno-Karabakh, which had broken out following the collapse of the Soviet Union. The war in Nagorno-Karabakh not only constituted an interstate war between Armenia and Azerbaijan, but also a war of secession, where Nagorno-Karabakh was trying to secede from Azerbaijan and be annexed by Armenia.

Russia's interests in developing its relationship with Armenia was to reassert its natural leadership role in the region and to establish a buffer region between its own borders and Iran and Afghanistan. It has therefore been motivated to continue its historically positive relationship with Armenia.

From the earliest post-Soviet days, Armenia pursued intensive bilateral negotiations with Russia. At the heart of these efforts was the ongoing Nagorno-Karabakh conflict, which had reemerged in the late Soviet period and which had drawn Russian mediation efforts from the early post-Soviet days. Armenia signed an all-important Treaty of Friendship and Cooperation with Russia (December 29, 1991), a document that included security arrangements reflective of bilateral goals set by the two sides. This treaty spelled out the principles of bilateral cooperation between the two countries. By the time Armenia signed a second friendship treaty with Russia in 1997, it had signed a plethora of other bilateral treaties with Russia. Moreover, this second friendship treaty was made all the more credible by being nested in other bilateral agreements such as the Treaty on the Russian Military Base on Armenian Territory.

Armenia was the most active Caucasus state in engaging Russia, signing 145 (Table 2.9). Initially, the focus of these treaties was military cooperation (e.g., transfer of FSU military equipment to Armenia, establishment of the legal status of Russian military forces on Armenian soil, and cooperation on the protection of CIS external borders) as well as the establishment of trade. Within a few years, however, this had widened to many related issues (e.g., cooperation in internal affairs, the defense industry, measures for emergency situations, and conduct of industrial military transportation for the defense of CIS members' external borders). In 1996, a treaty on the establishment of a Russian military base on Armenian territory signifies much stronger bilateral ties, with subsequent nested agreements addressing various aspects of the bases' operation. Especially suggestive of the burgeoning bilateral security relationship was the increased number of cooperative agreements on the joint training of Armenian and Russian troops, mutual planning of joint military operations, and mutual use of the countries' increasingly interconnected military infrastructure. These agreements, sometimes nested in other bilateral or CIS multilateral agreements, demonstrated increased cooperation not only in the sphere of military assistance, but also in the development of joint procedures for military operations of the two countries' armies. Further, as the relationship continued to grow, Russia and Armenia signed several treaties involving alleviating Armenia's debt to Russia in exchange for ownership of companies and industries that had been owned by Armenia's government.

Table 2.9.   Armenia-Russia Treaty Issues

Security	42
Economic	65
Integration	35
Total Bilateral Treaties	**145***

*Three of the treaties do not adhere to these classifications. Thus, the number of bilateral treaties signed are more than the sum of these three categories.

An analysis of the treaty network shows that there is one major sub-network (see Figure 2.4). As Figure 2.4 shows, the two Friendship Treaties provide the basis for most of the bilateral relationship between the two states. The Russian Military Base Treaty of 1996 is one of the most central treaties in their relationship, indicating the importance of security to Russia in the region. The small sub-network at the top of Figure 2.4 mainly has treaties addressing the alleviation of Armenian debt to Russia. On the left of the figure are issues that were important but not vital to building their relationship over time.

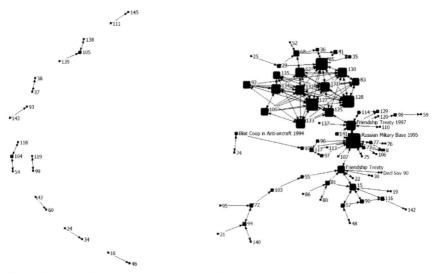

Figure 2.4. Russia-Armenia Treaty Network

Ultimately Russia and Armenia developed a mutually beneficial relation-ship over time. They cooperated over many different issue areas, and devel-oped a successful treaty network which led to mutual cooperation. While their motivations for cooperation were different, they created a mutual understand-ing for cooperation within the region. Armenia used Russia to bolster its posi-tion within the region especially vis-à-vis Azerbaijan. Russia was also able to develop a close ally and ensure its security in the region. I now turn to a more problematic relationship in the Southern Caucasus Region, specifically that of Russia's relations with Azerbaijan.

RUSSIAN-AZERI RELATIONS

While Russia and Armenia had a relatively positive relationship follow-ing the collapse of the Soviet Union, the relationship between Russia and Azerbaijan was much more complex. Russia's support of Armenia in the Nagorno-Karabakh led to more problematic relations between the two coun-tries (Lynch 2002; Tokluoglu 2011). Due to the special relationship between Russia and Armenia, Azerbaijan was very reluctant to cooperate with Russia (see Table 2.10).

As Table 2.10 shows, Azerbaijan was very reluctant to engage Russia and sign any treaties. They only signed 78 treaties as opposed to the 145 treaties signed by Armenia and Russia. The one area that Azerbaijan and Russia were able to cooperate on was economic issues and trade. This was mainly due to

Table 2.10.   Russian-Azeri Bilateral Treaties
by Issue Area

Security	23
Economic	40
Integration	16
Total Bilateral Treaties	**78***

*Certain treaties can address more than one issue area.
Thus, the total number of bilateral treaties signed is
not just the sum of the issue areas.

the fact that Azerbaijan needed Russian assistance in exporting its natural gas
to markets (Kjaernet 2010).

Azerbaijan and Russia cooperated in a very ad hoc manner, cooperating
on issues of mutual benefit without trying to build a cooperative relationship
(see Figure 2.5). As Figure 2.5 shows, while the Friendship and Cooperation
Treaty of 1992 and the Friendship and Cooperation Treaty of 1997 are central
to two different sub-networks, there is no tie between them. There is no con-
nection between the various sub-networks, indicating a reluctance to build a
relationship based on previous agreements.

While there was cooperation in economic issues, there was very little integrated cooperation dealing with security issues. Most of the security treaties
were stand-alone treaties that addressed individual issues, but did not build
toward a relationship. Overall, Figure 2.5 shows a relationship that shows
some cooperation, but is strained and has little hope of evolving into a cooperative relationship in the future. It is interesting to note that most of the

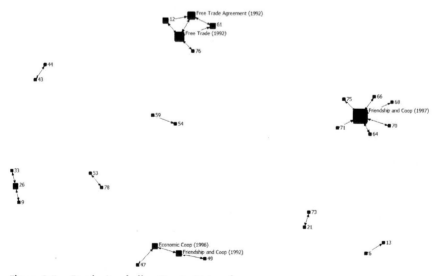

Figure 2.5.   **Russia-Azerbaijan Treaty Network**

limited cooperation ended around 1997, with the Friendship and Cooperation Treaty. That is not to say that there weren't treaties signed after 1997, merely that the treaties signed after 1997 tended to be stand alone treaties, and not part of building a relationship between Russia and Azerbaijan. I now turn to another problematic relationship in the Southern Caucasus Region, specifically the relationship between Georgia and Russia.

RUSSIAN-GEORGIAN RELATIONS

Russian-Georgian relations are most known for the war that occurred between them in 2008. However, even before that conflict, relations between the two states were strained. Russia had helped secessionist movements in South Ossetia and Abkhazia, and had stationed troops in these regions during the Georgian Civil War. These troops created de facto states in South Ossetia and Abkhazia, which only exacerbated the problems between them.

Between 1991 and 2005, Georgia and Russia signed 92 bilateral treaties. Interestingly, they signed almost as many security treaties as they did economic treaties (see Table 2.11). This is mainly due to the conflict and civil war which occurred in Georgia following the fall of the Soviet Union.

Table 2.11.   Russia-Georgia Bilateral Treaty Issue Areas

Security	30
Economic	39
Integration	26
Total Bilateral Treaties	**92***

*Certain treaties can address more than one issue area. Thus, the total number of bilateral treaties signed is not just the sum of the issue areas.

Many of the bilateral treaties addressed issues such as loans from Russia to Georgia as well as other issues such as the presence of Russian troops on Georgian territory (Figure 2.6). Similar to the case of the bilateral relationship between Moldova and Russia as well as Azerbaijan and Russia, there is an ad hoc approach to managing bilateral relations. Each sub network within the bilateral relationship addresses a different issue area, with no links between the issue areas. For example, on the bottom left of Figure 2.6, there is a sub network of treaties addressing the legal status of Russian forces on the territory of Georgia. All of these treaties address specific Russian forces that are present in Georgia such as Russian naval forces etc., Russian monetary support for these forces, jurisdiction over Russian soldiers, and Russia's ability to legally fly over Georgian air space. It is important to note that despite the fact that each of

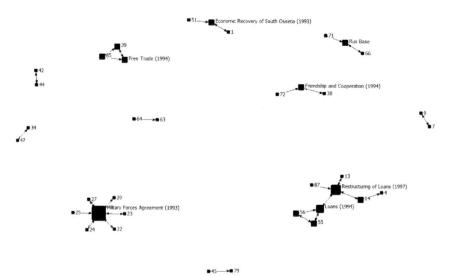

Figure 2.6. Russia-Georgia Treaty Network

these treaties are linked to the legal status of Russian forces treaty, they are not linked to the other treaty networks in the bilateral relationship.

Ultimately, the relationship between Russia and Georgia devolved into conflict. That is not to say that there was not some effort at conflict management between the two states, merely that Russia and Georgia were not able to build an effective relationship.

The Southern Caucasus Region is a very contentious region in post-Soviet space. While there were strategic goals that could have been achieved by all of the states in the region by cooperating with Russia, only Armenia actively pursued cooperation with Russia. Both Azerbaijan and Georgia were not able to build a cooperative relationship. Using the measure developed by Slobodchikoff (2013b), we can compare the relationships of each of the states in the region with Russia (see Table 2.12). Table 2.12 shows that by 2005, that only the relationship between Armenia and Russia was cooperative. The relationship between Azerbaijan and Georgia never got above the 1.0 threshold required for a relationship to be considered cooperative. Further, as Slobodchikoff (2013b) argues, it is much more likely for conflict to occur before the threshold is reached. Therefore, it would not be surprising to see more conflict between Russia and Georgia or Russia and Azerbaijan. This is especially worrisome if there is a flare-up in the conflict over the Nagorno-Karabakh region. While Azerbaijan was a weaker party during the initial conflict, it has been greatly strengthened through its wealth of natural resources,

Table 2.12.   Levels of Cooperation with Russia in Southern Caucasus Region by 2005

	Armenia	Azerbaijan	Georgia
Level of Cooperation	1.84	.56	.60

and now has a much stronger military. This situation is very troubling for the Southern Caucasus Region. I now turn to a discussion of the final region in the post-Soviet space, specifically the Central Asia Region.

CENTRAL ASIA REGION

In December 1991, Russia, Belarus and Ukraine met in Minsk and created the CIS. None of the Central Asian states had been invited to join. Yet the leaders of the newly independent Central Asian states met in Ashkhabad (the capital of Turkmenistan) and decided that despite the fact that they were not initially invited, that joining the CIS would be the best way to transition to independence (Olcott 1991, 2009). The next meeting of the CIS was then held in the Kazakh capital of Alma-Ata, where the former Soviet republics were declared sovereign states responsible for their own sovereignty, which included being responsible for their own natural resources. This declaration was extremely important for the states in the Central Asia Region, as they all had a wealth of natural gas reserves.

The Caspian Sea region has tremendous wealth in both oil and natural gas. Of these states, Kazakhstan had the largest energy reserves, with the potential of producing sixty five billion barrels of oil per year, second only in the region to Russia, which had the potential of producing ninety nine billion barrels of oil per year (Kalicki 2001). These vast energy reserves urged Western businesses, policy makers, and scholars to urge the United States to develop closer ties with Kazakhstan to try and lessen Western reliance on Russian energy (Alexandrov 1999; Allison 2004; Bahgat 2002; Macfarlane 2004). Despite the fact that many Western companies bought interests in some of the oil wells in Kazakhstan, the United States was largely unsuccessful in convincing Kazakhstan to lessen Russia's influence in the region by building pipelines that bypassed Russia. Instead, Kazakhstan was interested in actively engaging Russia and largely keeping the status quo by using pipelines going through Russia. Kazakhstan was not the only country in the region to have vast oil and gas reserves, but it was the country that had the most. I now turn to a discussion of relations between each of the states in the region with Russia beginning with relations between Russia and Kazakhstan.

RUSSIAN-KAZAKH RELATIONS

The West was mainly interested in Kazakhstan for its energy sources. However, Russia had more diverse interests in maintaining a cooperative bilateral relationship with Kazakhstan. Its interests were both economic and in security. Russia's main security interest was the Baikonur Cosmodrome, where all of the rockets for the space program were launched during Soviet times. While Russia could have built the infrastructure to maintain their space program and launch rockets from within Russia, the investment would have been extremely costly in terms of time and resources. Since the infrastructure was already intact in Kazakhstan, it was within Russia's strategic interests to maintain a cooperative relationship that would allow Russia to continue to have access to that vital infrastructure. In addition, Kazakhstan had nuclear weapons, and Russia was interested in ensuring their removal from Kazakhstan to Russia.

Kazakhstan was also extremely important to Russia's geopolitical strategy. Kazakhstan shares borders with many Islamic states. It is not far from Afghanistan. The geographical location of Kazakhstan offers an important buffer zone from those states that have many terrorists, and Russia wanted to ensure that the volatile situation to the south of Kazakhstan did not spread through Kazakhstan to Russia. These geopolitical interests pressed Russia to create a cooperative relationship with Kazakhstan.

An examination of the relationship between Russia and Kazakhstan highlights the importance of Kazakhstan as a geopolitical relationship that was vital to Russian security interests (see Table 2.13). While all of the previous bilateral relationships examined in this chapter have focused more on economic issues than security issues, the relationship between Russia and Kazakhstan clearly favored security issues. That is not to say that economic issues were not important to their relationship, as 85 of the treaties addressed economic issues.

An analysis of the treaty network between Kazakhstan and Russia shows that they indeed were very actively engaged (Figure 2.7). Figure 2.7 shows that some important treaties are central to the relationship between Kazakh-

Table 2.13.   Russia-Kazakhstan Bilateral
Treaties by Issue Area

Security	96
Economic	85
Integration	39
Total Bilateral Treaties	**203**

*Certain treaties can address more than one issue area. Thus, the total number of bilateral treaties signed is not just the sum of the issue areas.

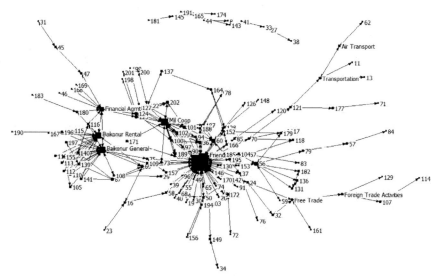

Figure 2.7. Russia-Kazakhstan Treaty Network

stan and Russia. Specifically the Friendship and Cooperation treaty is the most central treaty in the relationship. Contrary to Ukraine, which signed a friendship and cooperation treaty with Russia in 1997, Kazakhstan signed the Treaty of Friendship and Cooperation in May, 1992. Moreover, a great many treaties that followed the treaty constantly were nested within the Treaty of Friendship and Cooperation, giving it paramount importance in the relationship.

A further analysis of Figure 2.7 shows the importance of the Baikonur Cosmodrome to both Russia and Kazakhstan. Two important treaties dealing with Baikonur are central to the relationship. The first, labeled as Baikonur General in Figure 2.7 lays out the conditions of Russian forces using the cosmodrome for launching rockets and as a center for Russia's space program. The second central treaty dealing with Baikonur is labeled as Baikonur Rental in Figure 2.7. This treaty details the conditions and the amount of rent that Russia must pay to Kazakhstan to maintain control of the Baikonur Cosmodrome.

Figure 2.7 also shows how treaties addressing different issue areas fit into the treaty networks. For example, in addition to the treaties addressing Baikonur on the left of Figure 2.7, financial agreements related to military forces and the Agreement on Military Cooperation are also on the left side of the figure. On the right side of Figure 2.7 (closer to the bottom right) are a subset of the treaty network addressing trade treaties such as the Free Trade Treaty and the Agreement on Foreign Trade Activities. These treaties deal with minimizing tariffs on trade and addressing imports and exports between

Kazakhstan and Russia. The Agreement on Foreign Trade Activities deals
with how each state approaches trade in terms of third parties, specifically
CIS member states, in addition to agreeing how to address third party products that come through either Russia or Kazakhstan before being imported
into either one of the two states.

In the upper right corner of Figure 2.7 are treaties that address transportation. While the trade treaties in the lower right of the figure discussed
transportation of goods for import and export, the transportation treaties in
the upper right of the figure specifically addressed not only transportation of
goods, but also transportation for citizens.

Figure 2.7 illustrates the importance of the Treaty of Friendship and Cooperation between Kazakhstan and Russia. The treaty is not only the most
central treaty to this bilateral relationship, but it also is the treaty that allows
the deepening and extending of cooperation in different issue areas. Each of
the major issue areas (economic, security, and integrative) are connected by
treaty ties through the Treaty on Friendship and Cooperation.

Ultimately, the relationship between Russia and Kazakhstan has proven
to be extremely cooperative. The cohesiveness of the main treaty sub-
network illustrates the active effort of both Kazakhstan and Russia to build
a relationship as opposed to handling issues in an ad hoc manner. Kazakhstan was vital to Russia's strategic interests, and Russia was central to
Kazakhstan's regional interests. I now turn to examining the relationship
between Russia and Kyrgyzstan.

RUSSIAN-KYRGYZ RELATIONS

Contrary to the emphasis on security in the relationship between Russia and
Kazakhstan, the relationship between Russia and Kyrgyzstan was focused
more on economic issue areas than security (see Table 2.14). Further, as Table 2.14 shows, there were only 126 bilateral treaties signed between the two
countries as opposed to the 203 that were signed between Russia and Kazakhstan. Interestingly, many of the economic treaties between Kyrgyzstan and

**Table 2.14.   Russia-Kyrgyzstan Treaties by
Issue Area**

Security	34
Economic	53
Integration	40
Total Bilateral Treaties	**126***

*Certain treaties can address more than one issue area.
  Thus, the total number of bilateral treaties signed is
  not just the sum of the issue areas.

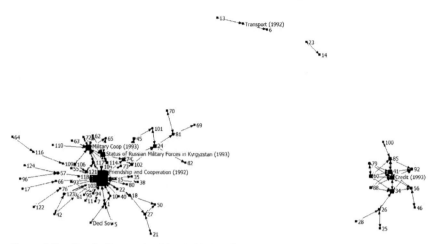

Figure 2.8. Russia-Kyrgyzstan Treaty Network

Russia mainly addressed loans from Russia to Kyrgyzstan, while the security treaties mainly addressed the status of Russian troops in Kyrgyzstan and the usage of Russian military hardware by the Kyrgyz military (see Figure 2.8).

As Figure 2.8 shows, there are two distinct sub-networks which make up the Russia-Kyrgyzstan treaty network. One is the main treaty network at the bottom left of the figure which includes the Friendship and Cooperation Treaty of 1992, as well as the security treaties which dealt with Russian troops being stationed on Kyrgyz territory and a treaty on military cooperation between Russia and Kyrgyzstan. Both of these security treaties were signed in 1993. The second main sub-network addresses loans and credit provided by Russia to Kyrgyzstan. Ultimately, the treaty network is relatively cohesive, and demonstrate an effort by both states to create a cooperative bilateral relationship. While the relationship was not quite as cooperative as that between Russia and Kazakhstan, nevertheless, it was a cooperative relationship instead of an ad hoc relationship. I now turn to a discussion of the relationship between Russia and Tajikistan.

RUSSIAN-TAJIK RELATIONS

The relationship between Russia and Tajikistan is similar to that of Russia and Kyrgyzstan. Clearly, Russia and Kazakhstan developed the best relationship in the Central Asian region, but the relationship between Russia and Tajikistan is nevertheless positive. An examination of the treaty areas addressed between the two states shows that Russia and Tajikistan mainly pursed issues related to economics (Table 2.15). Russia and Tajikistan signed far fewer

Table 2.15.   Russia-Tajikistan Bilateral
Treaty Issue Areas (1991–2005)

Security	28
Economic	43
Integration	24
Total Bilateral Treaties	**93***

*Certain treaties can address more than one issue area.
Thus, the total number of bilateral treaties signed is
not just the sum of the issue areas.

bilateral treaties than Russia and Kazakhstan. The main issue areas addressed in the economic treaties had to do with government debt and credit, while the main issue areas addressed in the security treaties had to do with the stationing of Russian troops in Tajikistan and the legal status of those forces while in Tajikistan.

An examination of the Russia-Tajikistan treaty network shows three main sub-networks (see Figure 2.9). Interestingly, despite the fact that Russia and Tajikistan focused mainly on economic treaties, the main sub-network on the right side of Figure 2.9 focuses on security issues such as the Military and Co-operation Treaty of 1993, the Treaty on the Legal Status of Russian Military Forces Stationed in Tajikistan (1993) and the Status of the Russian Military in Tajikistan (1999). One of the most central treaties to the treaty network is the Friendship and Cooperation Treaty (1993). Interestingly, this treaty is part of the sub-network involving security issues on the right side of Figure 2.9. This runs counter to the treaty network between Russia and Kazakhstan (Figure 2.7), where the Friendship and Cooperation Treaty was the basis for all of the treaties in the treaty network and brought together the various issue areas into one cohesive network.

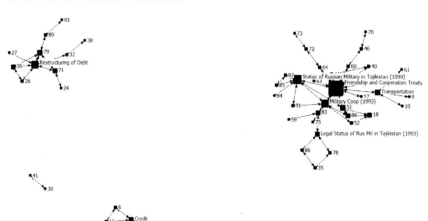

Figure 2.9.   Russia-Tajikistan Treaty Network

Further analysis shows that two of the sub-networks in the relationship deal with loans and credit from Russia to Tajikistan. The sub-network on the bottom of Figure 2.9 deals with Russia providing credit to Tajikistan, and the sub-network on the top left of Figure 2.9 addresses a restructuring of that debt. It is interesting that these sub-networks are not tied to each other since they address similar issues in the relationship. Further, it is also surprising that these sub-networks are not connected to the Friendship and Coopera-tion Treaty, which should serve as the most central treaty to the relationship, which sets the tone for the whole relationship. Finally, it is important to note that while the most central treaties in the relationship between Russia and Kazakhstan all were signed very early in their relationship, the Agreement on the Status of the Russian Military in Tajikistan was signed in 1999, which is much later than most of the central treaties. This indicates that the relation-ship between the states continued to evolve and change even as Russia had already built its relationship with other states in the region. I now turn to an examination of the least engaged relationship in the Central Asian region, specifically the relationship between Russia and Turkmenistan.

RUSSIAN-TURKMENI RELATIONS

Turkmenistan is a state that is much like Kazakhstan and the other states in Central Asia. It is located in the Caspian Sea region, and has an abundance of resources. Although Turkmenistan has fewer possible oil and natural gas wells than Kazakhstan, nevertheless Turkmenistan has tremendous reserves and is able to export large amounts of energy (Kalicki 2001). Despite pressure on Turkmenistan to try to build pipelines that bypass Russia, Turkmenistan chose to cooperate with Russia rather than anger Russia by choosing to en-gage Western interests over cooperating with Russia.

While Russia had many security interests in Kazakhstan such as maintain-ing access to the Baikonur Cosmodrome, Russia did not have the same level of security interests in Turkmenistan. There was no Russian military base within Turkmenistan's borders, and Turkmenistan wasn't as geographically strategically important to Russia as Kazakhstan. While Kazakhstan was cen-tral to Russian security and economic strategy, Turkmenistan was only im-portant to Russian strategic economic interests. Thus, it should be no surprise that there are less treaties in the bilateral relationship between Russia and Turkmenistan than there are between Russia and Kazakhstan.

Turkmenistan also wanted to be cautious toward Russia. While it wanted to maintain a relationship with Russia, it also wanted to be very independent of Russia's influence. Turkmenistan wanted to be seen as a "neutral" regional actor, where it could engage its neighbors on necessary issues, but not get entangled in any arrangements that were not of its own choosing. It was not hostile to any of its neighbors, but nevertheless had more of an isolationist mentality than Kazakhstan. In other words, Turkmenistan wanted to cautiously engage and cooperate with Russia, but it wanted to do so on its own terms. It could achieve selective cooperation in areas that it needed to cooperate without becoming over engaged.

An analysis of the issue areas addressed in the relationship between Russia and Turkmenistan illustrates the "neutral" approach toward Russia. Russia and Turkmenistan signed virtually equal numbers of bilateral treaties dealing with economic issues as security issues (see Table 2.16). This is surprising given that all of the other states in the region either signed more treaties related to security issues or more related to economic issues.

Table 2.16.   Russia-Turkmenistan Bilateral
Treaty Issue Areas (1991–2005)

Security	28
Economic	29
Integration	21
Total Bilateral Treaties	**77***

*Certain treaties can address more than one issue area.
 Thus, the total number of bilateral treaties signed is
 not just the sum of the issue areas.

An analysis of the bilateral treaty network between Russia and Turkmenistan shows that there was a deliberative and careful approach to relationship building between the two states (Figure 2.10). There are in fact two significant sub-networks. The main sub-network on the right side of Figure 2.10 addresses most of the issue areas addressed in the bilateral relationship. It should be noted that the Friendship and Cooperation Treaty is not the most central treaty to the relationship, rather the Treaty on the Inheritance of the Debt from the Soviet Union, where Russia assumed the Soviet Union's debt is the most central treaty to the relationship between Russia and Turkmenistan. Further, it should be noted that treaties addressing both security and economic issues are part of the main sub-network.

The second significant sub-network addresses Turkmenistan's debt to Russia. While the Debt Treaty is central to this sub-network, the most important sub-network is the one that is located on the right side of Figure 2.10. It should be noted that despite the low number of bilateral treaties signed between Russia and Turkmenistan, they built a fairly cohesive treaty network and built a cooperative, if cautious, relationship. I now turn to an examination of the relationship between Russia and the final Central Asian state, Uzbekistan.

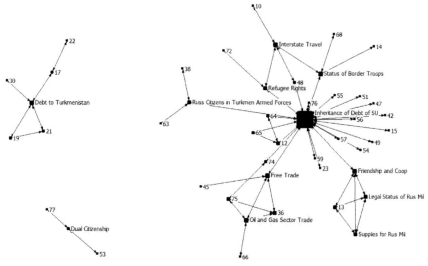

Figure 2.10.   Russia-Turkmenistan Treaty Network (1991–2005)

RUSSIAN-UZBEKI RELATIONS

The relationship between Russia and Uzbekistan was much more engaged than that between Russia and Turkmenistan. While they didn't sign as many treaties as Russia and Kazakhstan, nevertheless they signed more bilateral treaties than the other states in Central Asia did with Russia. While Kazakhstan was vital to Russian security interests, Uzbekistan was also important to Russia's economic interests. Thus, it is no surprise that Russia and Uzbekistan signed many more treaties that addressed economic issues than security issues (see Table 2.17).

Table 2.17.   Russia-Uzbekistan Bilateral Treaty Issue Areas (1991–2005)

Security	34
Economic	43
Integration	32
Total Bilateral Treaties	**109**

An examination of the treaty network between Russia and Uzbekistan shows that there is one main sub-network (see Figure 2.11). The main sub-network is on the right side of Figure 2.11, and combines both security and economic issues. For example, the Military Cooperation Treaty (1994) is in the same sub-network as the Economic Integration Treaty of 1994. Both Russia and Uzbekistan worked to build a cooperative relationship, and built

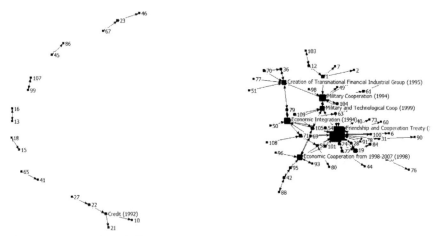

Figure 2.11.   Russia-Uzbekistan Treaty Network (1991–2005)

upon prior treaties. It is interesting to note that the treaty network shows that the centralized treaties were not all in the early years of the relationship. For example, the Economic Cooperation from 1998–2007 Treaty was signed in 1998, and the Creation of a Transnational Financial-Industrial Group was signed in 1995. In other words, the relationship consistently evolved over the time period from 1991 to 2005.

Turning to the Central Asian region as a whole, we can compare the level of cooperation of the bilateral relationships in the region using the measure proposed by Slobodchikoff (2013b) (Table 2.18). As Table 2.18 shows, the highest level of cooperation was between Russia and Kazakhstan, while the lowest level of cooperation was between Russia and Tajikistan. Contrary to the other regions in the post-Soviet space, there is no uncooperative bilateral relationship between Russia and any of the states in the Central Asian region. All of the relationships are greater than 1.0 on the level of cooperation measure, which indicate that all of the relationships are cooperative.

Ultimately, there is some regional variance in building cooperative relations among the states in the post-Soviet space. It is possible to analyze the level of cooperation among states and examine the regions to determine if

Table 2.18.   Central Asian Levels of Cooperation with Russia (1991–2005)

Bilateral Relationship	Number of Treaties Signed	Level of Cooperation
Russia-Kazakhstan	203	2.07
Russia-Kyrgyzstan	126	1.72
Russia-Uzbekistan	109	1.47
Russia-Turkmenistan	77	1.43
Russia-Tajikistan	93	1.31

Table 2.19.   Levels of Cooperation with Russia by Region in the Post-Soviet Space (1991–2005)

Bilateral Relationship	Level of Cooperation	Region
Russia-Kazakhstan	2.07	Central Asia
Russia-Armenia	1.84	Southern Caucasus
Russia-Belarus	1.80	European FSU
Russia-Kyrgyzstan	1.72	Central Asia
Russia-Ukraine	1.53	European FSU
Russia-Uzbekistan	1.47	Central Asia
Russia-Turkmenistan	1.43	Central Asia
Russia-Tajikistan	1.31	Central Asia
Russia-Georgia	.60	Southern Caucasus
Russia-Azerbaijan	.56	Southern Caucasus
Russia-Moldova	.41	European FSU

some regions are more problematic in cooperating with Russia than other regions (see Table 2.19). Table 2.19 creates a clear delineation between those relationships that are cooperative and those that can lead to conflictual relations. It is interesting to note that no Central Asian state has conflictual relations with Russia, while the Southern Caucasus region was the most problematic region in the post-Soviet space with two of the three states in the region having conflictual relations with Russia. Finally, it should be noted that Russia has created a cooperative relationship with at least one of the states in each region to ensure its regional presence in the post-Soviet space. As Table 2.19 shows, Russia's three most cooperative relationships are in each of the regions identified. In other words, Russia chose one state in each region that it had to have a cooperative relationship with so that it could build a regional security architecture.

Russia's approach to building its regional security architecture required it to develop cooperative bilateral relations with its neighbor states. However, it had to overcome great obstacles to building its relations with these states. First of all, it had to overcome the legacy of the Soviet Union, where it was distrusted by most of the states in the former Soviet Union. Second, Russia had to overcome the problem of power asymmetry. Despite the fact that Russia was the most powerful actor in the post-Soviet region, it could not build a regional security architecture on its own. It needed the cooperation of the other states in the FSU to achieve this regional security architecture.

Russia was able to overcome issues of mistrust and power asymmetry by creating these treaty networks of legalized treaties. By initiating these treaty networks, states in the region felt more secure in their relationship with Russia, and were more willing to build a cooperative relationship with Russia. This was certainly not the case with all of the states in the FSU.

While many of the states in the post-Soviet space chose to cooperate with Russia, three states cooperated only under extreme pressure, and really didn't develop a cooperative bilateral relationship. Those three states were Moldova, Georgia, and Azerbaijan.

Ultimately, Russia's strategy for creating a regional security architecture cannot only encompass bilateral relations in the FSU. It also had to create multilateral organizations that would help to create a regional security architecture. In fact, there are more multilateral organizations in the post-Soviet space than there are in any other region in the world (Volgy et al. 2008). While many scholars have been dismissive of the effectiveness of multilateral organization in the FSU (see Hansen 2013; Kramer 2008; Kubicek 1999, 2009; Miller and Toritsyn 2005; Olcott, Aslund, and Garnett 1999), I argue that multilateral organizations were vital to creating a regional security architecture. In the next chapter, I will discuss the main multilateral organizations in the post-Soviet space and discuss their strategic importance to Russia's regional security interests.

NOTE

1. A fourth geographical region of the FSU would be the Baltic States. However, they have become members of the EU, and self-selected out of the post-Soviet region. For that reason, they are not included in this analysis.

Chapter Three

Multilateral Relations in the Post-Soviet Space

While the previous chapter focused on bilateral relations between Russia and the former Soviet states, it is important to note that bilateral relations makes up only part of the security architecture of the post-Soviet space. As Russia is the regional hegemon, there must be some foreign policy vision that can tie together its relations with each of the states in the FSU. While not all of the states equally engage Russia and Russia's interests might not be the same in each of the FSU states, nevertheless, there must be some overarching goal of Russia's foreign and security policy towards these states. While effective bilateral relationships are one of the parts of creating a security architecture in the post-Soviet space, the bilateral relationships must be tied together by some grander architecture. In this book, I argue that Russia's multilateral organizations help to coordinate Russia's bilateral relations, and tie the relations together into a regional security architecture. The majority of scholars studying the post-Soviet space focus on Russia's bilateral relations with individual states and claim that the multilateral organizations in the post-Soviet space are not very important in regional governance, and are not very effective organizations (i.e. Hansen 2013; Kramer 2008; Kubicek 1999, 2009). Yet, there are more multilateral organizations in the post-Soviet space than in any other region in the world (Volgy et al. 2008). The puzzle then becomes, if there are so many multilateral organizations in the post-Soviet space, why do scholars believe that they are not important to the security architecture of the post-Soviet space. While I will specifically address the importance of multilateral organizations to the security architecture, in this chapter I will discuss the multilateral organizations in the post-Soviet space. I will first discuss general theories on multilateral organizations (specifically International Governmental Organizations), and then will discuss the main multilateral organizations in the post-Soviet states.

INTERNATIONAL GOVERNMENTAL
ORGANIZATIONS (IGO'S)

Much of the past debate between neoliberal institutionalists and realists has focused on whether or not multilateral institutions matter. Despite this disagreement, scholars have gone beyond that debate to specifically address the question of how institutions matter (Martin and Simmons 1998). Institutions can provide information, cut transaction costs, and facilitate interactions between states. While states remain the central actor in international relations, institutions have become very important actors in the international system.

Martin and Simmons (1998) suggest that institutions may simultaneously be causes and effects. In other words, states choose and design institutions that can resolve problems. However, once in place, "institutions will constrain and shape behavior, even as they are constantly challenged and reformed by their member states" (743). Further, literature on path dependence suggests that institutional patterns persist over long stretches of time and change is difficult and unusual (Capoccia and Kelemen 2007; Mahoney and Thelen 2010). The path dependence of institutional activity depends on the degree to which a particular IGO has been institutionalized. Prior to full institutionalization, it is much easier for member states to modify and adapt an IGO to specific needs. However, once an IGO has been fully institutionalized, it is very difficult to adapt the IGO. Thus, institutionalization of IGOs directly affect member state behavior. States first adapt the IGOs, but as the IGOs become more and more institutionalized, the IGOs begin to constrain the behavior of the member states.

It has been argued that the degree of IGO institutionalization has significant implications for interaction among states in various issue areas (Boehmer, Gartzke, and Nordstrom 2004; Hansen, McLaughlin Mitchell, and Nemeth 2008; Ingram, Robinson, and Busch 2005). Thus, it is extremely important to determine a measure of IGO institutionalization. To resolve this problem, Boehmer et al. (2004) develop a 3-point scale measure of IGO institutionalization ranging from minimalist to structured to interventionist. They argue that Minimalist IGOs are those institutions that have very little bureaucracy. Most of the decisions are made by the heads of state or government, and although they might meet regularly, there is no organizational bureaucracy. In other words, member states are able to easily adapt and change the IGOs to suit specific purposes. An example of a minimal IGO according to Boehmer et al. (2004) is the Central African Customs and Economic Union since it only has meetings of the heads of states.

Structured IGOs have more of a bureaucracy, and usually have a secretariat. They can make binding decisions on the member states, but they do not have a formal dispute settlement mechanism such as a court. While member states are somewhat constrained by structured IGOs, the lack of a formal dispute settlement mechanism means that member states can still choose whether or not to adhere to the binding decisions of the IGO. Structured IGOs provide legitimacy for IGOs as important actors in regional or international relations, yet still provide flexibility for the member states. According to Boehmer et al. (2004), examples of structured IGOs are the Arctic Council and the Central American Common Market.

Interventionist IGOs must have a formal dispute settlement mechanism. The presence of a formal dispute settlement mechanism constrains member states' behaviors, and thus make it very difficult for member states to adapt and change the IGOs. Instead, member states must work within the rules and order of interventionist IGOs to achieve their strategic goals. Boehmer et al. (2004) find that only highly institutionalized (interventionist) IGOs reduce the likelihood of militarized conflict.[1] Therefore, interventionist IGOs are extremely important to bring regional order and stability, and are vital to creating a regional security architecture. Further, Ingram et al. (2005) find that highly institutionalized IGOs have a greater impact on promoting trade. Thus, institutionalized IGOs are not only imperative in developing a regional security architecture due to the fact that they reduce conflict among states, but they also promote mutually beneficial trade among member states. The best known example of an interventionist IGO is the European Union.

The post-Soviet space not only has more IGOs than any other region (Volgy et al. 2008), but also has all three different types of IGOs. I will examine each of the main IGOs in the post-Soviet space and their importance to establishing a regional security architecture.[2] Also, it will be important to classify each of these IGOs according to type. First, I will examine the Commonwealth of Independent States (CIS).

THE COMMONWEALTH OF INDEPENDENT STATES (CIS)

The post-Soviet space is unique in many ways. The Soviet Union had been dominated by the Russian Republic. It was only natural that many of the newly independent states were wary of Russian intentions toward them. Many were worried that Russia wouldn't accept their sovereignty, while others worried that Russia would bully them into accepting terms for trade and security which benefitted Russian security and economic interests, but were not mutually beneficial. This high level of mistrust forced Russia to try to convince these states that relations could be formed that would be mutually beneficial. One of the ways to accomplish this was to develop a multilateral organization in the post-Soviet space which would facilitate interaction between the newly independent states.

The CIS was established originally by Belarus, Ukraine, and Russia on December 8, 1991. Russia as the successor state of the Soviet Union was far more powerful than the other former Soviet states. The CIS was therefore established as a means of facilitating the breakup of the USSR and developing a regional governance structure that would facilitate interaction between the three states and facilitate the breakup of the Soviet Union. The three states agreed that any former Soviet republic would be welcome to join the CIS as a member state.

Despite the fact that the Central Asian states were excluded from the original CIS treaty, the leaders of those states met in Ashkhabad (the capital of Turkmenistan) and decided that joining the CIS would be the best way to transition to independence (Olcott 1991, 2009). They became enthusiastic members as they saw the CIS as an important transition from the dissolution of the Soviet Union to guaranteeing their territorial sovereignty and independence. In fact, the next meeting of the CIS was then held in the Kazakh capital of Alma-Ata, where the former Soviet republics were declared sovereign states responsible for their own sovereignty, which included being responsible for their own natural resources. The Central Asian states believed that the CIS would allow for regional cooperation in trade, especially in exporting natural resources.

Not all of the FSU states joined the CIS (see Table 3.1). Specifically, the Baltic States (Estonia, Latvia and Lithuania) were never interested in joining the CIS. As Table 3.1 shows, Georgia was the last state to join the CIS in 1993, and the first state to officially withdraw from the CIS in 2008. While Ukraine was one of the first official members of the CIS, it did not ratify the CIS treaty, and thus became a de facto member. It was very active in the CIS up until the annexation of Crimea by Russia in 2014, and on March 14, 2014,

Table 3.1.   CIS Member States

State	Signed Treaty (Joined)	Withdrawn	Membership Status
Armenia	December 21, 1991	-	Official Member
Azerbaijan	December 21, 1991	-	Official Member
Belarus	December 8, 1991	-	Official Member
Kazakhstan	December 21, 1991	-	Official Member
Kyrgyzstan	December 21, 1991	-	Official Member
Moldova	December 21, 1991	-	Official Member
Russia	December 8, 1991	-	Official Member
Tajikistan	December 21, 1991	-	Official Member
Uzbekistan	December 21, 1991	-	Official Member
Turkmenistan	December 21, 1991	-	Unofficial Associate Member

a bill was introduced by Ukraine's parliament to officially withdraw from the CIS. Turkmenistan also officially signed the CIS Treaty on December 21, 1991, but also did not ratify the treaty. It became an unofficial member.

It is important to understand that not all of the member states were enthusiastic about the CIS and its purpose (Hansen 2013; Kramer 2008; Kubicek 1999, 2009). For example, the Central Asian states were very enthusiastic about the CIS (Marks 1996), while Moldova was very reluctant to join, even claiming that it only joined because it felt forced to by Russia (King 1994). Thus, certain states were more active in engaging the CIS for their needs than other states.

The CIS was established to closely resemble the EU in terms of its structure while being much more flexible than the EU. The supreme body within the CIS is the Council of the Heads of States. The Council is responsible for resolving principle questions of the CIS as well as setting the main goals of the CIS. It is important to note that decisions by the Council of the Heads of States are adopted by consensus.

In addition to the Council of the Heads of States are the Council of the Heads of Governments, the Council of Foreign Ministers, the Council of Defense Ministers, and the Council of Commanders-in Chief of Frontier Troops. The Council of the Heads of Governments works closely with the Council of the Heads of States to coordinate cooperation in trade as well as other important areas of common interests between the member states. The Council of Foreign Ministers works to ensure cooperation in foreign policy between member states to ease cooperation. The meetings of the Council of Foreign Ministers often adopt decisions between the meetings of the Councils of the Heads of States and Governments or at the discretion of those councils.

Of great importance to CIS member states is regional security. The Council of Defense Ministers is responsible for military cooperation between the CIS member states, and coordinates groups of military observers. In addition, the Council of Commanders-in-Chief of Frontier Troops are responsible for ensuring cooperation between the member states in guarding the external borders of CIS member states.

In addition to the aforementioned councils, the Inter-Parliamentary Assembly is an important aspect of the regional government structure of the CIS. Established in 1995, the Inter-Parliamentary Assembly was responsible for ensuring cooperation between the parliaments of the member states. This was similar to coordinating cooperation between the heads of state and government, but at the parliamentary level.

Dispute settlement within the CIS was to be handled by the Economic Court located in Minsk, Belarus. Any member state or CIS institution could bring a dispute to the Economic Court for adjudication. The court would be able not only to adjudicate on matters of economic dispute between member states, but also interpret international agreements to which CIS member states are a party. Further, courts of arbitration of member states could appeal directly to the Economic Court to request its interpretation of disputes. Once the court adjudicates a dispute, the adjudication is considered binding, yet enforcement of the ruling is left to the member states.

Beyond the charter bodies of the CIS which are mostly comprised of the member states themselves, the CIS has certain executive bodies which allow the organization to function independently of the member states. Specifically, there is the Economic Council, which ensures that decisions made by the Council of the Heads of State are properly implemented within the CIS structure, the Council of Permanent Plenipotentiary Representatives of the States-Participants of the Commonwealth, which is like the parliamentary body of the CIS, and finally the Executive Committee, which is responsible for coordinating the activities of the CIS and the organization of meetings among the councils, etc. Ultimately, the Executive Committee is like a secretariat that is a permanent bureaucratic organization responsible for many of the more mundane functions of the operations of the CIS.

Based on the criteria developed by Boehmer (2004), the CIS is an interventionist IGO. Not only does it have a professional bureaucracy, but it also has a dispute settlement mechanism. The Economic Court serves as the dispute settlement mechanism. While the CIS isn't as developed as the EU in terms of its bureaucratic organization, it is clear that it was not designed to be just like the EU. The member states would never have accepted such a powerful IGO.

Despite the fact that the CIS was a very structured organization, member states chose to use the CIS for their own purposes. For example, Russia used the CIS to try to reassert its regional hegemonic capabilities by trying to coordinate the tenor of cooperation with the weaker states in the post-Soviet space (Kramer 2008; Miller and Toritsyn 2005). The CIS was an ideal organization for doing this, as it could help to unify a foreign policy and coordinate a regional policy towards all of the member states. The CIS could also provide a very important function for the weaker states in the region, namely reinforcing their sovereignty and championing certain issues that were of vital importance to the smaller member states. More importantly, by joining the CIS, weaker states could coordinate their foreign policies toward Russia, and thus further constrain the regional hegemon (Willerton, Goertz, and Slobodchikoff 2012; Willerton, Slobodchikoff, and Goertz 2012; Willerton et al. 2006).

While the CIS was originally established to mainly allow economic cooperation, security was nevertheless an important component of regional cooperation. Issues like cooperating on defense and military issues were extremely important to CIS member states. To ensure that Russia did not dominate the security and economic aspects of the CIS, the CIS developed a "flexible" design structure which allowed member states to sign only those multilateral agreements which they deemed beneficial to their own interests. Thus, rather than requiring enforcement of agreements among all member states (the EU model), the CIS allowed states to choose whether or not they wanted to sign an agreement, and only required implementation of those agreements which were signed by the member state. For example, if a border treaty was signed by 9 of the CIS members and other CIS member states did not choose to sign the treaty, then only the 9 member states would be responsible for implementing the agreement. Those states that did not sign the agreement would not be required to implement the agreement.

According to the criteria established by Boehmer et al. (2004), the CIS is an interventionist IGO. This is due to the Economic Court as an official dispute settlement mechanism. While Russia wanted to use the CIS to reestablish its own regional hegemonic status, other states in the region saw the CIS as an opportunity to constrain Russia and ensure their own sovereignty. The CIS was able to do both as an interventionist IGO.

While the CIS was one of the most important multilateral organizations established in the post-Soviet space, it was not the only one. In fact, it was not even the only interventionist IGO in the post-Soviet space. I next turn to an examination of the Eurasian Economic Community (EurAzEC).

EURASIAN ECONOMIC COMMUNITY (EURAZEC)

The Eurasian Economic Community is a very important organization in the post-Soviet space. Originally the Eurasian Economic Community was an emanation from the CIS. EurAzEC was formed from the Central Asian Cooperation Organization. The original members were Kazakhstan, Kyrgyzstan, Tajikistan, Uzbekistan, and Russia (see Table 3.2). Turkmenistan chose not

Table 3.2. **EurAzEC Member States**

State	Membership Status
Belarus	Official Member
Kazakhstan	Official Member
Kyrgyzstan	Official Member
Russia	Official Member
Tajikistan	Official Member
Uzbekistan	Suspended Membership
Armenia	Observer
Moldova	Observer
Ukraine	Observer

to participate. In addition to the member states, Moldova and Ukraine were granted observer status in 2002, and in 2003, Armenia was also granted observer status. By 2008, Uzbekistan decided to suspend its membership.

EurAzEC is incorporated as a legal body. That means that it has the power to sign binding treaties under its own authority. As part of its legal status, it joined the United Nations (UN) as an official observer, granting it a special status within the framework of the UN. Further, in 2007, the UN adopted a special resolution calling for special cooperation between the UN and EurAzEC.

The original purpose of EurAzEC was to try and create a single market and trade zone. Member states worked to create free trade zones in EurAzEC, and to lower barriers to trade. Among the goals of EurAzEC was to help its member states integrate into the global economy and not only increase trade among its member states, but also to increase trade between its member states and the rest of the world (Linn and Tiomkin 2006; Shadikhodjaev 2008; Zhalimbetova and Gleason 2001a, 2001b). This was one of the reasons that it declared itself a legal body, as it could then legally sign trade agreements with other countries and IGOs on behalf of the organization and not just on behalf of each of the member states.

The structure of EurAzEC is similar to that of the CIS in that it also has an interstate council that is composed of the member states. This is the supreme body of the organization. The heads of state and government serve on the interstate council, and determine the guiding principles of the IGO. The decisions of the Interstate Council must be made by consensus, and the states are required to execute the decisions of the Interstate Council by passing the required national regulations that would allow decisions to be effectively implemented.

In addition to the Interstate Council, EurAzEC established the Integration Committee. The Integration Committee is composed of the deputy heads of governments of the member states. Their prime responsibility is to ensure free trade among the member states as well as identifying further possibilities for integration. The Integration Committee also monitors the implementation of joint projects as well as the budget of the IGO. Contrary to the Interstate Council, the Integration Committee does not need to have each decision be unanimous. Instead, a formula was developed for the decision making process. First of all, decisions by the Integration Committee require a ⅔ vote to pass. However, each state does not have an equal vote. Instead the number of votes are apportioned according to the amount that each state pays toward the budget of EurAzEC (see Table 3.3). As Table 3.3 shows, Russia pays the most towards the budget of EurAzEC, and therefore has 40 votes. Kyrgyzstan and Tajikistan pay the least, and only have 10 votes each.

Much like the CIS, EurAzEC has an Inter-parliamentary Assembly. It is responsible for ensuring cooperation between the legislative bodies of the

Table 3.3. Number of Votes for Member States
in the Integration Committee of EurAzEC

State	Number of Votes
Russia	40
Belarus	20
Kazakhstan	20
Kyrgyzstan	10
Tajikistan	10

member states. The Assembly is also responsible for creating national legislation among the member states that is necessary to ensure compliance with decisions in the Interstate Council.

EurAzEC also has a dispute settlement mechanism. The Community Court settles economic disagreements among member states as well as resolving disputes regarding the implementation of decisions of the Interstate Council. Thus, based on the criteria established by Boehmer et al. (2004), the EurAzEC is an interventionist IGO.

While the CIS and EurAzEC are the only two interventionist IGOs in the former Soviet space, there are many other IGOs that are not as structured. I will now turn to a discussion of the "Structured IGO" category proposed by Boehmer et al. (2004) and those IGOs in the post-Soviet space which fit the structured IGO category.

It is important to note that the structured category for IGOs means that IGOs often have a professional staff. In other words, structured IGOs are more functional than merely their member states. Often structured IGOs declare themselves as legal entities under international law. The main difference between structured IGOs and interventionist IGOs is that structured IGOs do not have formal dispute settlement mechanisms that are used to resolve disputes among their member states. This means that structured IGOs cannot bind states with their decisions. While technically decisions of the IGO might be legally binding, with no arbitration court to resolve disputes, it is in reality very difficult to enforce binding resolutions. I now turn to the first structured IGO in the post-Soviet space, specifically the Organization of Black Sea Economic Cooperation (BSEC).

THE ORGANIZATION OF BLACK SEA
ECONOMIC COOPERATION (BSEC)

The BSEC was founded in June of 1992, when several former Soviet states as well as other states that bordered the Black Sea met in Istanbul to discuss

Table 3.4.   BSEC Member States

State	Post-Soviet Space?	Membership Status
Albania	No	Founding Member
Armenia	Yes	Founding Member
Azerbaijan	Yes	Founding Member
Bulgaria	No	Founding Member
Georgia	Yes	Founding Member
Greece	No	Founding Member
Moldova	Yes	Founding Member
Romania	No	Founding Member
Russia	Yes	Founding Member
Turkey	No	Founding Member
Ukraine	Yes	Founding Member
Serbia	No	Member (Joined 2004)
Austria	No	Observer
Belarus	Yes	Observer
Croatia	No	Observer
Czech Republic	No	Observer
Egypt	No	Observer
France	No	Observer
Germany	No	Observer
Israel	No	Observer
Italy	No	Observer
Poland	No	Observer
Slovakia	No	Observer
Tunisia	No	Observer
United States	No	Observer

cooperation. The Summit Declaration and the Bosphorus Statement were signed on June 25, 1992, forming the BSEC. The founding member states were Albania, Armenia, Azerbaijan, Bulgaria, Georgia, Greece, Moldova, Romania, Russia, Turkey and Ukraine (see Table 3.4). It is interesting to note that contrary to the two interventionist IGOs in the post-Soviet space, the BSEC member states included more than just states in the former Soviet Union.

The goal of the BSEC was to foster good relations among those states that bordered the Black Sea and to increase economic cooperation among those states. The idea was that the BSEC would create cooperation through economics and trade, which would in turn lead to peaceful relations between the member states (Ozer 2002; Stribis 2003). The BSEC was extremely important to other states because the BSEC region was second only to the Persian Gulf in oil and natural gas production, and has served as a very important corridor for trade to reach Western Europe. This is the reason that so many Western European states have requested observer status with the BSEC. It is interesting to note that Belarus is the only FSU state that has requested observer status and not requested to become a member state.

Despite the fact that the Charter establishing the BSEC was signed in June 1992, the secretariat of the BSEC was only established in 1994 (Black Sea Economic Cooperation 1998). The headquarters of the secretariat was to be in Istanbul, Turkey. Even though the secretariat was established in 1994, the actual Charter of the BSEC did not go into effect until 1999 due to the fact that the Charter could not go into effect until all the member states had ratified the Charter.

Once the Charter took effect, the BSEC acquired an international legal identity, meaning that it could sign treaties and become an observer in other organizations. The BSEC actively sought to sign treaties with other organizations, especially the United Nations and other smaller regional organizations. Further, the BSEC allowed other organizations to become observer organizations in the BSEC (see Table 3.5). As Table 3.5 shows, the BSEC is interested in promoting trade not only among its member states, but facilitating trade and cooperation among other states and organizations. While sectoral dialogue partner states and organizations do not have the status of observers, nevertheless they play an important role in more focused cooperation between the BSEC and other states and organizations.

Table 3.5. BSEC Observer Organizations and Sectoral Dialogue Partners

State or Organization	Status
International Black Sea Club	Observer Organization
Energy Charter Secretariat	Observer Organization
Black Sea Commission	Observer Organization
European Union	Observer Organization
Hungary	Sectoral Dialogue Partner State
Iran	Sectoral Dialogue Partner State
Japan	Sectoral Dialogue Partner State
Jordan	Sectoral Dialogue Partner State
South Korea	Sectoral Dialogue Partner State
Montenegro	Sectoral Dialogue Partner State
Slovenia	Sectoral Dialogue Partner State
United Kingdom	Sectoral Dialogue Partner State
Black and Azov Seas Port Association	Sectoral Dialogue Partner Organization
Black Sea International Shipowners Association	Sectoral Dialogue Partner Organization
Black Sea Region Association of Shipbuilders and Shiprepairers	Sectoral Dialogue Partner Organization
Black Sea Universities Network	Sectoral Dialogue Partner Organization
Union of Road Transport Association in the Black Sea Cooperation Region	Sectoral Dialogue Partner Organization
Conference of Peripheral Maritime Regions for Europe	Sectoral Dialogue Partner Organization
Danube Commission	Sectoral Dialogue Partner Organization

One of the big projects of the BSEC was the development of the Black Sea Trade and Development Bank. Founded in 1997, the bank was responsible for financing both public and private projects that would foster economic development and cooperation in the region. The bank tries to bring in foreign direct investment as well as financing regional projects. Unlike the International Monetary Fund, the Black Sea Trade and Development Bank does not have any policy conditions that it attaches to its financing. In other words, its financing only applies to specific projects, and not trying to influence policy within its member states. The bank's headquarters is in Thessaloniki, Greece.

The structure of the BSEC resembles that of many of the interventionist IGOs. It has a Council of the Heads of State and Governments. As with most IGOs, this council is responsible for the main decisions regarding the BSEC. This council is responsible for the overall agenda of the BSEC and guiding the organization.

The Council of Foreign Ministers of the BSEC is the main decision-making body of the organization. It decides on which states can gain membership or observer status. Not only does it decide on matters related to the functioning of the BSEC, but it also has the ability to establish subsidiary organs.

There is also a Chairman of the BSEC. The Chairman of the BSEC is responsible for implementing the decision of the Council of Foreign Ministers. The Chairman position shall be assumed by a member state on a rotating basis, with the term of the Chairman being six months.

One of the unique structural features of the BSEC is the "Troika" system. The current Chairman of the BSEC, the predecessor to the Chairman of the BSEC, and the next Chairman of the BSEC form a special consultative group that can meet at the request of the Chairman to resolve problems related to the activities of the BSEC and its relations with other states and organizations.

The BSEC also has a Committee of Senior Officials. These members are basically the designees of the Committee of Foreign Ministers. Their responsibility is basically to prepare and submit the budget to the Committee of Foreign Ministers and to review the actions of the subsidiary organizations.

The BSEC has a Parliamentary Assembly. These are representatives of the parliaments of the member states, and are only a consultative body. They are not responsible for decision making for the organization.

The reason that the BSEC is classified as a structured IGO is that it has the Permanent International Secretariat (PERMIS). PERMIS is only responsible to the organization and not to any government official. This separation allows the IGO to be its own entity as opposed to merely reflecting the power structure and goals of its member states. PERMIS is responsible for the day-to-day function of the BSEC.

It should be noted that the BSEC does not have a formal dispute settlement mechanism. This is the reason that the organization is classified as a structured IGO and not an interventionist IGO. Despite the fact that BSEC is not an interventionist IGO, they have been very successful in securing cooperation among member states, especially in trade and academic cooperation. The BSEC has established special affiliated centers, which help in policy analysis and facilitates cooperation among member states. For example, the International Center for Black Sea Studies (ICBSS) is a non-profit organization that is dedicated to providing policy analysis and research to BSEC member states to encourage multilateral cooperation. The ICBSS is affiliated with the BSEC, and operates as the BSEC "think tank," yet it also operates and conducts its own research projects for other interested parties.

Another affiliated organization with the BSEC is the BSEC Coordination Center for the Exchange of Statistical Data and Economic Information. This organization is under the Turkish Statistical Institute, yet is nevertheless affiliated with the BSEC. The purpose of this organization is to provide statistical data to member states to help coordinate policy and further cooperation among the member states.

The BSEC actively accepted its role as an international juridical personality. Not only has it signed treaties with other organizations such as the United Nations, but it has also developed relationships with other organizations. For example, it was granted observer status with the UN. Further, it has signed treaties of cooperation with such organizations as the EAEC, the World Trade Organization, the World Bank, the United Nations Development Program, and many other organizations.

Ultimately, while the BSEC is not an interventionist IGO, it has been able to effectively facilitate cooperation not only among its member states, but also between global organizations as well as regional organizations. The BSEC is more of a facilitating organization than one that can constrain the behavior of its member states. It has been very useful in encouraging trade of information as well as goods between Russia, the FSU, and the West. I now turn to a discussion of another organization that serves as a bridge between the FSU and another region, specifically, the Shanghai Cooperation Organization.

THE SHANGHAI COOPERATION ORGANIZATION (SCO)

Much like the BSEC, the Shanghai Cooperation Organization (SCO) is an organization that bridges the FSU and another region. Specifically, the SCO tries to bring together Russia, China, and Central Asia. Whereas, the BSEC is an economic organization focusing on trade, the SCO is a security organization. That is not to say that the SCO does not want to promote trade, merely that its focus is on security. Specifically, the focus of the SCO was to combat three specific threats to regional security, namely ethnic separatism, religious extremism, and international terrorism (Yuan 2010).

From the Chinese perspective, the SCO was an opportunity to begin to develop bilateral relations with newly independent Central Asian states, while continuing to work closely with Russia (Chung 2006; Cohen 2006; Huasheng 2004). It was determined that security would be one of the best ways of establishing cooperation, and that would later lead to cooperation in trade as well as other issue areas between the member states.

Some critics of the SCO claimed that it was an organization that was built to promote and anti-Western agenda (Germanovich 2008; Laruelle and Peyrouse 2009). Other critics argued that the SCO promoted authoritarian values (Ambrosio 2008). However, some have argued that the SCO has been a big success, and one of its greatest successes has been the fact that it has lessened the security risks between the member states, especially in terms of border disputes (Guang 2009). In fact, Guang (2009) argues that in the span of a decade, Russia and China had solved all of their border disputes along their long shared border. It was due to the SCO that they were able to resolve these disputes.

The SCO was originally relatively weak, and not very institutionalized. In fact, China often viewed the SCO as a chance to reproduce Chinese norms and create both economic and security ties to the FSU (Chung 2006), whereas Russia viewed the SCO as an opportunity to deepen relations with China and Asian states in general. Russia realized that it would not be able to rely on the West for all of its strategic interests, and had to begin building relationships with Asian states for both security and economic reasons.

The SCO was first formed as the Shanghai Five in April 1996, with five member states (see Table 3.6). From its inception, the focus of the SCO was security, and the original treaty founding the SCO was the Treaty on Deepening Military Trust in Border Regions. As Table 3.6 shows, in 2001, the Shanghai Five expanded by granting Uzbekistan membership status. Following Uzbekistan's ascension, the Shanghai Five became known as the SCO.

It is interesting to note that the only state affiliated with the SCO that is not in Asia is Belarus. When Belarus requested formal ties to the SCO, it was originally told that admittance would only be for states in Asia, yet the SCO nevertheless decided to grant Belarus the status of Dialogue Partner. Further, Turkey is the only NATO member state that also is affiliated with the SCO.

The SCO has tried to build relations with other international organizations. For example, the CIS has worked with the UN and with many of its emanations. Further, the SCO has a good working relationship with the CIS,

Table 3.6.   SCO Member States, Observers, and Dialogue Partners

State	Date Joined	Membership Status
China	04/26/1996	Founding Member
Kazakhstan	04/26/1996	Founding Member
Kyrgyzstan	04/26/1996	Founding Member
Russia	04/26/1996	Founding Member
Tajikistan	04/26/1996	Founding Member
Uzbekistan	06/15/2001	Member
Afghanistan	06/06/2012	Observer
India	06/05/2005	Observer
Iran	06/05/2005	Observer*
Mongolia	06/17/2004	Observer
Pakistan	06/05/2005	Observer
Belarus	06/15/2009	Dialogue Partner
Sri Lanka	06/15/2009	Dialogue Partner
Turkey	12/05/2012	Dialogue Partner

*On March 24, 2008, Iran applied to become a full-time member, but due to UN sanctions, cannot yet be admitted as a full-time member

EurAzEC, the Collective Security Treaty Organization (CSTO), and the Association of Southeast Asian Nations (ASEAN). Despite the fact that the SCO was founded as a security organization, it nevertheless has worked with both the CIS and EurAzEC to sign trade agreements and try to increase trade among their member states, in addition to trying to develop a regional multilateral energy policy (Scheineson 2009).

In 1998, Iran applied for full member status to the SCO. While UN sanctions prevent Iran from becoming a full member, nevertheless, the prospect of Iran joining the SCO is intriguing. Theoretically, the SCO would be able to constrain Iran's foreign policy and bring it more into the global order (Scheineson 2009). However, questions remain as to Iran's reliability as a partner, and accepting Iran as a member state would only reinforce the idea that the SCO is an anti-Western organization.

The SCO's institutional design resembles that of many of the international organizations in the post-Soviet space. Its top decision-making body is the Heads of State Council. The Council meets at least once a year, at special SCO Summits. The SCO Summits alternate between the capital cities of the member states. The Heads of State Council is responsible for determining the overall goals of the organization.

The Heads of Government Council also must meet on an annual basis. They are responsible for determining new areas of multilateral cooperation. The Heads of Government Council is also responsible for approving the annual budget of the organization.

The Council of Foreign Ministers also meets as needed and discusses the reaction of the SCO to international issues. Further, it is responsible for external relations with other states and organizations. For example, the Council of Foreign Ministers works very closely with the CIS and EurAzEC to ensure regional multilateral governance.

In addition to the other councils, the SCO has the Council of National Coordinators. This council has mechanisms for meetings of different levels of government officials. These government officials in turn coordinate domestic policies of their member states to be in compliance with the SCO framework.

Instead of one professional secretariat like the BSEC and other IGOs in the post-Soviet space, the SCO has two professional governing bodies. One is the SCO Secretariat. The Secretariat is headquartered in Beijing. The Secretariat of the SCO is responsible for the day-to-day governance of the SCO. In addition, there is a Chairman of the Secretariat who is appointed by the Heads of States Council.

The second professional governing body of the SCO is the Regional Anti-Terrorist Structure (RATS). This Structure is headquartered in Tashkent. The purpose of RATS is to coordinate member states' policies against terrorism, extremism, and separatism. Each member state sends a representative to RATS, and then RATS elects a Head of RATS for a three-year term.

Much like with the BSEC, there is no official dispute settlement mechanism in the SCO. This means that it is a structured IGO and not an interventionist IGO. While the lack of a dispute settlement mechanism have caused some scholars to question the effectiveness of the SCO, the lack of an official dispute settlement mechanism has actually provided flexibility in melding very different foreign policies and helped to manage great power competition in Central Asia. In fact, despite the fact that the SCO was primarily founded as a security organization, it has nonetheless begun to evolve and facilitate economic and cultural cooperation as well as cooperation in security.

To facilitate economic cooperation, the SCO developed the SCO Business Council. This is a non-governmental organization which works closely with and under the SCO framework. The goal of the Business Council is to facilitate economic cooperation among the SCO member states through bringing together business and industry leaders of the member states and facilitating their interactions.

One of the main areas of economic cooperation identified by the Business Council is in the energy sector. As such, the Business Council developed the SCO Energy Club, which would create a joint energy policy for the SCO. it is important to note that the Business Council has the ability to make decisions independently of the SCO. So while the Business Council facilitates cooperation within the framework of the SCO, it is nevertheless an independent organization.

In addition to the Business Council, the SCO established the SCO Interbank Consortium. The purpose of the Consortium was to raise money to help finance initiatives with the SCO member states. The SCO Interbank Consortium is very similar to the Black Sea Trade and Development Bank. The Interbank Consortium is headed by a bank of one of the member states on a rotating basis.

Interestingly, the SCO specifically cites the need to develop cultural and educational opportunities. The SCO has worked on several cultural exchanges, and has been working on developing an SCO university that will draw upon the resources of many of the best universities in Russia including Moscow State University and other very good universities in Russia and the member states.

Ultimately the SCO is still evolving. While it was first established as only dealing with security issues, it has evolved beyond just a security organization. In the future, the SCO will have to continue to evolve and will have to develop new means of cooperation and integration. If the SCO can truly develop close cooperation among its member states in energy, the SCO will become a very powerful regional organization. I now turn to a discussion of another structured IGO which was formed to address regional security. Specifically, I will now discuss the Collective Security Treaty Organization (CSTO).

THE COLLECTIVE SECURITY
TREATY ORGANIZATION (CSTO)

Unlike the BSEC and the SCO, the Collective Security Treaty Organization (CSTO) is not a bridge from the post-Soviet space to other regions. Instead, several member states in the CIS recognized that while the CIS was an organization that could effectively manage the breakup of the Soviet Union, the member states had to now address their security needs. Thus, Armenia, Belarus, Kazakhstan, Kyrgyzstan, Russia, and Tajikistan signed the Collective Security Treaty (CST) on May 15, 1992. In 1993, Azerbaijan, Georgia, and Uzbekistan also signed the treaty. In 1994, the treaty actually took effect. The initial treaty was given a term of five years, with the opportunity to renew the treaty.

The initial goal of the CST was to ensure regional stability and peace by identifying collective security threats. Further, while those states that signed the CST were wary of Russia's regional hegemony, they were also extremely apprehensive about NATO's intentions, especially as NATO began its east-ward expansion. If other member states were apprehensive about NATO's intentions, then Russia was threatened by NATO's actions. While the United States had promised not to expand NATO initially, they withdrew that prom-ise, and began expanding the alliance. It is no wonder that Russia and the FSU felt the need to further develop a regional collective security organization.

In 1999, six of the nine original signatories of the CST decided to renew the CST. Only Georgia, Uzbekistan, and Azerbaijan decided not to renew the original treaty. In 2001, they decided to formalize their agreement into the Collective Security Treaty Organization (CSTO) (see Table 3.7). As Table 3.7 shows, Uzbekistan originally signed the CST, chose not to renew it after five years, but nevertheless decided to join the CSTO when it became a for-mal organization in 2001.

Table 3.7.   CSTO Member States

Member State	Status in CSTO
Russia	Founding Member
Armenia	Founding Member
Belarus	Founding Member
Kazakhstan	Founding Member
Kyrgyzstan	Founding Member
Tajikistan	Founding Member
Uzbekistan*	Founding Member
Afghanistan	Observer State
Serbia	Observer State
Iran	Possible Candidate

*Uzbekistan originally signed the CST, declined to re-new after five years, but agreed to join the CSTO in 2001. Uzbekistan withdrew from the CSTO in 2012.

Since its inception, the CSTO has continued to evolve. In 2005, joint military exercises were held, and in 2007, the CSTO signed an agreement to cooperate in security, crime, and drug trafficking. Further, in 2007, CSTO developed peacekeeping forces that could be used in the FSU to ensure peace and stability and prevent the spread of interstate and intrastate conflict. This peacekeeping force could be deployed by UN mandate or without a mandate provided that the peacekeeping force was stationed within the borders of one of the member states.

In 2009, CSTO developed the Collective Rapid Reaction Force. The goal of the force was to be able to repulse an invasion from an outside force, re-spond to terrorist attacks and natural disasters, and fight transnational crime and drug trafficking. Not all of the member states were in favor of developing the force, specifically Uzbekistan and Belarus initially opposed the force. Belarus eventually signed the Collective Rapid Reaction Force Agreement, while Uzbekistan refused to sign it.

Much like with the SCO, Iran has applied for membership to the CSTO. Since Iran is currently under United Nations sanctions, Iran cannot become a member state. However, Iran joining the CSTO is intriguing, as it would definitely mean that the tenor of the organization would drastically change. No longer would CSTO be a regional security organization confined to the FSU, but it would begin to spread into a more interregional security organization.

CSTO has two observer states, Afghanistan and Serbia. Further, CSTO has observer status with the UN. This means that CSTO has a juridical personality, and has the ability to sign its own international agreements.

The institutional design of CSTO resembles the institutional design of the SCO. Specifically, there is a Council on Collective Security. This Council is composed of the Heads of State of the member states. The Council on Collective Security serves as the highest organ of the organization.

There is a Council of Foreign Ministers and a Council of Defense Ministers. Each of these councils are also composed of the foreign and defense ministers of their respective member states. They are mainly advisory councils in their respective spheres. For example, the Council of Foreign Ministers advises the Council on Collective Security on issues regarding diplomatic relations, and the Council of Defense Ministers advises the Council on Collective Security on issues regarding military cooperation.

There is also a Committee of Secretaries of the Security Council. This Committee serves to assist coordination among the member states. They also advise the respective member states on the best approach to joint operations and activities involving state security.

Like many of the IGOs in the post-Soviet space, the CSTO has a professional secretariat, meaning that it is a structured organization. The secretariat is responsible for the day-to-day operations of the organization, and for drafting official responses and draft decisions related to the organization. The head of the secretariat is the Secretary-General, who is elected for a three-year term by the Council of Foreign Ministers. The secretariat is located in Moscow, Russia.

Ultimately, the CSTO is a very important organization in the post-Soviet space in that its sole focus is collective security. It is the natural counterbalance to NATO, and can be very useful in this role. However, since states in the post-Soviet space are generally wary of Russian hegemonic power, the CSTO must remain a relatively weak organization. If Russia is to control the CSTO too aggressively, then it risks having member states withdrawing from the organization. It should be noted, however, that without Russia's membership, the organization would not be at all viable. I now turn to a discussion of the only IGO in the post-Soviet space in which Russia is not a member, the GUAM Organization of Democracy and Development.

THE GUAM ORGANIZATION OF
DEMOCRACY AND DEVELOPMENT (GUAM)

The GUAM Organization of Democracy and Development (GUAM) is an organization that was founded specifically to try to limit Russia's regional influence. The goal of the organization was to have the weaker states collectively work together so that Russia's power and influence would be diminished. The name GUAM came from the initials of the founding member states, Georgia, Ukraine, Azerbaijan, and Moldova (see Table 3.8). As Table 3.8 shows, the original member states expanded to include Uzbekistan, and the organization was renamed GUUAM. However, Uzbekistan chose to leave GUUAM, and the name of the organziation reverted back to GUAM.

Table 3.8.   GUAM Member States

Member State	Member Status
Georgia	Founding Member
Ukraine	Founding Member
Uzbekistan	Joined in 1999, Withdrew in 2005
Azerbaijan	Founding Member
Moldova	Founding Member
Turkey	Observer State
Latvia	Observer State

   Specifically, the member states stated that their goals were to increase democracy and democratic governance in the region, ensuring regional stability, ensuring regional security, and working towards European integration with the EU. In other words, the goals of GUAM were to limit Russia's power and influence, and to work towards joining the EU.

   In 2006, GUAM further changed its name to GUAM Organization for Democracy and Economic Development. The idea was that this change would be welcoming to new member states, and that GUAM would attract new member states. However, no new states have applied for membership since the name change. Further, GUAM recommended developing its own peacekeeping force that could be used in regional conflict. In 2014, GUAM condemned Russia's actions in Ukraine, and passed a resolution affirming Ukraine's territorial integrity.

GUAM's structure closely resembles that of most of the IGOs in the post-Soviet space. It also has a Council of the Heads of State of the member states. This is the main decision making body of the organization. Further there is a Council of Ministers of Foreign Affairs, Council of National Coordinators, and Council of Permanent Representatives. Each of these councils serve as advisors to the Council of the Heads of State.

GUAM also has a Parliamentary Assembly. The Parliamentary Assembly passes resolutions and thus advises the Council of the Heads of State of the member states. In addition to the Parliamentary Assembly, GUAM has the Business Council.

The Business Council facilitates the implementation of GUAM agreements in the member states. In addition, the Business Council works to create more economic cooperation among the member states. It does this by representing GUAM to various business sectors and helping member states match their specific needs with other states or industries. The Business Council also promotes GUAM and its member states at specialized exhibitions and seminars.

GUAM also has a professional secretariat located in Kiev, Ukraine. The secretariat is responsible for the day-to-day operation of the organization, and is headed by a Secretary General.

GUAM is an international legal personality, so it has the ability to sign treaties with other states and organizations. As such it has worked closely with the United States, especially in the development of the Virtual Law Enforcement Center and a project on trade and transportation. GUAM also has worked closely with Japan and Poland as well as the UN and the Organization for Security and Cooperation in Europe (OSCE).

In addition to cooperating with other states and organizations, GUAM has developed working groups that are specifically designed at fostering cooperation in certain specific industries. For example, GUAM has established working groups on transportation, trade and economics, telecommunications, tourism, and culture.

Ultimately, GUAM must rely on its outside partnerships in regional cooperation due to the fact that the regional hegemon is not a member state. This makes coordination and regional governance very difficult to achieve, yet allows GUAM a level of flexibility to cooperate with other organizations and states that it would not have if Russia were a member state. While GUAM's evolution has been relatively slow and it has not enticed any new member states, its level of cooperation with outside states and organizations make it an important organization in the post-Soviet space, and one that will counter Russian efforts at establishing a regional security order.

One of the aspects that ties together all of these IGOs in the post-Soviet space is that all of them are either interventionist or structured IGOs. They all have at the very least an international legal personality and a professional secretariat that manage the day-to-day operations of the organizations. Where they have differed have been in whether or not they have an official dispute settlement mechanism.

Most of the IGOs have had Russia as the central member state (with the exception of GUAM). Further, most of the IGOs do not have the supranational capabilities that the EU has in terms of forcing their member states to adapt to decisions made by the organization. In fact, by institutional design, the member states still have a lot of flexibility and are not constrained by the actions of the IGOs. In fact, the institutional design features have been purposely designed in this manner to manage the mistrust that many of the FSU states have toward Russia. However, a new IGO has been created that will more closely resemble the EU than any of the other IGOs in the post-Soviet space. I now turn to a discussion of this organization, the Eurasian Customs Union.

EURASIAN CUSTOMS UNION

Scholars generally believe that most of the multilateral organizations in the post-Soviet space have failed (Blockmans 2008; Carbone 2013; Dwan and Pavliuk 2000; Hansen 2013; Kubicek 1999; Rowe and Torjesen 2008; Torjesen 2008). Some of the reasons for the perceived failure has been that the FSU states have been very wary of Russian hegemonic strength. Despite the fact that the Commonwealth of Independent States helped to dissolve the Soviet Union in an orderly fashion and helped to rebuild relations among the FSU (Slobodchikoff 2013b; Willerton, Goertz, and Slobodchikoff 2012; Willerton, Slobodchikoff, and Goertz 2012), nevertheless, the majority of cooperation in the FSU occurred at the bilateral level within the multilateral framework established by the CIS and other regional organizations.

The framework established by the CIS was a means of restraining the regional hegemon and allow trade and economic cooperation without entailing true regional integration. After all, the Soviet Union had just dissolved, and none of the states wanted to recreate that experience and relinquish their new found sovereignty. Thus, the institutional structure of the CIS and the other multilateral organizations in the post-Soviet space reflected the necessity of facilitating cooperation without promoting integration.

The growth and expansion of the European Union and NATO to Russia's traditional sphere of interest caused a distinct change in Russian foreign policy toward the FSU (Ponsard 2006). Russia made clear that the FSU was within its sphere of influence and that it would not tolerate the West trying to gain influence within the FSU. It established its own version of the Monroe Doctrine, where it would not allow any further expansion (Slobodchikoff 2013a).

Part of Russia's new orientation on the FSU was the understanding that the regional security structure would have to be able to compete with the EU or many of the FSU states would be drawn in to join the EU and NATO and would therefore hinder Russia's own strategic interests. Naturally, the CSTO was one way to oppose NATO. However, none of the other multilateral institutions could really provide competition to the EU. They had been specifically designed as a way to maximize the flexibility for weaker states instead of integration into a supranational organization. Thus, the Economic Union was created.

Given that Russia was moving toward membership in the World Trade Organization (WTO), it made logical sense that the new Economic Union would resemble the WTO and create a new organization that was specifically designed to integrate the economies of its member states. This would in turn create a powerful trading bloc that would be a rival to the European Union (Henley 2014; Tarr 2012).

Russian President Vladimir Putin has described the Eurasian Union as being the best aspect of the Soviet Union, while those in the West, such as then Secretary of State Hillary Clinton described the Eurasian Union as being an attempt to recreate the Soviet Union (Henley 2014). However, it is very difficult to predict the effectiveness of this new organization as well as its new evolution. It seems clear that there is reluctance to creating a new Soviet Union among the FSU states, but some of the states are certainly more opposed to economic integration than others.

Initially the Eurasian Union came out of a bilateral customs union which was developed by Russia and Belarus. The idea was to integrate their economies further and create a free trade zone as well as a customs union. Tariffs could be imposed on outside goods, and there would be increased trade between the two countries. However, the idea to create the Eurasian Economic Union was not officially proposed until 2001.

On November 18, 2011, the presidents of Russia, Kazakhstan, and Belarus signed an agreement which would establish the Eurasian Union by 2015 (Guneev 2014; Henley 2014). They established a Eurasian Commission which was modelled on the European Commission in the European Union (see table 3.9).

As table 3.9 shows, since the initial agreement, several other FSU states have showed an interest in joining. Specifically, Kyrgyzstan and Tajikistan. In 2013, Armenia announced its intention to become a member. Georgia has also considered the possibility of joining, but has reiterated its desire

Table 3.9. **Prospective Member States of the Eurasian Union**

State	Status
Russia	Prospective Member State
Belarus	Prospective Member State
Kazakhstan	Prospective Member State
Armenia	Prospective Candidate State
Kyrgyzstan	Prospective Candidate State
Tajikistan	Prospective Candidate State
Ukraine	Prospective Observer State

to pursue membership in the EU, so is unlikely to join. Ukraine submitted a request to join as an observer in August of 2013, however, it was told that it could not sign an association agreement with the EU and become an observer of the Eurasian Union. With the coup d'état, which replaced Ukrainian President Viktor Yanukovych in 2014 with a government much less sympathetic to Russia, it seems unlikely that Ukraine will request to become a member state in the near future.

While Russia has claimed that the Eurasian Union is necessary to improve the economies of many of the FSU states and will greatly improve the quality of life of the citizens of the member states, the United States has expressed its opposition to the formation of this organization. The United States believes that the Eurasian Union is a means to recreating the Soviet Union, and that it must be prevented from fully forming. In fact, during the Ukrainian crisis in 2014, the United States and the EU tried to entice Ukraine from joining the Eurasian Union to ensure that Ukraine would not become a possible member state.

The future of the Eurasian Union is not clear. While Putin has championed its cause and gained supporters in many of the FSU states, it remains to be seen whether the Eurasian Union can effectively overcome the fundamental mistrust of Russia that many states in the FSU still retain. To be effective, the Eurasian Union will need to overcome this mistrust if the member states will ever agree to integrate economically into a supranational organization like the EU. Too many of their sovereign powers would be ceded to the supranational organization, so until there is enough trust built up, the Eurasian Union will remain a work in progress.

Ultimately, the Eurasian Union is not the only IGO in the post-Soviet space which must remedy the lack of trust of Russia as the regional to become an effective organization. In fact, almost all of the IGOs in the region except for GUAM have this problem to overcome. GUAM has a more difficult problem to overcome to become an effective organization, namely that it does not have a powerful enough member state to be able to make it an effective organization. There is no state that is able to be the driving force behind the organization.

The lack of trust is fundamentally the reason that the IGOs in the post-Soviet space have been considered to be relatively ineffective by scholars. Taken out of context, the IGOs certainly resemble ineffective organizations. Yet, the organizations are actually vital to developing a regional security structure.

First, the organizations resemble concentric waves of water which radiate from a given point when a small rock is thrown into calm water. In this case, Russia resembles the rock. It is the force behind each of these organizations (waves). Each wave, or in this case organization reflects the power of Russia as the regional hegemon. That is why the post-Soviet space has those organizations which only have FSU states as their member states, while other IGOs are more open and bridge the gap between different regions. For example, in figure 3.1, Russia is the most powerful actor, creates the CIS, and in turn creates the SCO for managing relations with China in Central Asia. A similar figure could be made for illustrating the relationship between Russia, the CIS, and the BSEC.

It should be noted that IGOs are not the only means of establishing a security architecture within the region. To establish a security architecture in the post-Soviet space, Russia needed to use both bilateral and multilateral means. The multilateral means were necessary to create the general rules of behavior and establish the general order, while the bilateral treaties and agreements then

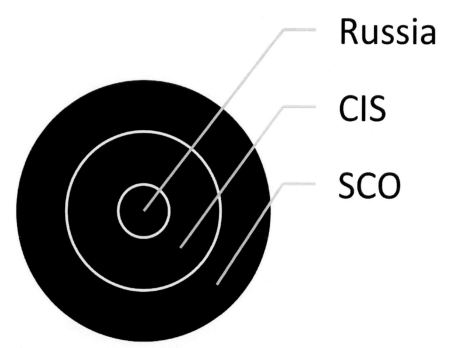

Figure 3.1.   IGOs in the post-Soviet Space as Concentric Circles

became necessary to solidify and clarify the place and behavior of each state within the regional order and hierarchy. In the next chapter, I will discuss how to examine the regional security architecture in light of both a multilateral and bilateral approach to creating the regional order by Russia.

NOTES

1. Such IGOs have the ability to collect and disseminate valuable information, intervene and involve in costly signaling (2004, 16).

2. By main IGOs, I mean that they are not solely established to deal with one issue. The IGOs must be established to address more than one issue area, and they must be active IGOs in the post-Soviet space.

Chapter Four

The Troika Option

Combining Multilateral and Bilateral Relations

In the previous two chapters, I have discussed Russia's bilateral relationships with the FSU states and the multilateral organizations within the post-Soviet space. I have approached each chapter as being distinct from the other. In other words, I have presented a bilateral approach to Russian foreign policy in the FSU and a multilateral approach to Russian foreign policy in the FSU. In this chapter, I will argue that in order for Russia to build its regional security architecture, it must in fact embrace both bilateral and multilateral approaches. Instead of being two different approaches, I argue that bilateral and multilateral treaties are actually a cohesive foreign policy strategy that are used in combination to achieve foreign policy goals. Only through a combined approach to foreign policy in the post-Soviet space can it hope to create a strong regional security architecture. In this chapter, I will first examine both bilateral and multilateral theories of international relations, then examine those theories in the post-Soviet space. I will then introduce an approach that combines both bilateralism and multilateralism as a way in which a hegemon can build a regional security architecture. Finally, I will explain how social network analysis can help to show the process of building a regional security architecture. In the next chapter, I will actually show how Russia has created its regional security architecture.

HEGEMONIC POWER AND
BUILDING A SECURITY ARCHITECTURE

One of the great debates about the global hegemon's approach to power among neoinstitutionalists in international relations is between multilateralists (Keohane 1989; Ruggie 1994; Ruggie 1993; Weber 1991) and bilateralists (Hemmer and Katzenstein 2002; Okawara and Katzenstein 2001). Multilateralists argue that although there is one hegemon in the world system, it is to the benefit and stability of the world that other states are treated as equals (Ruggie 1993). Multilateralists state that organizations such as the North Atlantic Treaty Organization (NATO) are proof that the United States uses multilateralism to achieve its goals of world stability according to its world order (Ruggie 1993). Bilateralists argue that although NATO is an example of multilateralism, the relationship between the United States and NATO is the exception rather than the rule (Hemmer and Katzenstein 2002). They state that the United States mainly uses bilateralism as its approach to international relations. According to bilateralists, the United States uses multilateralism only in the circumstances where the norms and shared culture are similar, and uses bilateralism with regional powers to achieve its goals when a shared sense of culture and norms are not present (Hemmer and Katzenstein 2002).

Both multilateralists and bilateralists believe that either multilateralism or bilateralism is used, but not in combination. That is not to say that states cannot join multilateral organizations if their foreign policy strategy is predominantly bilateral, just that the hegemonic state focuses on one over the other. In other words, if a state has a specific foreign policy outcome, it can choose to pursue this outcome either through multilateral or bilateral means. However, can it really be that states can only predominantly focus on one strategy or the other? Is there no ability or incentive for states to use a combination of both approaches? I argue that there are in fact three strategies that hegemons can use in their approaches to international relations. They can use a multilateral approach, a bilateral approach, or they can use a combination of the two, which I refer to as the troika option. The main method that states can use the troika option is through the use of treaty networks.

In the literature on institution building, previous work has tended to focus on individual treaties rather than on conglomerations of related treaties. The method for determining whether a hegemonic state's approach to international relations is either bilateral or multilateral is to count the number of bilateral treaties signed between the universal hegemon and another state and compare that sum to the number of multilateral treaties signed between the universal hegemon and other states in an international organization to determine whether the hegemon uses a multilateral or bilateral approach. For example, between 1992 and 2004 Russia signed 144 multilateral CIS security treaties and only 34 bilateral treaties with Georgia (Willerton et al. 2006). According to this, Russia is using a multilateral approach and not a bilateral one in its regional relations.

The problem with this method is that it doesn't examine the content of the treaties themselves or how significant any individual treaty might be. For instance, the treaty establishing NATO is equal to many bilateral agreements in terms of influence, resources, etc. Without examining the content of treaties, scholars miss the point that any given treaty may build upon previous multilateral and bilateral treaties. For example, of the 34 bilateral security treaties that Russia signed with Georgia, 19 of them are nested within other treaties, meaning that the treaty might not only have a bilateral approach, but could be a combination of multilateral and bilateral approaches. Moreover, not only are these treaties nested, but these treaties are part of the treaty network. The importance of the bilateral treaty network was examined in Chapter 2, where I examined Russia's bilateral relations with the FSU. Of importance for this discussion is that the denser a bilateral treaty network, the less likely that relationship is likely to devolve into violent conflict. By examining the relationship among treaties, scholars can achieve a more detailed understanding of the complex relationship between states.

Although Russia is the regional hegemon, Russia must react to Western expansion into its sphere of influence, and there are limits to its ability to unilaterally dictate the policies of the other states in its region. According to the bilateralists and multilateralists, Russia must therefore use either a predominantly multilateral strategy through the Commonwealth of Independent States (CIS) or a bilateral strategy through its interactions with member states of the CIS. However, is it possible that Russia is able to use a combination of both approaches?

With the fall of the Soviet Union, Russia has had to rebuild its relationships with CIS member states. Therefore, Russia is the perfect state to examine whether or not states use a combination of multilateral and bilateral approaches in their relationships with other states in their region. In this chapter I will first examine the literature on multilateralism versus bilateralism, then I will examine Russia as a regional hegemon and its relations with other states in its region focusing on CIS member states. I will then examine a complete set of bilateral and multilateral security treaties between Russia and CIS member states to determine whether or not Russia uses a combination of multilateral and bilateral approaches in its relations with CIS member states.

MULTILATERALISM VS. BILATERALISM

John Ruggie has been one of the most influential scholars to highlight multilateralism as a novel idea of diplomacy in the latter part of the twentieth century. Ruggie (1994; 1993) studies Europe, and more specifically focuses on NATO. He asserts that multilateralism is the United States' method for ensuring its global hegemonic status for two reasons. First, by treating many countries as equal and working together to achieve goals, the great powers remain satisfied with the current world order. Second, he states that multilateralism mirrors the domestic structure of the United States in that the federal government must work with the states to maintain effective governance, and that the states are treated as more-or-less equal partners in governance. Although these two reasons effectively explain why the US would prefer to use multilateral principles, a problem arises in that they are not able to explain why in some cases such as NATO the US uses multilateralist principles, whereas in other cases such as its approach to the Southeast Asia Treaty Organization (SEATO), it uses more of a bilateral approach. According to this hegemonic theory, the US should simply use multilateralist principles in all of its foreign policy, especially with other multilateral organizations it is a member of such as SEATO.

A second perspective of multilateralist principles argues that a unipolar world system is inherently unstable and that the most stable world system is multipolar (Weber 1991). Weber (1991) asserts that by using multilateralist principles in Europe, the United States is actually trying to establish an independent center of power that is not reliant upon the power of the US. By creating an independent center of power, the United States is creating a multipolar system, which in turn leads to increased stability. However, Weber's (1991) theory about the creation of a multipolar system doesn't explain why multilateralism is not more evident in other regions besides Europe or the North Atlantic. Multilateralist principles should be evident in other regions of the world like Asia, where the US mostly focuses on bilateral principles of diplomacy.

Bilateralists argue that the multilateral approach to NATO is the exception rather than the rule. Hemmer and Katzenstein (2002) assert that multilateralism is very difficult to accomplish in that it requires a shared sense of collective identity among all of the parties. They argue that this was possible in Europe – because of shared history and a sense of equality – but not possible in Asia. Moreover, they argue that the NATO collective security article which states that an attack on any NATO member is the same as an attack on all member states, and this led to the use of multilateralist principles, whereas SEATO's collective security agreement states that an attack on any member of SEATO is a threat to peace and safety. By examining SEATO, they argue that the US mostly tried to organize SEATO through bilateral agreements with Japan instead of using multilateralist principles with all of the member states. Instead of having an independent power base consisting of all SEATO members, the US instead wanted to establish Japan as the power base within SEATO, with the rest of the members relying on Japan's leadership and power.

Interestingly, Hemmer and Katzenstein (2002) stress that different approaches are utilized by the US in different regions. They argue that regions are not geographical, but rather are politically constructed. Thus, different approaches to diplomacy are needed in different regions depending on the needs or the beliefs of the hegemon. Although their theory pertains to the global hegemon, it can be expanded to regional hegemons as well for two reasons. First, according to Lemke (2002), although there is a universal hegemon, there are also regional hierarchies. Regional hierarchies are headed by regional hegemons, which display the same behaviors as the universal hegemon. Theories pertaining to the universal hegemon can thus be applied to regional hegemons. Second, the Soviet Union was one of two universal hegemons, and Russia as the successor state to the Soviet Union could be examined using universal hegemonic theory. Thus, it is possible to examine the CIS and see if Russia, the regional hegemon, utilizes multilateralism or bilateralism or a combination of the two in its approach to the CIS and the CIS member states.

One of the biggest problems with both multilateralist theory and bilateralist theory is that it is a dichotomous approach to diplomacy. The hegemon either uses multilateralist principles or bilateralist principles, but never a combination of both. This belief stems from the fact that most scholars see treaties as individual entities without examining the whole treaty complex. If scholars examined treaty complexes, they would be able to determine that in most relationships between the hegemon and other international organizations such as NATO and SEATO, that the hegemon actually uses a combination of multilateralist and bilateralist approaches to diplomacy. Specifically regarding the CIS, Russia is the regional hegemon, and uses a combination of multilateralist and bilateralist approaches to diplomacy within the CIS. By understanding that a combination of approaches can be used, scholars can more precisely understand interactions between states.

RUSSIA AND THE CIS

Following the fall of the Soviet Union, the Russian Federation had to work to rebuild the power structure and its influence with the former Soviet republics. Although Russia was still the regional hegemon, it was forced to begin relationships anew, and relied on treaty construction and treaty nestedness to achieve this goal. No other state has initiated as many bilateral and multilateral treaties as Russia, and this treaty activism covers a wide range of issue areas (Slobodchikoff 2013b; Willerton, Slobodchikoff, and Goertz 2012; Willerton et al. 2006). Although Russian strategies evolved over the last two and a half decades, one of the driving forces behind Russian treaty activism was its desire to reestablish its sphere of influence in what it referred to as the "near abroad." Where other states saw the establishment of the CIS as an institution to dismantle the remnants of the Soviet Union, Russia also saw the establishment of the CIS as a way in which to rebuild its influence, and with the establishment of the CIS, chose to construct both multilateral and bilateral treaties and use treaty nestedness to further increase their influence in the region. In fact, a vast majority of bilateral treaties between Russia and the other CIS member states in this study are nested, making treaty nestedness one of the most important tools in treaty construction.

One of Russia's first acts after the dissolution of the Soviet Union was to declare itself the successor state to the Soviet Union (Olcott, Aslund, and Garnett 1999). In doing this, Russia sent a signal to all of the other states that it was the regional hegemon. Russia possessed the necessary infrastructure and capability to assume that role, whereas the other states did not.

The dissolution of the Soviet Union also presented many challenges to Russia. First, a newly independent Russia possessed a complex set of security concerns. One of the security concerns had to do with the borders of the new Russian Federation. During the Soviet period, borders between the republics did not need to be patrolled as vigorously as the external borders of the Soviet Union. Moreover, although Soviet military troops were stationed within the borders of Russia, many soldiers were stationed in outer republics closer to the external borders of the Soviet Union. With Russia declaring itself the successor state to the Soviet Union, technically all of the troops became Russian troops. However, they became Russian troops stationed in newly independent states.

Further complicating the issue of military forces was that the newly independent states needed militaries of their own. The former Soviet military could not just be dismantled with each state getting the rights to the military that was stationed on its territory. To dismantle the military in that fashion would have placed Russia at a tremendous disadvantage relative to the former republics. Moreover, since the Soviet military was composed of soldiers from all of the former republics, citizens of one newly independent state might find themselves serving in a defunct state's army while stationed in a different sovereign territory.

In short, to address security concerns, Russia had to address the issue of the status of military forces with the members of the CIS. It had to first determine to whom the military belonged and then determine whether or not the troops would remain stationed in the new independent state. With vital security interests in different areas coupled with a lack of infrastructure to barrack a military of that size, it was in Russia's interest to ensure that portions of its military could remain stationed in the former Soviet republics. However, it was not necessarily in the interest of the former republic to have Russian troops stationed within its borders.

Since Russia saw the purpose of the CIS as both to dissolve the Soviet Union and to build up its own power and influence, it is logical that Russia would pursue status of forces agreements multilaterally through the CIS. Russia would seek to gain recognition of its hegemonic power and take control of most of the former Soviet military troops and apparatus. However, once the general status of forces agreements had been decided multilaterally, it was logical that Russia would then use bilateral agreements to determine specific stationing of troops in specific states. Thus, in the case of stationing of troops, I would expect that Russia would use a combination of multilateralism and bilateralism by using nested treaties. The initial status of forces agreements would be multilateral, then bilateral treaties would be nested within the initial multilateral treaties, and finally more bilateral treaties would be nested within bilateral treaties.

In addition to the status of forces being one of the major security issues that Russia needed to resolve, Russia also wanted to resolve the question of the status of nuclear weapons. It was not in Russia's interest that many states in its region would become nuclear powers, and thus wanted to ensure that nuclear weapons remained Russian possessions. Thus, I would expect Russia to have used a similar strategy to that expected for stationing of troops: using a combination of multilateralism and bilateralism by using nested treaties in a treaty network. Again, the initial agreements would be multilateral, then bilateral treaties would be nested within the initial multilateral treaties.

Similar to security concerns, Russia also possessed many strategic concerns. These were concerns that would allow it to retain its regional power as well as to gain great power status universally (Olcott, Aslund, and Garnett 1999). Some of the security concerns overlap with strategic concerns such as status of forces and control over nuclear weapons, but the strategic concerns build upon the security concerns. Whereas security concerns are mostly for protecting power, strategic concerns are mostly for projecting power.

One of the main strategic concerns was the ability to retain military bases in former Soviet republics. For example, all of the Soviet Union's naval bases on the Black Sea were in Ukraine and not Russia. If Russia wanted to retain the Black Sea Fleet and not lose control of a vital part of its naval forces including ships, weapons, and troops, it had to find a way to retain those naval bases and all of the military hardware associated with those bases. To relinquish them would have been a tremendous loss of strategic power. Although Russia did have naval ports in Arkhangelsk and St. Petersburg in the North and Khabarovsk and Vladivostok on the Pacific Ocean, the Black Sea fleet was vital for maintaining interests in the Mediterranean and Middle East.

Similar to security concerns, I would expect Russia to use a combination of both multilateralism and bilateralism in the resolution of its strategic concerns. Russia would want to develop a multilateral agreement detailing the strategic concerns that needed to be addressed by all of the CIS member states, but then move to bilateralism when addressing specific concerns such as naval bases and the Black Sea Fleet in Ukraine.

In addition to security and strategic concerns following the breakup of the Soviet Union, Russia had serious concerns regarding its infrastructure. Over seventy years of a planned economy had wreaked havoc with state production. Factories were not functioning at capacity, and there was a shortage of products available in the marketplace. Despite Russia possessing a tremendous wealth of natural resources, the capability to bring the natural resources to market needed to be drastically upgraded. For example, natural gas pipelines bringing natural gas to Western Europe had to pass through Ukraine, and this became a big problem with the dissolution of the Soviet Union.

One of the biggest problems facing Russia regarding infrastructure was that the Soviet government had spread vital infrastructure among its republics (Hewett 1988). For example, steel that was necessary to produce rockets was produced in Magnetogorsk (central Siberia), rocket fuel was produced in Armenia, Ukraine, and Kazakhstan, and rockets were assembled and sent to outer space from the Baikonur Cosmodrome in Kazakhstan. This system of spreading vital infrastructure among the republics was extremely inefficient during the Soviet period, but became virtually unworkable once the republics gained their freedom.

Once Russia had established its status as the regional hegemon and resolved the most vital security and strategic concerns, Russia could then seek to ensure that it did not lose access to vital infrastructure. This was especially important for retaining access to sites such as the Baikonur Cosmodrome which was vital if Russia wanted to maintain its space program. Thus, Russia could pursue two approaches to ensure its access to vital infrastructure. First, Russia could either target specific states through bilateral treaties, or it could use a combination approach where it could establish multilateral agreements on joint use of infrastructure among all CIS member states and then further refine those agreements through bilateral treaties nested within the multilateral treaties.

Although Russia was the dominant member in the CIS, Russia did not have the power to unilaterally dictate policy to other member states. CIS member states saw a decrease in Russian capabilities, and wanted to ensure that they were able to keep Russia from regaining too much power. Thus, they determined that it was in their best interest to have good relations with Russia and to codify agreements with Russia and other CIS member states through legal treaties (Garnett and Trenin 1999). By addressing Russia multilaterally, CIS member states were able to ensure that all of the member states could collectively ensure equitable treatment and given the status of important regional actors, whereas by engaging Russia bilaterally, the CIS member states ensured that they could sign more specific agreements. The combination of both multilateral and bilateral approaches ensured that the CIS member states were important regional actors rather than vassals the way they had been under the Soviet system. By signing treaties with Russia, CIS member states were also protecting themselves. The treaties could constrain Russia and clearly establish spheres of influence and protection. In addition, since nested treaties explicitly refer to and can be constrained by prior treaties, it was in the interest of CIS member states to use nested treaties as a means of constraining Russian hegemonic power. This strategy would not work with an inflexible regional power with the capabilities to unilaterally set regional policy, but with Russia's decreased capabilities, Russia was forced to become a flexible regional power willing to use different methods to achieve its objectives (Garnett and Trenin 1999). These different methods included both multilateralism and bilateralism to achieve its objectives.

Given these complicated issues and complex array of policy interests, a more focused examination of which strategies a regional hegemon will use in its relationship with other member states in that region is required. In the next chapter, I will examine all of the bilateral and multilateral relationships in the post-Soviet space using social network analysis. The purpose of this study is merely to build a theory that can be tested in the future among all member states of the CIS. In this chapter I examine the bilateral relationships between Russia and four member states of the CIS, namely Kazakhstan, Moldova, Ukraine and Uzbekistan. The purpose of this examination is to show how these security treaties are nested within the larger multilateral organizations, which is important to understanding how a regional security architecture is built by the regional hegemon. These four cases were chosen using three criteria: geographical diversity, number of bilateral treaties with Russia, and geographical contiguity. First, two of the states are in Europe (Moldova and Ukraine), while two are in Asia (Kazakhstan and Uzbekistan). Also, one of the European states is large (Ukraine) while one is relatively small (Moldova) in terms of the amount of bilateral treaties with Russia, and the same holds true for the two Asian states (Kazakhstan-large, Uzbekistan-small). Finally, one of the two European states is contiguous to Russia (Ukraine) while the other is not (Moldova), and the same holds true for the two Asian states (Kazakhstan-contiguous, Uzbekistan-non-contiguous). Moldova was chosen because it is in Europe, has a relatively small number of bilateral treaties with Russia, and is non-contiguous. Ukraine, on the other hand, was chosen because it is in Europe, has a large number of bilateral treaties with Russia, and is contiguous. In Asia, the two countries chosen were Kazakhstan because it has a large number of bilateral treaties with Russia and is contiguous, whereas Uzbekistan has a small number of bilateral treaties with Russia and is non-contiguous. By defining the scope according to these criteria, a relatively representative sample is achieved in an effort to limit selection bias. Thus, the bilateral relationships between Russia and Kazakhstan, Moldova, Ukraine and Uzbekistan provide an ideal scope to examine whether or not a regional hegemon can use a combination of multilateralism and bilateralism in its relationships with other states within its region.

METHODOLOGY

The data used for this analysis are taken from all bilateral and multilateral security treaties between Russia and each of the four states between 1990 and 2005. In other words, the data are a systematic and complete set of bilateral and multilateral security treaties among the CIS member states. It should be noted that since the focus of this study is on the relationship between the regional hegemon and the other states in the region, the bilateral treaties examined are those between Russia and each of the other states in this study. For example, bilateral treaties between Russia and Ukraine are examined, whereas bilateral treaties between Ukraine and Uzbekistan are not examined in this study.

I have previously argued that states can combine multilateralist and bilateralist approaches to international relations through the use of treaty nesting. For this study, I define a treaty as being nested within a prior treaty if the treaty explicitly mentions the prior treaty in its content. In most cases, a nested treaty will specifically state both the name and the date that the prior treaty was signed. Thus, it is possible to determine in which specific treaties a treaty is nested within.

When examining nested treaties, the first step is to determine whether or not a specific treaty is nested. Then the nested treaty is further examined to determine whether it is nested within a multilateral or bilateral treaty. A bilateral treaty nested within another bilateral treaty provides evidence of bilateralism, whereas a bilateral treaty nested within a multilateral treaty provides evidence of a combination of multilateralism and bilateralism. The possible combinations of nested treaties are as follow: a bilateral treaty nested in another bilateral treaty; a bilateral treaty nested in a multilateral treaty; a multilateral treaty nested in a bilateral treaty; a multilateral treaty nested in a multilateral treaty; or not nested at all. In addition treaties can be nested in multiple treaties. A nested treaty can thus be nested within multilateral treaties and bilateral treaties as well. Thus, the unit of analysis is the individual bilateral security treaty, and the population is all of the bilateral security treaties signed between Russia and the CIS member states.

In addition to examining whether or not a treaty is nested, each bilateral treaty was coded according to the issue areas it addressed. Bilateral treaties can address more than one issue area, and thus each of the treaties was coded accordingly. Each issue area was coded dichotomously for each treaty so that it would be possible to analyze all of the different issue areas addressed to determine which issue areas are addressed by the bilateral treaties.

DATA AND ANALYSIS

According to multilateralist and bilateralist theory there should be evidence of either multilateralism or bilateralism within the treaties of the CIS. However, I argue that Russia as the regional hegemon can utilize both bilateralism and multilateralism in combination. If Russia were to use both bilateralism and multilateralism in combination, it would have to use nested treaties. Indeed, Russia uses large numbers of nested treaties in its bilateral relationships with Kazakhstan, Moldova, Ukraine, and Uzbekistan (see Table 4.1). In fact, in three out of the four bilateral relationships, close to 80% of the bilateral treaties are nested either in bilateral or multilateral treaties. It is evident that Russia indeed uses nested treaties in its bilateral relationships. However, the fact that a majority of bilateral treaties are nested does not specifically

Table 4.1. Percentage of Bilateral Treaties Nested in Bilateral or Multilateral Treaties

Bilateral Relationships	Percent of Treaties Nested (Total # of Nested Treaties)	Total Number of Bilateral Treaties
Kazakhstan-Russia	79 (75)	95
Moldova-Russia	23 (5)	22
Ukraine-Russia	83 (65)	78
Uzbekistan-Russia	82 (28)	34

address whether or not Russia uses a combination of multilateralism and bilateralism in its relationships with other CIS member states. It merely states that Russia utilizes the necessary tool to combine both approaches.

To determine whether or not Russia uses a combination of multilateralism and bilateralism, the nested treaties must be examined in more depth. If bilateral nested treaties are nested within multilateral treaties, then there is evidence that Russia indeed combines multilateralism and bilateralism. By examining nested treaties among the four bilateral relationships, I find that Russia does combine multilateralism and bilateralism (see Table 4.2). In this table, it should be noted that a bilateral treaty nested within another bilateral treaty is merely evidence of bilateralism, whereas a bilateral treaty nested within a multilateral treaty provides evidence of the combination of multilateralism and bilateralism. In fact, in three of the four bilateral relationships, between 42% and 52% of the bilateral nested treaties are nested within multilateral treaties. Interestingly, in the bilateral relationship between Russian and Uzbekistan, bilateral treaties nested in multilateral treaties outnumber the bilateral nested treaties. In all of the other bilateral relationships, bilateral nested treaties slightly outnumber treaties nested in multilateral treaties.

Table 4.2.   Distribution of Bilateral and Multilateral Nesting Treaties

	# of Parent Bilateral (nesting treaties) (%)	# of Parent Multilateral (nesting treaties) (%)	Total # of Nesting Treaties***	Total # of Bilateral Treaties
Kazakhstan-Russia	143 (76%)	44 (24%)	188	95
Moldova-Russia	4 (57%)	3 (43%)	7	22
Ukraine-Russia	81 (58%)	57 (42%)	139	78
Uzbekistan-Russia	39 (48%)	42 (52%)	81	34

*Table entries represent number of nesting treaties
**Total number of nesting treaties may not equal the sum of parent bilateral treaties and parent multilateral treaties due to nesting treaties that are not CIS related.
***Total Number of Nested Treaties can exceed total number of treaties due to multiple nesting

Since I am examining bilateral relationships, if Russia were to use only bilateralism in its relations, the percentage of bilateral nested treaties nested within multilateral treaties would be zero. In fact, if that were the case, the percentage of bilateral nested treaties nested within other bilateral treaties would be extremely high, but the percentage of bilateral nested treaties nested within multilateral treaties would be extremely low. However, the data show that a large percentage of bilateral nested treaties are nested within multilateral treaties, which shows strong evidence for the fact that Russia uses a combination of multilateralism and bilateralism.

Since I have shown that Russia uses a combination of multilateralism and bilateralism in its relations with CIS member states, the question now arises as to whether Russia used multilateralism to generally solve complicated issues and then use bilateralism to enact specific policies outlined in the multilateral treaties. If that is the case, then the data should show that the percent of bilateral treaties nested in multilateral treaties should be higher in the early years than in later years in Table 4.2. To test this, I sampled the number of treaties nested in bilateral treaties and the number of treaties nested in multilateral treaties at four different points. The four different years were chosen according to historical importance in Russia. I chose to compare treaties in 1993, 1996, 2000, and 2004.

In 1993, then President Yeltsin ordered Russian troops to attack the Russian White House in a standoff between the President and the Duma, which ensured an extremely strong executive branch. The reason this year was chosen was to see if there was a difference between approaches to international relations prior to the strong executive as well as after. The other years were chosen for the fact that they were years in which a presidential election took place. What I find is that the number of bilateral treaties nested within multilateral treaties was indeed higher between 1990 and 1993, and generally the proportion declined through the rest of the years (see Table 4.3). This is true for all of the bilateral relationships except for Russia and Uzbekistan. In that bilateral relationship, the percentage of bilateral treaties nested within multilateral treaties remains consistently high for all of the years examined.

It is interesting to note that although the proportion of treaties nested within multilateral treaties decreased significantly in the Kazakhstan-Russia bilateral relationship, all of the other bilateral relationships showed a relatively stable proportion during the years examined. In fact, most of the percentage of treaties nested within multilateral treaties remained between 40% and 50%, indicating that the bilateral relationships used a combination of bilateralism and multilateralism during the whole period of study.

Although these data seem to show that the trend is for bilateral treaties to be nested in more multilateral treaties early in the relationship and less with the passage of time, it is clear that a combination of bilateralism and multilateralism is used in all of the bilateral relationships. However, it is not clear what issues are addressed in these bilateral treaties and whether certain issues lend themselves more to a bilateral or multilateral approach. Since I argue that security, strategic, and infrastructure concerns should drive treaty formation between Russia and the CIS member states, it is important to examine the issue areas addressed by the treaties.

Table 4.3. Temporal Examination of Treaties Nested Within Bilateral and Multilateral Treaties (1993–2004)

		Through 1993	*Through 1996*	*Through 2000*	*Through 2004*
Kazakhstan-Russia	# Nested in Bilateral	10	73	111	126
	(%)	(33%)	(72%)	(74%)	(75%)
	# Nested in Multilateral	20	29	40	42
	(%)	(67%)	(28%)	(26%)	(25%)
Moldova-Russia	# Nested in Bilateral	2	4	4	4
	(%)	(50%)	(67%)	(67%)	(57%)
	# Nested in Multilateral	2	2	2	3
	(%)	(50%)	(33%)	(33%)	(43%)
Ukraine-Russia	# Nested in Bilateral	16	33	67	78
	(%)	(35%)	(45%)	(55%)	(58%)
	# Nested in Multilateral	30	40	55	56
	(%)	(65%)	(55%)	(45%)	(42%)
Uzbekistan-Russia	# Nested in Bilateral	0	13	26	36
	(%)	(0%)	(46%)	(42%)	(49%)
	# Nested in Multilateral	1	15	36	38
	(%)	(100%)	(54%)	(58%)	(51%)

*Table entries represent # of treaties nested in bilateral and multilateral treaties

Issue Areas

In examining the issue areas addressed by the individual treaties, it is important to examine the issue areas in each bilateral relationship separately. For ease of reporting purposes, I first examine the overall results of the issue areas addressed and whether they lend themselves to a bilateral, multilateral, or combination approach. Then I discuss each bilateral relationship according to the number of bilateral treaties signed in the bilateral relationship. If my suppositions hold true, then security, strategic, and infrastructure concerns should be the main issue areas addressed in the bilateral relationships.

According to the results, the data support my suppositions (see Table 4.4). In all of the bilateral relationships, the evidence is strong that Russia indeed uses a combination of multilateralism and bilateralism across all issue areas. Although the number of issue areas addressed differs depending on the bilateral relationship, most of the issue areas show a combination of multilateralism and bilateralism. Moreover, there seems to be a fairly even divide between those treaties that are nested in bilateral treaties and those treaties nested in multilateral treaties.

Interestingly, the treaties in the bilateral relationship between Russia and Ukraine seem to address the widest variety of issue areas, whereas the bilateral relationship between Russia and Moldova addresses the least variety of

Table 4.4. Security Issue Areas Addressed by Nesting

		Stationing of Troops and Bases	Nuclear Weapons	Chemical Weapons	Conventional Weapons	Small Arms	Terrorism	Natural Disaster	Natural Resource Management	Immigration	Interstate Crime	Drug Trafficking	Interstate War	Intrastate War	Territorial Disputes	Peacekeeping	Financing	Infrastructure and Administration	Friendship and Cooperation	No Security Issues
Kazakhstan-Russia	# of Bilateral treaties	35	5	0	0	0	0	1	2	0	0	0	0	0	0	0	5	69	23	0
	% Nested in Bilateral	82	100	—	—	—	—	50	60	—	—	—	—	—	—	—	62	78	70	—
	% Nested in Multilateral	18	0	—	—	—	—	50	40	—	—	—	—	—	—	—	38	22	30	—
	Total # Nested	71	6	—	—	—	—	1	10	—	—	—	—	—	—	—	13	144	30	—
Moldova-Russia	# of Bilateral treaties	0	0	0	0	1	0	0	0	0	1	0	2	0	6	1	0	0	0	8
	% Nested in Bilateral	—	—	—	—	0	—	100	—	—	33	—	100	—	100	0	—	—	—	0
	% Nested in Multilateral	—	—	—	—	0	—	0	—	—	67	—	0	—	0	0	—	—	—	100
	Total # Nested	—	—	—	—	0	—	1	—	—	3	—	1	—	2	0	—	—	—	1
Ukraine-Russia	# of Bilateral treaties	31	19	1	30	2	2	6	4	9	3	7	0	2	5	0	42	26	22	2
	% Nested in Bilateral	68	58	67	53	67	80	56	100	53	83	60	—	14	75	—	55	58	49	67
	% Nested in Multilateral	32	42	33	47	33	20	44	0	47	17	40	—	86	25	—	45	42	51	33
	Total # Nested	63	55	3	60	6	5	9	5	19	6	15	—	7	8	—	78	55	39	3
Uzbekistan-Russia	# of Bilateral treaties	0	0	—	9	2	5	0	1	1	6	2	0	0	0	0	5	0	9	4
	% Nested in Bilateral	—	—	—	56	57	54	—	100	100	32	22	—	—	—	—	30	—	61	89
	% Nested in Multilateral	—	—	—	44	43	46	—	0	0	68	78	—	—	—	—	70	—	39	11
	Total # Nested	—	—	—	18	7	13	—	2	1	19	9	—	—	—	—	20	—	18	9

issue areas. This variation among the bilateral relationships should be examined in greater depth according to the individual bilateral relationship. I now turn to examining each relationship in greater depth.

Kazakhstan-Russia

The relationship between Kazakhstan and Russia is extremely important for a couple of major reasons. The first reason is that many Soviet troops were stationed in Kazakhstan at the time of the dissolution of the Soviet Union. Many of these troops were "rocket troops" meaning that they were assigned control of mobile nuclear weapons. In addition, many of these troops were stationed at the Baikonur Cosmodrome and other facilities involved in the Russian space program. This fact supports the supposition that the stationing of troops is an important issue that Russia needed to address, and the data corroborate this supposition. In fact, 35 treaties address stationing forces, with 33 of them being nested.

Although the stationing of troops was an important issue area addressed in the bilateral relationship, it was surprising that there weren't many treaties addressing nuclear weapons between Russia and Kazakhstan. There were only 5 treaties. Since the nuclear arsenal was under the control of the Soviet strategic rocket forces prior to the collapse of the Soviet Union, Russia and Kazakhstan had to resolve questions about ownership of the nuclear weapons, which country would control them, and many other issues related to the nuclear arsenal. Even more surprising is the finding that even though all of the other issue areas in the Kazakhstan-Russia bilateral relationship show signs of bilateral treaties nested in multilateral treaties, none of the treaties addressing nuclear weapons show a mixed approach. In fact, all of the nested treaties were nested within bilateral treaties.

The second reason that Kazakhstan was so important to Russia's interests was the Baikonur Cosmodrome mentioned earlier. It was vital for Russia to maintain its hegemonic status by continuing to be greatly involved in outer space. Russia did not want to cede outer space solely to the Americans, and felt that it had inherited the legacy of Sputnik and Gagarin. By inheriting this legacy, Russia still had to be competitive in the space race, which meant that it either had to build up its own infrastructure or try to utilize the current infrastructure in Kazakhstan. Thus, there is a situation where the regional hegemon did not possess the current infrastructure to maintain its current status, and thus needed to address this infrastructure deficiency. The data seem to support this contention. In fact, the vast majority (72%) of bilateral treaties between Russia and Kazakhstan address infrastructure. Of these 69 treaties that address infrastructure, 56 are nested, which gives further support for this contention.

Finally, although the issue areas addressed in this bilateral relationship show evidence of a combination of multilateralism and bilateralism, the majority of the nested treaties in this relationship show evidence for bilateralism. In other words, most of the treaties that are nested are nested within bilateral treaties rather than multilateral treaties. This is surprising as many of the other relationships are more evenly balanced between treaties nested within bilateral treaties and treaties nested within multilateral treaties. Despite this finding, it should be stressed that there is still strong evidence that Russia uses a combination of bilateralism and multilateralism in this bilateral relationship.

Ukraine-Russia

The relationship between Russia and Ukraine covers almost all of the issue areas covered by this study. Moreover, the combination of a multilateralist and bilateralist approach is extremely evident in this relationship. High percentages of bilateral treaties are nested within multilateral treaties. This finding provides direct support for the supposition that through the use of nested treaties, hegemons can choose a combination of multilateralism and bilateralism.

Similar to the bilateral relationship between Kazakhstan and Russia, the data seem to support my contention that the stationing of troops should be one of the major issue areas addressed by treaties. Many Soviet troops were stationed in Ukraine prior to 1991. Moreover, the Black Sea Fleet was stationed in Odessa. Russia did not want to fully relinquish its claim to the Black Sea Fleet, either sailors or ships. Thus, a substantial amount of treaties had to lay the groundwork for the reassignment of the Black Sea Fleet to either the Ukrainian or Russian Navy.

To divide the Black Sea Fleet, troops had to be reassigned and new military ports had to be updated or created. Bilateral treaties range from the creation of dry-docks to the exact number of ships that each state would receive. Due to the technical nature of the reapportionment of the Black Sea Fleet, each successive treaty is constrained by prior treaties related to the Black Sea Fleet, which would explain treaty nestedness in the bilateral treaties between Russia and Ukraine in the stationing troops issue area.

Unlike the bilateral relationship between Russia and Kazakhstan, the bilateral relationship between Russia and Ukraine also shows evidence supporting my contention that there should be many treaties addressing nuclear weapons, and that those treaties should be largely nested. In fact, of the 19 treaties that address nuclear weapons, 17 (89%) of them are nested. Moreover, where

100% of the nested treaties in the Kazakhstan-Russia bilateral relationship were nested in bilateral treaties, there is a much more even split in the bilateral relationship between Russia and Ukraine. In fact, 42% of nested treaties addressing nuclear weapons between Russia and Ukraine are nested in multilateral treaties.

One very surprising result according to these data is the number of treaties that address financing. In fact, there are 11 more treaties addressing financing than the stationing of troops. Of the 42 treaties that address financing, 35 of them are nested. The logical question that arises in this case is what kind of financing is addressed. Once again, the answer seems to deal with the Black Sea Fleet. With the cost of war ships, submarines, and aircraft carriers, a great deal of financing had to be arranged to keep both states happy with the results. The states could not simply split the navy in half, so financing became extremely important to ensure a mutually beneficial bilateral relationship. Again, 42% of nested treaties in the bilateral relationship that address financing are nested within multilateral treaties.

The only other potentially non-military issue area of significant importance in the bilateral relationship between Ukraine and Russia involves the infrastructure. However, this could be misleading. One of the major reasons for so many infrastructure treaties is that Russia did not have a major port on the Black Sea that would be able to serve as the home port for the Black Sea Fleet. Ukraine did possess the necessary naval bases, and Russia needed access to them. This situation is similar to that of the bilateral relationship between Kazakhstan and Russia, except in this case it is a lack of the necessary military infrastructure in Russia that led to so many treaties addressing infrastructure.

Finally, similar to the bilateral relationship between Kazakhstan and Russia, friendship treaties also were numerous. However, only 77% of the friendship treaties were nested, whereas in the other major issue areas the percentage of nested treaties was between 80% and 90%. Interestingly, there were more bilateral treaties nested within multilateral treaties (51%) than bilateral treaties nested within other bilateral treaties (49%) in this issue area.

Uzbekistan-Russia

The bilateral relationship between Uzbekistan and Russia is one of the smaller bilateral relationships in this study. However, it is also a very important relationship. It is extremely important for three reasons. The first reason is that because of Uzbekistan's geographical location and the fact that the majority of its citizens are Muslim, this makes Uzbekistan extremely important in terms of terrorism. Russia and Uzbekistan have cooperated in the war on terrorism, and Uzbekistan has often been targeted by terrorist groups. More-over, with United States involvement in the war on terrorism, Russia might be worried about its sphere of influence in that area of the world. Thus it is not surprising that the data show that terrorism is an important issue area ad-dressed by the treaties and that 100% of them are nested. Also, it is interesting that the combination approach is also used in this bilateral relationship related to terrorism rather than the approach being mostly bilateral.

Similar to the terrorism issue area, many treaties between Uzbekistan and Russia address military cooperation. A lot of these treaties have to do with joint military training of troops and sharing military information. With terror-ist groups infiltrating Uzbekistan, military training and preparedness becomes all that more important.

The second reason for strong relations between Russia and Uzbekistan is because of crime. Smuggling and drug trafficking are big problems in Uz-bekistan, and many of the drugs end up in Russia. Thus, a strong bilateral relationship between the two countries is needed to combat international crime and smuggling. Thus, it is not surprising that interstate crime is such an important issue in the bilateral relationship between Russia and Uzbeki-stan where it is not as important in other bilateral relationships among CIS member states.

It should be noted that fighting terrorists and interstate crimes requires both conventional weapons and a tremendous amount of money. Thus, it is not surprising that both conventional weapons and financing are important issue areas in the bilateral relationship between Russia and Uzbekistan. It is surprising, however, that neither nuclear weapons nor troop placement are important issue areas addressed.

Moldova-Russia

The relationship between Moldova and Russia is the most problematic of the four bilateral relationships studied in this analysis and thus requires a deeper understanding. Relations between Russia and Moldova are extremely contentious. Despite their contentious relationship, and Russian involvement within Moldova's borders, Moldova and Russia were able to sign twenty-two bilateral treaties, with five of them (22%) being nested (see Table 4.1).

Since 1940, the Soviet Union had tried to create ethnic cleavages between Moldova and Romania. One of the prime examples of this policy was to cre-ate a Moldovan language[1] by using Cyrillic instead of the traditional Latin alphabet (King 1994). More importantly, they ignored the ethnic cleavage between the population living in the Transnistria Region and those living in Moldova. While Moldovans held cultural affiliations with Romania, those living in Transnistria were more culturally tied to ethnic Russians. Over 60% of the population was ethnic Russian, and once ethnic Moldovans gained power in Moldova in 1991, Transnistria declared independence from Moldova and looked to Moscow for assistance.

Russia urged for the secession of the ethnic Russian region of Transnistria, which led to a civil war. With Russian troops already stationed in Transnistria, Russia was not only able to advocate secession for Transnistria, but was also able to use their forces to initiate a cease-fire between the warring factions, thus granting de-facto independence to Transnistria (King 1994). Thus, it is not surprising that the greatest number of treaties (32%) between Russia and Moldova have to do with Transnistria.

A further examination of the bilateral treaties between the Russian Federation and Moldova indicates that of the total 22 bilateral security documents in our treaty population, 11 (or 50%) were negotiated in the years 1990–1994. The first treaty was a September 1990 agreement on the establishment of relations between the two countries. However, it was not until almost two years later, in July 1992, that another treaty was signed. Unsurprisingly, this treaty dealt with establishing a military cease-fire between the Transnistria Region and Moldova. Moreover, this treaty established de facto independence for Transnistria, with Russian forces acting as peacekeepers to ensure that there would be no renewed fighting.

The substantive focus (73%) of the bilateral treaties between the Russian Federation and the Republic of Moldova has to do with the Russian military forces stationed in Moldova. Most of those treaties have to do with (1) arrangements governing Russian forces on Moldovan territory (9 treaties); (2) Transnistria (7 treaties); (3) joint military operations (4 treaties); and (4) exchanges of military hardware and weapons systems (3 treaties). Other issues addressed were border security, methods of handling confidential information, and joint crime control efforts.

One of the most interesting aspects of the relationship between Russia and Moldova is that it does not follow the normal pattern of development in bilateral treaty formation. Many of the other bilateral treaties between Russia and the other members of the CIS involve laying the foundation for relations between the two states, signing treaties of mutual understanding and friendship, and then beginning to address substantive issues. Although the first bilateral treaty between Russia and Moldova involves a mutual declaration of sovereignty, it is not until 2001 that the first friendship treaty between Russia and Moldova is signed. Most of the bilateral treaties involved substantive issues, and very few of the treaties (5 treaties) showed any signs of treaty nestedness. In fact, in 2001, Russian-Moldovan relations improved as Russian-Transnistrian relations deteriorated, however, in 2003 the relations soured again with the failure of Moldova and the Transnistria region to sign the Kozak Memorandum, which would have provided a resolution to the conflict.

The failure of both parties to sign the Kozak Memorandum was a pivotal moment in Russian-Moldovan relations (Tolkacheva 2006). By not signing the Kozak Memorandum, Moldova signaled its intention that it preferred to work with the European Union and not with Russia to resolve the conflict, which set relations back between the two states back even further.

Despite the fact that the overall number of bilateral treaties between Russia and Moldova declined after 2000, relations between the two states actually improved. There was more of an effort to maintain a dialogue, and both states seemed to be content with maintaining the status quo in Transnistria. With the Georgian invasion of South Ossetia, there is renewed interest in the status of Transnistria. In fact, in September, 2008, the Russian Foreign Minister, Sergei Lavrov, reiterated to the Moldovans that as long as the status quo was maintained in Transnistria and that Moldovan forces would not move into the disputed territory, that Moldova had nothing to fear from Russia. Ultimately, I would have expected more treaties and specifically nested treaties if there was no separatist movement in Moldova with Russian peacekeeping troops ensuring de facto independence of Transnistria.

Neoinstitutionalist liberals have a long standing debate about the direction of international relations in the latter part of the twentieth century. Scholars like Ruggie (1994; 1995) claim that multilateralism is the preferred approach to international relations and point to international organizations such as NATO as confirmation of this position. Other scholars, on the other hand, argue that very few organizations function like NATO, and that in fact, international relations is bilateral (see Hemmer and Katzenstein 2002). However, neither the multilateralist scholars nor the bilateralist scholars argue that both approaches can be used in combination.

The problem with both the multilateralist and bilateralist school of thought is that a dichotomization occurs. Much as in a statistical analysis where the dichotomization of a continuous variable leads to a decrease in variance, and thus the reliability of predictive or descriptive results, important conceptual information is being lost in this case as well. The truth is that approaches to international relations can be either multilateral, bilateral, or some combination of the two.

Russia presents a very interesting conundrum to both the multilateralists and the bilateralists. On the one hand, it is seen as carrying a big stick as the regional hegemon that is willing to unilaterally force its neighbors into acting in accordance with its wishes. On the other hand, Russia is seen as a state that has to cooperate with its neighbors to resolve a power vacuum that was left after the collapse of the Soviet Union.

I have shown in this analysis that contrary to Western perceptions, Russia is actually a flexible regional power willing to use different methods to achieve its goals. In this way, Russia defies multilateralists and bilateralists both, for it does not use just one or the other method in its relations with its neighbors, it uses both in combination by using nested treaties.

Ultimately the combination of bilateral and multilateral approaches to international relations through treaty nestedness was prevalent among most of the four bilateral relationships in this study. In fact, as we shall see in the next chapter, treaty nestedness is prevalent in all of Russia's relationships with the FSU. In the next chapter, I will show how treaty nestedness, and specifically the combination of a multilateral and bilateral approach to building a regional security architecture is vital to all of the relationships in the post-Soviet space. Using network analysis, I will show how certain foundational bilateral and multilateral treaties serve as the lodestone treaties for creating a regional security architecture.

Finally, not all states in bilateral relationships choose to utilize treaty nestedness. The case of the bilateral relationship between Moldova and Russia illustrates this point well. There is a lack of nesting it the bilateral relationship that probably is attributed to the problematic and antagonistic nature of their relationship. Initial data indicate that the cause of treaty nestedness and overall treaty formation might be due to Russia's support of Transnistria which in turn antagonizes the Moldovan government. Moldova in turn has turned toward the West rather than the Russians hoping that the West will help solve their internal dispute. Seeing how the West has continuously expanded both the EU and NATO, Moldova is hoping that it will be able to join both of these organizations and will be able to leave Russia's sphere of influence. This is especially true beginning in 2013, where the EU actively wooed Ukraine, Moldova and Georgia into signing cooperation agreements with the EU to ensure that those states would not be within Russia's sphere of influence. Naturally, Russia has resented the geopolitical interference of the West, and has set up its own Monroe Doctrine in the post-Soviet space. The geopolitical conflict between Russia and the West only highlights the importance of creating a regional security architecture to bring order and predictability to the states within the region.

Although I have found that there is middle ground in the debate between multilateralism and bilateralism, the question remains as to what motivates regional hegemonic states to choose its approach to international relations. Is it just a question of capabilities? If so, then one would presume that the more power a regional hegemon has, the likelier the hegemon is to act bilaterally (if not unilaterally). Whereas if a regional hegemon has less relative power, it should then choose to act multilaterally. However, this would indicate that the regional hegemon is not necessarily choosing its approach to international relations, but that the relative power of the other actors will dictate the hegemon's approach to international relations. Future research should examine the ways in which a hegemon is allowed to choose the approach to international relations.

Ultimately this chapter has shown that Russia indeed uses a combination of multilateral and bilateral means in building not only its relationships with other FSU states, but also in creating its regional order. Specifically, this chapter has demonstrated that Russia uses this combination method in creating the regional order, but the chapter has not shown how Russia has built the regional order using this combination. In the next chapter, I will show how Russian multilateral and bilateral treaties combine to create the regional security architecture and promote regional governance and stability.

Russia's quest to build a regional security architecture has been a deliberative and long term strategy. Russia's leaders have worked to build relations with the FSU states in ways that not only ensure regional stability, Russia's continued hegemonic status, yet also seeks to create predictability in the post-Soviet space. Its approach allows for a region-specific approach to its foreign policy while allowing a certain level of flexibility to account for those states that are more or less eager to work with Russia. It should not be forgotten that while Russia is the most powerful state in the region and is often seen as the neighborhood bully, that it must work in conjunction with the weaker states in the region to ensure its regional security architecture. Certain states like Moldova present challenges to Russia's building the regional security architecture, while other states like Kazakhstan are much more eager to cooperate. Thus, Russia as the regional hegemon, must be very flexible in how it constructs not only its bilateral relations, but also how it constructs the multilateral organizations in the region as well as the combination of the two. In other words, creating the regional security architecture is not an easy task. It requires cooperation from the other regional states, in addition to a deliberative plan to create the regional architecture. Following events in Ukraine in 2013 and 2014, many of the states in the post-Soviet space are even more wary of Russia and its hegemonic status in the post-Soviet space. Russia will need to continue to provide flexible bilateral and multilateral relationships with the weaker states in the region to continue to illicit cooperation from these states.

NOTE

1. Although Soviet linguists claimed that the Moldovan language was distinct, most other linguists agreed that there was no distinct Moldovan language, but that it was actually Romanian.

Chapter Five

Building a Regional IGO Network

In Chapter 2, I discuss Russia's bilateral relations with the FSU states. It is possible to determine which relationships were more cooperative than others, and based on network analysis, it was possible to determine which relationships were more likely to devolve into violent conflict than other relationships. In Chapter 3, I introduce Russia's multilateral relationships in the post-Soviet space. Specifically, Russia has been very active in its multilateral strategy. Yet, scholars have all noted the relative ineffectiveness of these regional IGOs at multilateral governance. Instead, scholars have often noted that Russia has been more effective at pursuing a bilateral strategy with the FSU states. In Chapter 4, I argue that a dichotomous approach to examining international relations by determining whether a hegemon pursued more of a bilateral or multilateral strategy set up a false premise. Actually, hegemonic states pursue a combination of a multilateral and bilateral strategy of international relations when creating regional order and stability. I show that Russia uses treaty nesting to combine bilateralism and multilateralism. This approach allows Russia to create its regional security architecture, establish its regional order, and create a stable regional environment that promotes predictability for all of the regional states.

In Chapter 1, I introduce the theoretical framework for understanding regional order and the fact that a regional order is nested in the global order (see Figure 5.1). In the case of Russia, following the collapse of the Soviet Union, Russia had to recreate the regional order, nested within the global order mandated by the global hegemon, the United States. Thus, we should expect to see Russia's regional security architecture nested within the broader global order. As Figure 5.1 shows, the global order is established by the United States, which establishes its rules, principles, and institutions. Then the regional hegemon, in this case Russia, establishes a regional order which

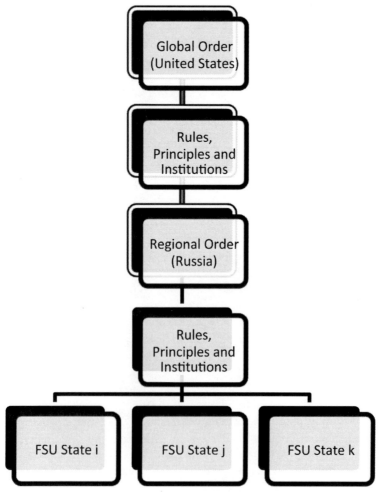

Figure 5.1.   Russia's Regional Order Nested in the Global Order

falls under the global order. In the regional order, Russia establishes its own rules, principles, and institutions. Finally, the FSU states must then abide by those rules, principles, and institutions.

While it is clear that the regional and global orders should be related, it is not necessarily apparent as to how they are related. To determine how they are related, it becomes necessary to examine the rules, principles and institutions in the regional order. By analyzing these institutions for nesting, we should be able to determine how the regional rules, principles and institutions are tied to the global rules and institutions. Further, we can then determine and examine how a regional order is created by the regional hegemon.

The way in which I will examine the regional order is by analyzing all of the treaties (both bilateral and multilateral) between Russia and the other FSU states between 1991 and 2005. These years are the critical years for building regional order, so should show how the regional order is created. I will further examine each treaty for signs of nesting. The first step is to determine whether or not a specific treaty is nested in another treaty or treaties. This can be done by carefully reading a treaty and seeing whether or not it specifically refers to another treaty. If it does, then it is nested within the treaty/treaties to which the specific treaty refers.

Once each treaty has been analyzed for evidence of nesting, then the treaty must be classified according to which treaty/treaties it is nested within. Specifically a treaty can be nested within at least one bilateral treaty, or a multilateral treaty, or any combination of the two. Each treaty is given either a specific name or unique identification number and then is carefully read and coded to determine its relationship to other treaties. Again, it should be noted that a treaty is related to another treaty if and only if it mentions a specific treaty within the text of the treaty. If a treaty merely deals with the same issue area addressed by a prior treaty without referring to a specific treaty within its text, then that treaty is not considered to be nested at all and thus is unrelated to any other treaty.

Once the relationship between the treaties is established it is possible to use social network analysis to analyze the relationship between the treaties. For example, we can use degree centrality measures to determine which specific treaties are the most central to relationships within the post-Soviet space. Specifically, I can examine a specific multilateral IGO and its member states to further examine the regional order. Since this research seeks to examine the post-Soviet space, I will only examine those multilateral IGOs specifically within the post-Soviet space (See Table 5.1). As Table 5.1 shows, since both the SCO and BSEC have member states that are not within the post-Soviet space, those two IGOs will not be a part of this analysis. In this chapter, I will first examine each of the IGOs with only FSU member states to see how they fit in to the regional security architecture. In the next chapter, I will examine the regional architecture as a whole, and

Table 5.1.   IGO's in the Post-Soviet Space

IGO's with Only FSU Member States	IGO's with Outside FSU Member States
GUAM	BSEC
CSTO	SCO
EurAzEC	
Eurasian Union	
CIS	

discuss how it was created. I now turn to an examination of GUAM and how it fits in to the security architecture.

GUAM

Chapter 2 contains a more detailed discussion of GUAM and its institutional design features. However, it is important to note that the goals of GUAM were to limit Russian regional influence. Thus, we should expect the member states to not actively take part in the regional order that Russia created following the collapse of the Soviet Union. That is not to say that they did not participate, since they were the weaker states and had to engage Russia. However, they were much less active in their engagement of Russia than many of the other FSU states (see Table 5.2). As Table 5.2 shows, the relationships between Georgia and Russia, Moldova and Russia, and Azerbaijan and Russia, are the least cooperative relationships. In fact, the three relationships are more likely to have violent conflict occur between them than the other relationships in the FSU (Slobodchikoff 2013b). While the relationships between Russia and Ukraine and Russia and Uzbekistan are more cooperative than those of the other GUAM member states, nevertheless they are problematic.

Table 5.2.   Measure of Cooperative Bilateral Relationship Among GUAM Member States with Russia 1991–2005

Bilateral Relationship	Cooperative Relationship
Russia-Ukraine	1.53
Russia-Uzbekistan	1.47
Russia-Georgia	.60
Russia-Azerbaijan	.56
Russia-Moldova	.41

Given the relative lack of cooperation among the GUAM member states with Russia, it is logical to expect that there is a reluctance to accept the regional order (see Figure 5.2). In fact, since the goal of many of the GUAM member states is to seek to join the EU and NATO, it should not be surprising that many of the most central treaties in the treaty network are neither bilateral treaties between Russia and any of the GUAM member states. Instead, many of the most central treaties in the network are treaties that involve Western powers and are much more international in scope.

As Figure 5.2 shows, one of the most central treaties in this network is the Helsinki Act. It is located in the bottom of Figure 5.2. The Helsinki Act was the final act signed in 1975 when Finland called together the Conference on

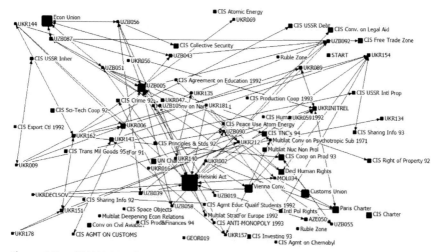

Figure 5.2. GUAM Member States' Treaty Network in Regional Order

Security and Cooperation in Europe. The idea of this conference was that those who were responsible for peace in Europe (both Western Europe and the Communist Bloc) would gather and try to come to agreement on how to improve relations between Western Europe and the Communist Bloc. Over thirty five states attended this conference including the United States and the Soviet Union.

The importance of the Helsinki Act is that it recognizes territorial sovereignty and the inviolability of a state's borders. Further, the states agreed in the Helsinki Act to refrain from using force against another state in Europe, or even from the threatening the use of force. In addition, states agreed on respecting human rights including the right to self determination. Finally, the Helsinki Act called for a peaceful resolution to all international disputes.

The reason that these FSU states chose to specifically nest many of their agreements within the Helsinki Act was because of the lack of the resource of trust with Russia. In other words, they wanted to ensure that Russia would abide not only by their agreements, but also would continue to recognize their sovereignty, the inviolability of their borders, and would try to peacefully resolve disputes between them and Russia.

Another treaty that is central to the relationship between the GUAM member states and Russia is the Vienna Convention. The Vienna Convention outlined the supremacy of treaties and defined the fact that states could not only negotiate treaties, but that those treaties were the foundations of modern international law. Further, many states including Russia and the FSU states recognized the primacy of international law, meaning that international law took precedence over domestic law. In other words, if a domestic law and

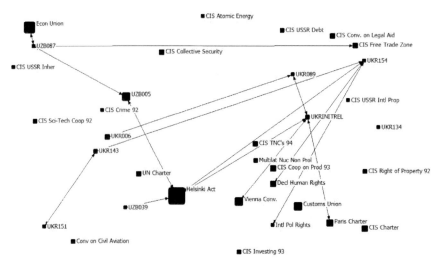

Figure 5.3.   More Central Treaties among GUAM Member States and Russia 1991–2005

international law were in conflict, then the domestic law would be changed
to be in concert with international law.

A closer examination of the most central treaties among GUAM member
states and Russia shows that some other treaties such as the UN Charter and
the Paris Charter also were central to the treaty network (see figure 5.3). Especially important to the GUAM member states is the Paris Charter, which
was signed in 1990.

The Paris Charter is nested within the framework of the Helsinki Act, except that it was signed just after the fall of the Communist Bloc. It recognized
that security was threatened with the collapse of the Soviet Union and that an
agreement needed to be reached quickly to bring the old Communist states
into the Western legal system. Thus, most of the European countries in addition to the United States and Canada attended a summit for European security
which ended with the signing of the Paris Charter.

One of the major accomplishments of the Paris Charter was the formation
of the Organization for Security and Cooperation in Europe (OSCE). The
OSCE is the predominant security organization in Europe whose member
states encompass both former Communist states and Western states. The
OSCE is responsible for arms control, human rights, freedom of the press,
and is often responsible for monitoring free and fair elections.

The Paris Charter also set up a professional secretariat and became an
international organization interested in securing peace and cooperation in
Europe. One of its stated goals was to bring the former Communist countries
into Western ideology and the Western legal framework. Thus, it is no sur-

prise that the Paris Charter would be one of the most central treaties in the GUAM member states' treaty network with Russia.

In addition to nesting its relationship to Russia within a Western legal framework, the GUAM member states' treaty network also has a couple of other more post-Soviet region treaties as being central to their relationship. For example, the Customs Union Treaty and the Economic Union Treaty are extremely central to their relationship (located at the bottom right and top left of Figure 5.3). Interestingly, the CIS Free Trade Zone Treaty is tied to the Economic Union Treaty in this relationship.

Since most of the post-Soviet regional treaties that are central to the relationship involve economics and trade, it shows that there is a realization among the GUAM member states that they must engage Russia on economic issues, but are still very wary of its intentions. Even economic cooperation must be tied to the Western legal framework to overcome the lack of trust by the GUAM member states of Russia (see Table 5.3). As Table 5.3 shows, the central treaties of the GUAM treaty network are mostly tied to the Western legal framework with some regional treaties also being central to the GUAM treaty network.

Table 5.3. Central Treaties of the GUAM Treaty Network (1991–2005)

Lodestone Global Order Treaties	Lodestone Regional Order Treaties	Lodestone Bilateral Treaties
Helsinki Act	Customs Union	UKR006
Paris Charter	Economic Union	UZB005
UN Charter	Collective Security Treaty	
Vienna Convention	CIS Charter	
International Declaration of Human Rights	CIS TNC Agreement	
Treaty of Non-Proliferation of Nuclear Weapons	CIS Convention on Legal Aid	
	CIS Production Coop	
	CIS Right of Property	
	CIS Atomic Energy	

Finally, Figure 5.3 clearly shows that none of those states that have non-cooperative relationships with Russia have any bilateral treaties that are central to the relationship of the GUAM member states and Russia. A couple of bilateral treaties between Uzbekistan and Russia and Ukraine and Russia are central to the relationship. Specifically, the bilateral treaties are the basis for international relations between Russia and Uzbekistan and Russia and Ukraine respectively. Both of the bilateral treaties are located in the center left of Figure 5.3 (UKR006 and UZB005).

The GUAM member states are much more wary of their place within the regional order established by Russia. Yet they have cautiously engaged the regional order. Their insistence on tying the relationship to Western legal values grants legitimacy to the regional order as being nested within the global regional order. This is certainly one way to carefully manage regional cooperation and coexistence within the regional order. I now turn to an IGO that is more accepting of Russia's hegemonic status and right to create the regional order, specifically the Collective Security Treaty Organization (CSTO).

COLLECTIVE SECURITY TREATY ORGANIZATION (CSTO)

Contrary to the GUAM member states, the purpose of the CSTO was not to limit Russia's regional hegemony, but rather to develop a coordinated defensive military alliance. That is not to say that mistrust of Russia isn't an important obstacle to cooperation within the military alliance. In fact, it is due to the region's mistrust of Russia that scholars deem the CSTO to be a relatively unsuccessful IGO.

Examining the relationship between the CSTO and its member states using social network analysis provides a very different result than that of the GUAM member states (see Figure 5.4). As Figure 5.4 shows, the Helsinki Act is also central to the CSTO treaty network (bottom left of Figure 5.4). However, it is not as central to the relationship as it was to the GUAM treaty network. In addition to the Helsinki Act, the Paris Charter is also central to the relationship (bottom right of Figure 5.4).

Like the GUAM treaty network, the UN Charter is also central (top middle of Figure 5.4), as is the Declaration of Human Rights (top left of Figure 5.4). In other words, the CSTO, like GUAM, is grounded in a Western legal framework and Western ideals. Much as with GUAM, the CSTO stresses the idea of state sovereignty as being a fundamental aspect of relations among the member states as well as the inviolability of member states' borders. By nesting the relationship of CSTO in the Western legal framework, CSTO is able to manage the problem of mistrust of Russia while also nesting the regional organization within the global order.

Figure 5.4 also shows that CSTO has a much denser treaty network than GUAM. There is much more interaction between the Western legal framework and regional treaties, IGOs, as well as bilateral treaties. In fact, besides the Western legal treaties, some of the most important lodestone treaties are the Economic Union Treaty (top middle of Figure 5.4) and the Customs Union Treaty (top right of Figure 5.4).

An examination of a more detailed network map that shows only more central treaties to the treaty network shows the importance of security treaties to the CSTO treaty network (see Figure 5.5). This is logical due to the fact that

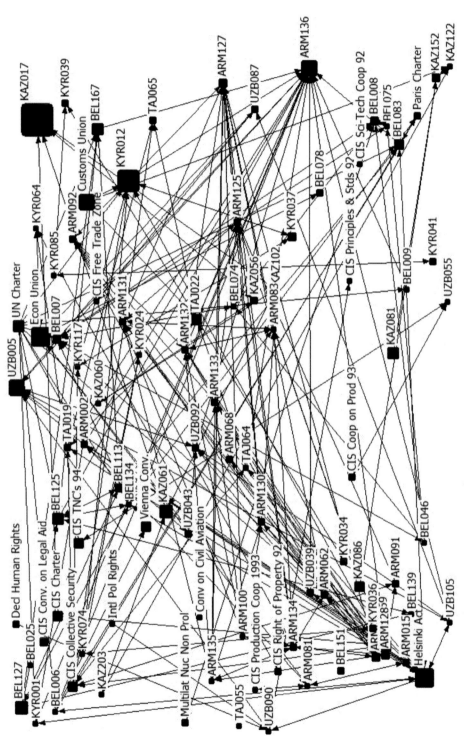

Figure 5.4. CSTO Member States' Treaty Network (1991–2005)

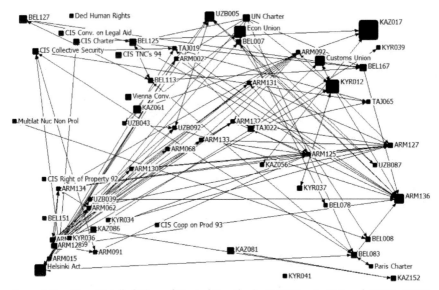

Figure 5.5.   More Detailed View of Central Treaties in CSTO Treaty Network (1991–2005)

CSTO is a defensive alliance. In addition, the Treaty on Non-Proliferation of Nuclear Weapons is also central to the CSTO alliance.

Certain bilateral security treaties also serve as central lodestone treaties to the CSTO treaty network. For example, the Treaty on Military Cooperation between Kazakhstan and the Russian Federation (KAZ061 top left of Figure 5.5) is central to the CSTO treaty network. Not only is this treaty important to the bilateral relationship between Russia and Kazakhstan, but it is also tied to the multilateral CSTO treaty network.

It is important to ascertain which are the most vital lodestone treaties to the CSTO treaty network. By only examining the most central treaties in the CSTO treaty network, we can determine the most vital treaties (see Figure 5.6). Figure 5.6 shows the interaction between bilateral treaties, multilateral regional treaties as well as their place within the Western legal structure.

Figure 5.6 very clearly shows the Helsinki Act at the bottom left as one of the most vital central treaties to the CSTO treaty network. Further, the Vienna Convention and the UN Charter are the other Western treaties which nest the CSTO treaty network within the Western legal framework.

The Collective Security Treaty, Customs Union Treaty, Economic Union Treaty, and the CIS Charter serve to nest the CSTO within the regional order in the post-Soviet space. It should be noted, that the Collective Security

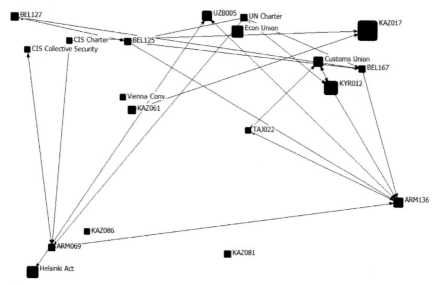

Figure 5.6. Most Vital Treaties to CSTO Treaty Network (1991–2005)

Treaty focuses solely on regional security issues while the Economic Union Treaty and the Customs Union Treaty focus on regional economic issues. Finally, the CIS Charter addresses both security and economic issues.

Bilateral treaties further solidify the relationships between Russia and the other CSTO member states into the regional order. In contrast to the GUAM treaty network, the CSTO treaty network has at least one bilateral lodestone treaty from each member state. Armenia has two bilateral treaties that are central to the CSTO treaty network. The first is the Treaty on the Russian Military Base in Armenia (ARM069 bottom left of figure 5.6), which was signed March 16, 1995. This treaty established a Russian military presence in Armenia and allowed Russia to lease the territory upon which its troops would be stationed.

The second bilateral treaty between Armenia and Russia that was central to the CSTO treaty network was The Agreement between Armenia and Russia on the Protection of State Secrets (ARM136 right side of figure 5.6), which was signed on November 5, 2002. This treaty was intended to safeguard state secrets between the two states and ensure intelligence cooperation between the states.

There were three bilateral treaties between Russia and Belarus that served as lodestone treaties for the CSTO treaty network. Specifically, all three bilateral treaties established a bilateral union between Russia and Belarus and are central to the CSTO treaty network (BEL125 and BEL127 top left of figure 6, and BEL167 top right of figure 5.6). These bilateral treaties created a union which would function like an IGO, and would facilitate cooperation in both economic and security issues between the two states. The treaties established a professional secretariat and had a formal structure beyond just meetings beyond the two member states.

There were four bilateral treaties between Kazakhstan and Russia which were central lodestone treaties to the CSTO treaty network. The first is the most central treaty to the CSTO treaty network. It is the Treaty of Friendship and Cooperation between Kazakhstan and Russia (KAZ17 on the top right of Figure 5.6). Kazakhstan is central to Russian security and economic interests, so it is not surprising that a bilateral treaty between Kazakhstan and Russia would be so central to the CSTO treaty network. Further, the treaty lays the groundwork for cooperation in such security matters as the Baikonur Cosmodrome, which is central to Russia's space infrastructure.

The second bilateral treaty between Kazakhstan and Russia that serves as a lodestone treaty to the CSTO treaty network is the Military Cooperation Treaty signed March 28, 1994 (KAZ061 on the top left of Figure 5.6). This treaty laid the groundwork for allowing Russian troops in Kazakhstan as well as outlining future cooperation with the Baikonur Cosmodrome.

The final two bilateral treaties between Russia and Kazakhstan that are central to the CSTO treaty network both directly address the Baikonur Cosmodrome. Specifically, The Agreement on Education Processes at the Baikonur Cosmodrome signed August 30, 1994 (KAZ081 in the bottom center of Figure 5.6) and the Agreement to Rent the Baikonur Cosmodrome signed December 10, 1994 (KAZ086 on the bottom left of Figure 5.6). Both treaties address specific aspects of the Baikonur Cosmodrome and its use by Russia.

The bilateral relationship between Kyrgyzstan and Russia provides one treaty that is a lodestone treaty for the CSTO treaty network. Specifically the Treaty of Friendship and Cooperation between Kyrgyzstan and Russia (KYR012 right side of Figure 5.6) lays the groundwork for future cooperation both in security and economic issues. This is an omnibus treaty that sets the initial relations and direction of cooperation between the two states.

Similar to the Treaty of Friendship and Cooperation between Kyrgyzstan and Russia, the Treaty of Friendship and Cooperation between Tajikistan and Russia also is a central treaty in the CSTO treaty network (TAJ022 in the middle of Figure 5.6). It also lays a broad groundwork of cooperation between Russia and Tajikistan.

Finally, the Treaty on International Relations and Friendship between Russia and Uzbekistan (UZB005 at the top of Figure 5.6) is the final bilateral treaty which is central to the CSTO treaty network. It also helps lay the groundwork for both security and economic cooperation between Russia and Uzbekistan.

It should be noted that all of the Friendship and Cooperation treaties between Russia and each of the CSTO member states are fairly similar. They recognize the sovereignty of each of the states, discuss the adherence to the rule of law and order, and begin to identify broad areas of cooperation in security and economic issues that would benefit both states. They are often very vague as they serve to guide the relationship between the two states, build trust, and facilitate future cooperation. It is not by accident that so many bilateral Friendship and Cooperation treaties are so central to the CSTO treaty network. Russia has actively pursued economic and security cooperation with each of the CSTO member states, and has actively created a regional order that includes the lodestone Friendship and Cooperation Treaties as the basic building blocks for future cooperation in more specific areas.

Ultimately, Russia has actively pursued cooperation from each of the CSTO member states. While there is still mistrust among the member states, nevertheless Russia possessed a cooperative bilateral relationship with each of the member states (see Table 5.4). As Table 5.4 shows, contrary to several of the GUAM member states, all of the CSTO member states had cooperative bilateral relationships with Russia between 1991 and 2005.

Table 5.4. Cooperative Relationships between Russia
and the CSTO Member States

Bilateral Relationship	Cooperative Relationship
Russia-Kazakhstan	2.07
Russia-Armenia	1.84
Russia-Belarus	1.80
Russia-Kyrgyzstan	1.72
Russia-Uzbekistan	1.47
Russia-Tajikistan	1.31

Russia actively built its relationships with each of these states to create its regional order. It nested its relationship with the CSTO member states within three distinct levels (see Table 5.5). As Table 5.5 shows, it nested the relationship with the CSTO member states within the global order by creating a system based on the Western legal system. Therefore the regional order is nested within the global order. Second, Russia nested its relationship with the CSTO member states within the regional order by tying in the CSTO to regional treaties. Finally, Russia nested the relationship further by tying bilateral treaties between Russia and each of the member states to the CSTO relationship. This created a strong relationship for cooperation. I now turn to a discussion of the Eurasian Economic Community, which Russia used to build a similar regional order.

Table 5.5.   **Three Levels of Nesting Within CSTO Regional Order**

Lodestone Global Order Treaties	Lodestone Regional Order Treaties	Lodestone Bilateral Treaties
Helsinki Act	Customs Union	ARM069
Paris Charter	Economic Union	ARM136
UN Charter	Collective Security Treaty	BEL125
Vienna Convention	CIS Charter	BEL127
International Declaration of Human Rights		BEL167
		KAZ17
Treaty of Non-Proliferation of Nuclear Weapons		KAZ061
		KAZ081
		KAZ086
		KYR012
		TAJ022
		UZB005

EURASIAN ECONOMIC COMMUNITY (EURAZEC)

The member states of EurAzEC and CSTO are very similar. Therefore, we would expect to see a very similar treaty network for EurAzEC as we did for CSTO (see Figure 5.7). Upon first glance, Figure 5.7 shows a very similar network, except it is denser than that of CSTO, which indicates an even higher level of cooperation among the member states than the member states of CSTO. The treaty network seems much more interconnected and dense than that of the CSTO and certainly denser than the treaty network of GUAM member states.

A closer examination of the EurAzEC treaty network showing only the more central treaties shows a similar nesting strategy to that used in the CSTO treaty network (see Figure 5.8). Much like in the CSTO treaty network, the EurAzEC treaty network is grounded in Western legal framework. The most central Western treaties are the Helsinki Act (top middle of Figure 5.8), the UN Charter (bottom left of Figure 5.8), the International Declaration of Human Rights (top of Figure 5.8), the Vienna Convention (bottom right of Figure 5.8), and the Treaty of Non-Proliferation of Nuclear Weapons (top left of Figure 5.8).

Similar to the CSTO treaty network, the EurAzEC also is nested within broader regional treaties. This has the effect of tying EurAzEC to the regional order. Specifically, the CIS Charter (bottom of Figure 5.8), Customs Union Treaty (bottom of Figure 5.8), the Economic Union Treaty (upper right of Figure 5.8), and the Treaty on Collective Security (right side of Figure 5.8) are central to the EurAzEC treaty network as well as the CSTO treaty network.

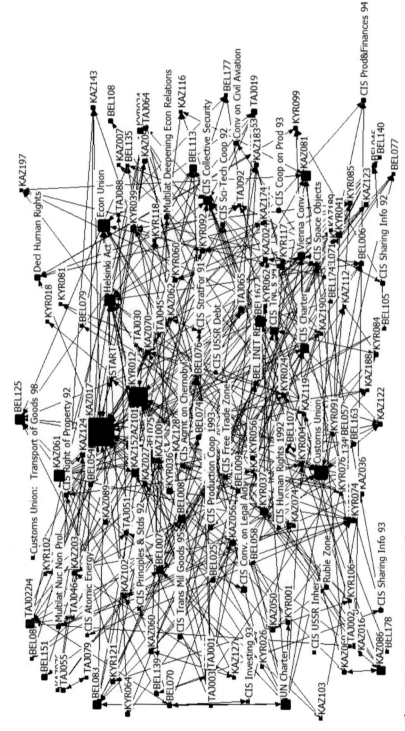

Figure 5.7. EurAzEC Treaty Network

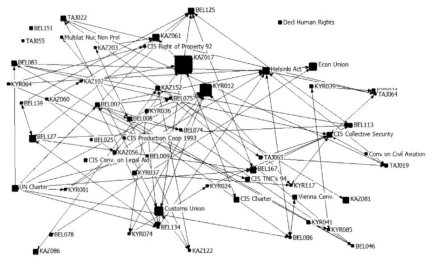

Figure 5.8.   Central Treaties in EurAzEC Treaty Network

In addition to the regional treaties that are central to both the CSTO treaty network and the EurAzEC treaty network, several other regional treaties are central only to the EurAzEC treaty network. First, the CIS Agreement on Trans-National Corporations (TNC) from 1994 (bottom center of table 5.8) paves the way for CIS member states to have corporations easily conduct business in other CIS member states. This treaty was instrumental for companies such as Gazprom, the Russian natural gas company, to work with the governments of the other CIS member states as well as other companies in the region to gain access to natural resources and pipelines.

Another regional treaty that is central to the EurAzEC treaty network is the CIS Convention on Legal Assistance and Legal Relations in Civil, Family, and Criminal Matters (CIS Convention of Legal Aid left side of figure 5.8). This treaty was very important to the EurAzEC treaty network because it established a regional jurisdiction for the legal systems of each of the member states. It coordinated cooperation among the various member states' courts, and ensured that citizens of the member states would have legal representation in the other states. Further, it allowed cooperation among the various law enforcement agencies of the member states.

Another regional treaty that is central to the EurAzEC treaty network is the Agreement on the General Condition for Support of the Development of Production, Cooperation of Enterprises and Sectors of Commonwealth of Independent States Participating States (CIS Production Coop center of figure 5.8). This agreement was extremely important in trying to develop economic cooperation in various sectors and industries. The idea was to facilitate cooperation and create economic ties that would benefit all of the member states.

One of the central questions regarding the breakup of the Soviet Union was how to handle property. States had to settle property rights for each of the FSU states, and as privatization was occurring in the early 1990s, it became important to resolve which property rights would not only be afforded to the states, but also which rights could be bestowed upon individuals and institutions. Thus, it is not surprising that the CIS Agreement on the Recognition and Regulation of Property Rights (CIS Right of Property top of Figure 5.8) is one of the central regional treaties to the EurAzEC treaty network.

Like the CSTO treaty network, the EurAzEC treaty network has several bilateral treaties that are central. Specifically, many of the same bilateral treaties are some of the most central treaties to both treaty networks. However, there are more bilateral treaties that are central to the EurAzEC treaty network than to the CSTO treaty network. For example, the Treaty between Tajikistan and Russia on a Russian Military Base on the Territory of Tajikistan (TAJ065 middle of Figure 5.8) provided the authority for Russia to station military forces and rent a military base for those forces.

TAJ065 is not the only bilateral security treaty which is central to the treaty network. The Agreement between the Russian Federation and Kazakhstan on the Use of Air Force Bombing Range Number 929 on the Territory of Kazakhstan (KAZ102 top left of Figure 5.8) allowed Russian military planes to train and bomb targets within Kazakhstan.

It should be noted that not only bilateral security treaties served as the central bilateral lodestone treaties in the EurAzEC treaty network. For example, the Agreement on Economic Cooperation between Russia and Kazakhstan for the period of 1998–2007 (KAZ152 middle of Figure 5.8) created a blueprint for economic cooperation between Russia and Kazakhstan that also served as a model for cooperation among the other EurAzEC member states.

Ultimately, much like in the CSTO treaty network, Russia actively pursued a treaty network that combined both economic and security treaties into a cohesive treaty network that allowed cooperation among the member states. The treaty network began building the resource of trust among the member states to allow further cooperation and integration of the member states' economies.

It is important to note that Russia actively nested the EurAzEC treaty network within the global order (see Table 5.6). Further, regional treaties and bilateral treaties served as lodestone treaties which further solidified the regional order that Russia wanted to create. All of the treaties created a synergy that was designed to facilitate cooperation, broaden security, and create

Table 5.6.   Three Levels of Nesting Within EurAzEC Regional Order

Lodestone Global Order Treaties	Lodestone Regional Order Treaties	Lodestone Bilateral Treaties
Helsinki Act	Customs Union	ARM069
Paris Charter	Economic Union	ARM136
UN Charter	Collective Security Treaty	BEL125
Vienna Convention	CIS Charter	BEL127
International Declaration	CIS TNC Agreement	BEL167
of Human Rights	CIS Convention on Legal Aid	KAZ17
Treaty of Non-Proliferation	CIS Production Coop	KAZ061
of Nuclear Weapons	CIS Right of Property	KAZ081
		KAZ086
		KYR012
		TAJ022
		UZB005
		TAJ065
		KAZ102
		KAZ152

predictability among the EurAzEC member states. I now turn to a discussion of the Eurasian Union and its treaty network in the regional order.

EURASIAN UNION

An examination of the treaty network of the Eurasian Union shows a network that is denser than the others examined so far in this chapter (see Figure 5.9). In fact, it is so dense that it is very hard to analyze the architecture of the treaty network. However, what Figure 5.9 illustrates is how interconnected the treaties are in the treaty network. It should be noted that Armenia, Kyrgyzstan, Tajikistan, and Uzbekistan are not currently members of the proposed Eurasian Union. Therefore, while the treaty network of the Eurasian Union might look similar to that of EurAzEC, it is nonetheless quite different.

To better analyze the treaty network, it is paramount to examine a diagram of the treaty network which can actually illustrate the most central treaties in the relationship (see Figure 5.10). Figure 5.10 shows a similar pattern to the previous treaty networks examined in this chapter. Basically, the treaty network is nested within the Western legal framework. In this case, the treaty network is nested within the Treaty of Non-Proliferation of Nuclear Weapons (bottom left of Figure 5.10), the Helsinki Act (bottom left of Figure 5.10), the Vienna Convention (middle of Figure 5.10), and the UN Charter (bottom of Figure 5.10). It should be noted that two important Western legal treaties

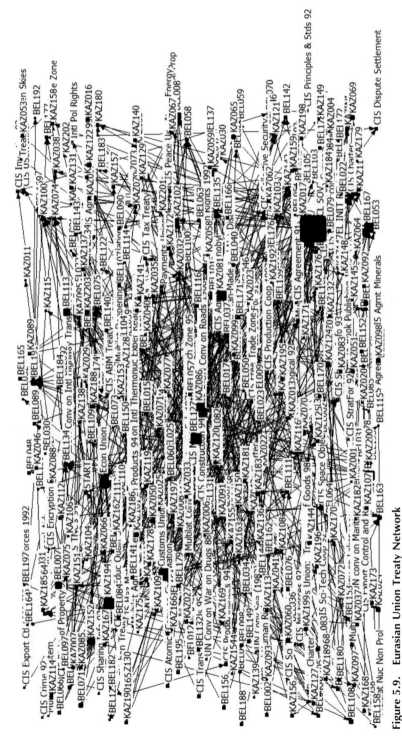

Figure 5.9. Eurasian Union Treaty Network

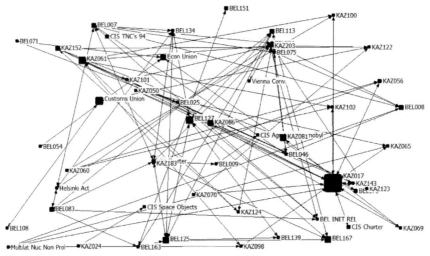

Figure 5.10.   Most Central Treaties in Eurasian Union Treaty Network

are not central to this treaty network. Specifically, the Paris Charter and the International Declaration of Human Rights are not central to this treaty network, whereas they were in the EurAzEC treaty network. While this pattern is very similar to how it has been in the previous treaty networks that have been examined previously in this chapter, what is surprising is the fact that they are less central to the Eurasian Union Treaty Network than they were to the treaty networks analyzed previously. I have created the nodes in all of the figures in this chapter to be set to size dependent upon their degree centrality to the treaty network. In comparing the previous networks to Figure 5.10, it is evident that the Western legal framework treaties are less central to the Eurasian treaty network than they were to the previously discussed treaty networks.

Regional treaties also are central to the Eurasian Union treaty network. Much like the previous treaty networks examined in this chapter, the Customs Union, Economic Union, CIS TNC Treaty, and CIS Charter are central to the treaty network. In contrast to the previous treaty networks, the Customs Union treaty is more central to the treaty network than the Economic Union treaty, whereas in the previous treaty networks the Customs Union treaty is less central to the treaty networks than the Economic Union treaty. Interestingly, the Collective Security Treaty, the CIS Convention on Legal Aid, the CIS Production and Cooperation Treaty, and the CIS Right of Property Treaty are not central to this treaty network the way they were to the EurAzEC treaty network. While this might be because the Eurasian Union is still relatively new, it also highlights the fact that the initial member states of the Eurasian

Union have a relatively cooperative relationship amongst themselves, and can focus on using a lot of bilateral treaties to achieve their integration goals.

Another regional treaty that is central to the Eurasian Union treaty network is the CIS Space Objects Treaties, which paves the way for cooperation in rocketry and established the basis for bilateral cooperation between Kazakhstan and Russia on the Baikonur Cosmodrome. Still another regional CIS treaty that facilitated bilateral cooperation was the CIS Agreement on Chernobyl, which specified how to continue to try to resolve the ecological and health disaster which occurred after the nuclear reactor exploded at the Chernobyl nuclear plant in Belarus. The CIS Agreement on Chernobyl facilitated bilateral cooperation between Russia and Belarus.

Perhaps one of the most surprising aspects of the Eurasian Union treaty network is the fact that so many bilateral treaties are central to the treaty network. Besides those bilateral treaties that have been central to those treaty networks discussed previously in this chapter between Kazakhstan and Russia and Belarus and Russia, there are several bilateral treaties that are central only to the Eurasian Union treaty network. For example, the Treaty on Military Cooperation between Belarus and Russia (BEL007 top left of Figure 5.10) and the Agreement between Belarus and Russia on the Temporary Stationing of Russian Strategic Forces on the Territory of Belarus (BEL008 right side of Figure 5.10). Both of these treaties set the precedent for Russian military cooperation with Belarus, and allowed Russian military forces to be stationed in Belarus.

The Friendship and Cooperation Treaty between Belarus and Russia (BEL083 bottom left of Figure 5.10) is also a central bilateral treaty in the Eurasian Union treaty network. This treaty was an omnibus treaty that detailed the different issues areas of cooperation between the two states.

Belarus and Russia also signed the Treaty on the Equality of Business Entities (BEL151 top of Figure 5.10). This treaty allowed businesses that were based in each of the states to operate on an equal basis in the other country. In other words, a company like Gazprom could operate in Belarus and have the same rights and privileges as a company based in Belarus and vice versa.

Russia and Kazakhstan also had several lodestone treaties that were central to the Eurasian Union treaty network. This was especially true for Russia's interests in gaining access to the Baikonur Cosmodrome. Therefore, the Agreement on Renting the Baikonur Cosmodrome between Russia and Kazakhstan (KAZ183 middle of Figure 5.10) was central to the Eurasian Union.

Finally, the Agreement on Economic Cooperation between 1998 and 2007 (KAZ152 upper left of Figure 5.10) laid the foundation for further economic cooperation between Russia and Kazakhstan. Further, the agreement set a precedent for further economic cooperation among the current and future members of the Eurasian Union.

While the Eurasian Union has not fully been established yet, the West is worried about its potential to reintegrate many of the FSU states into a newer version of the Soviet Union. It is early to make such predictions, yet we can ascertain certain aspects of the Eurasian Union which are very important. First, the Eurasian Union has been discussed and prepared for many years. The groundwork has been laid by this treaty network. Its foundation is pretty secure. What remains is to iron out more details in terms of actual integration.

Second, the Eurasian Union is based much less within the Western legal framework than the previous organizations examined in this chapter (see table 5.7). That is not to say that the Eurasian Union is not based within the Western legal framework, merely that it is not as nested within the Western legal framework as the previous treaty networks examined in this chapter.

Ultimately, the Eurasian Union is still an unknown as to whether or not it will become the Russian version of the European Union. However, a firm foundation has already been created. I now turn to an examination of the final multilateral treaty network in the post-Soviet space, specifically that of the Commonwealth of Independent States (CIS). This is the most inclusive of the regional IGOs and was designed to ease the dissolution of the Soviet Union. However, the CIS morphed into a version of regional governance, and it is very important to the establishment of the regional order.

Table 5.7. Three Levels of Nesting Within Eurasian Union Regional Order

Lodestone Global Order Treaties	Lodestone Regional Order Treaties	Lodestone Bilateral Treaties
Helsinki Act	Customs Union	BEL125
UN Charter	Economic Union	BEL127
Vienna Convention	CIS Charter	BEL167
Treaty of Non-Proliferation	CIS TNC Agreement	KAZ17
of Nuclear Weapons	CIS Space Objects Treaty	KAZ061
	CIS Agreement on Chernobyl	KAZ081
		KAZ086
		KAZ102
		KAZ152
		BEL007
		BEL008
		BEL083
		BEL151
		KAZ183
		KAZ152

COMMONWEALTH OF INDEPENDENT STATES (CIS)

The CIS was originally established as a way in which the Soviet Union could quickly be dissolved in a fair and equitable manner. Yet, it also became a regional IGO that could be used for regional governance purposes and a way to facilitate cooperation between FSU states. While some countries were reluctant to join the CIS since they saw it as an IGO that would be used to promote Russian hegemony, nevertheless, many states did join the CIS.

One of the methods that the CIS used to entice reluctant member states was to create flexible treaties, where only those member states that wanted to cooperate on a single treaty could sign, and those member states that did not want to sign an individual treaty were not bound to the provisions of the treaty (Willerton, Goertz, and Slobodchikoff 2012). However, many of the CIS treaties served as lodestone treaties for the many regional organizations in the post-Soviet space as well as for many of the bilateral relationships between Russia and the rest of the FSU states.

Upon first examination of the CIS treaty network, it resembles that of the Eurasian Union in that it is very interconnected and does not easily lend itself to interpretation (see Figure 5.11). It is instead necessary to examine the treaty network that has only the most central treaties shown for ease of interpretation (see Figure 5.12).

In Figure 5.12, I have shown only those treaties which have a degree centrality of 20 or higher.[1] This allows an easier interpretation and visual aid in understanding Russia's approach to creating regional governance through the CIS and more specifically the creation of its regional order. For this analysis, I will first show the most central treaties beginning with a degree centrality score of 20 or higher, and then continue to show lower degree centrality to illustrate how the CIS treaty network was built.

Figure 5.12 really shows the importance of the Western legal basis for establishing the CIS. In fact, the Helsinki Act has the highest degree centrality of 62 (middle of Figure 5.12). In addition to the Helsinki Act, the Vienna Convention (middle of Figure 5.12) and Paris Charter (right side of Figure 5.12) are very central to the CIS treaty network.

The fact that the Helsinki Act has the highest degree centrality of all of the treaties in the treaty network shows the deliberate process with which Russia and the FSU constructed the FSU to be based within the Western legal basis. Yet, since the Soviet Union was a fundamental actor in creating the Helsinki Act, the Helsinki Act is the perfect treaty to bridge an organization that established itself on a Western legal basis with a deliberate Russian character.

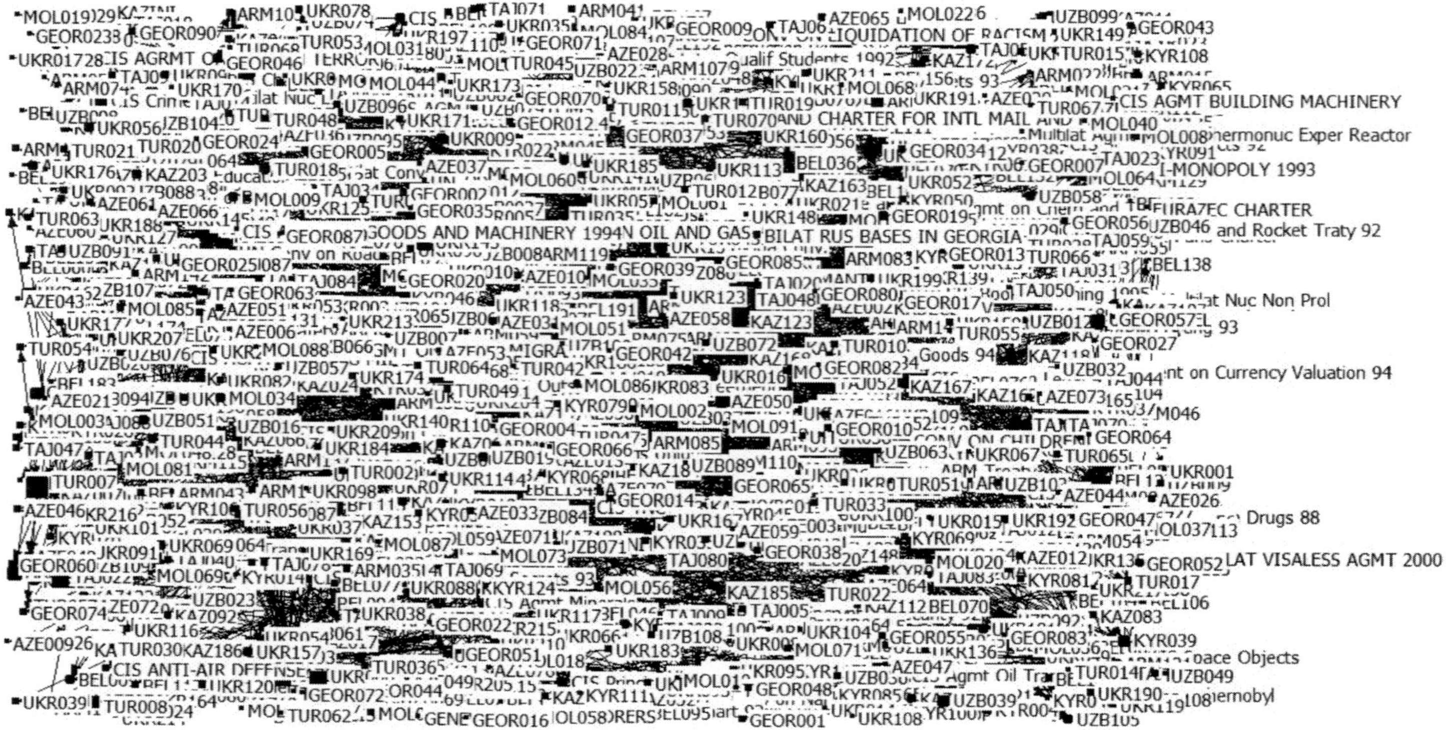

Figure 5.11. CIS Treaty Network (1991–2005)

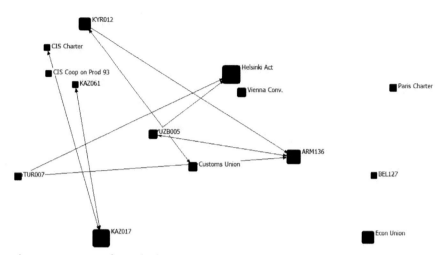

Figure 5.12. Central Treaties in CIS Treaty Network with Degree Centrality 20 or higher

Of those treaties that are most central to the CIS treaty network, several are CIS regional treaties. Specifically, treaties like the CIS Charter (upper left of Figure 5.12), the Customs Union Treaty (center of Figure 5.12), the Economic Union Treaty (bottom right of Figure 5.12), and the CIS Treaty on Cooperation in Production (upper left of Figure 5.12) are the most central regional treaties. Many of these regional treaties are also the most central treaties in the EurAzEC treaty network as well.

There are several bilateral treaties that are most central to the CIS as well. Of these bilateral treaties, the friendship and cooperation treaties are extremely important since they set the direction for bilateral cooperation between Russia and each of the member states. For example, KAZ017, is the Friendship and Cooperation Treaty between Kazakhstan and Russia (bottom left of Figure 5.12), the Agreement on Friendship and Cooperation between Kyrgyzstan and Russia (KYR012 top left of Figure 5.12), UZB005, the Initial Relations and Friendship and Cooperation Treaty between Russia and Uzbekistan. Each of these treaties laid the groundwork for further cooperation between each of the FSU states and Russia.

KAZ061, on the other hand, is the Military Cooperation Treaty between Kazakhstan and Russia (top left of Figure 5.12). This treaty laid the foundation for military cooperation between the two states, especially laying the groundwork for future cooperation in rocketry and space.

The Agreement between Armenia and Russia on State Secrets (Arm136 middle of Figure 5.12) is an important central bilateral treaty because it provides a blueprint for dealing with state secrets and international intelligence cooperation. This became ever more important as technology advanced over the time period of this analysis and the internet became widely used as a medium for exchanging state secrets and intelligence.

TUR007 (left side of Figure 5.12) specifically addressed the issue of the debt of the Soviet Union. Later, this treaty would become the basis for the CIS agreements on the USSR's debt and also the CIS Inheritance Treaty.

Finally, BEL127 (right side of Figure 5.12) addressed the bilateral union between Belarus and Russia. This treaty was extremely important as it became the foundation for the Eurasian Union. The treaty outlined future bilateral cooperation, but really stressed an integrative process, which became the blueprint for how to develop the Eurasian Union.

Each of the treaties discussed form the most central of the treaties in the CIS treaty network. By examining the treaty network with a degree centrality of 10 or higher, we can begin to discern how the CIS treaty network was built and how it became part of the regional order (see Figure 5.13).

Specifically, more treaties that tied the CIS to a more Western legal system became central between a degree centrality of 10 and higher. For example, the International Declaration of Human Rights (top of Figure 5.13), the Convention on International Political Rights (bottom right of Figure 5.13), the Treaty of Non-Proliferation of Nuclear Weapons (right side of Figure 5.13), and the UN Charter (bottom of Figure 5.13) all are central to the CIS treaty network if the degree centrality is examined at 10 or higher. These treaties further tie the CIS to a Western legal system, which has two main goals. First, by tying the CIS to the Western legal system, CIS member states would not fear Russian hegemony as much, which would facilitate cooperation among the member states. Second, nesting the CIS within the global order ensured

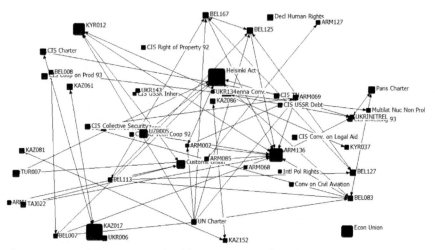

Figure 5.13.   CIS Treaty Network with Degree Centrality of 10 or Higher

that the United States and other great powers would not question Russia's intent in creating a regional order by using its hegemonic power.

More regional treaties are central to the CIS treaty network with a degree centrality of 10 or higher. For example, the CIS USSR Inheritance Treaty (middle of Figure 5.13) and the CIS USSR Debt Treaty (middle of Figure 5.13) are very central to the CIS treaty network. This is mostly due to the fact that these two treaties were instrumental in dissolving the Soviet Union and determining that Russia would become the successor state to the Soviet Union while also splitting many of the former assets of the Soviet Union.

In addition, there is the CIS Collective Security Treaty (left side of Figure 5.13). Not only is this the foundational document of the CSTO, but it also sets the parameters of regional security cooperation among the FSU states. It should be noted that the Collective Security Treaty is central to almost all of the regional IGOs in the post-Soviet space.

Finally, the CIS Right of Property Treaty (top of Figure 5.13) is a central regional treaty in the CIS treaty network. This treaty is an extremely important transitional treaty in the CIS expansion from an organization which was merely responsible for handling the dissolution of the Soviet Union to becoming an organization responsible for setting the agenda for regional governance. While treaties such as the USSR Debt Treaty and the CIS USSR Inheritance Treaty were responsible for the division of the USSR's assets, the CIS Right of Property Treaty began to build up a new regional order that had to resolve such fundamental issues as who would have fundamental property rights in the post-Soviet space.

In addition to regional treaties being central to the CIS treaty network, several bilateral treaties should also be analyzed when the degree centrality is examined at a level of 10 or higher as opposed to 20 or higher. Specifically, many of these bilateral treaties are related to those bilateral treaties which have a degree centrality measure of 20 or higher. For example, while there were three Friendship and Cooperation Treaties which were central at a level of 20 or higher, TAJ022 (bottom left of Figure 5.13) , the Treaty of Friendship and Cooperation between Tajikistan and Russia, and BEL083 (bottom right of Figure 5.13), the Treaty of Friendship and Cooperation between Belarus and Russia, are also central to the CIS treaty network when the degree centrality is examined at a level of 10 or higher.

KAZ152 (bottom of Figure 5.13) is a treaty that addresses economic cooperation between Kazakhstan and Russia from 1998 to 2007. This treaty established built upon previous treaties of economic cooperation between Kazakhstan and Russia to really create a reliable cooperative economic relationship. Moreover, this treaty served as a blueprint for many of the other bilateral economic cooperation treaties between the other FSU states and Russia.

The Bilateral Union between Russia and Belarus served as an important predecessor to the Eurasian Union. It was also important to show other states how regional integration could benefit the other FSU states. Therefore, it should not be surprising that more treaties addressing the Bilateral Union are central to the CIS treaty network when examining degree centrality of 10 or higher. In addition to BEL127, which was central even when examining the treaty network with a degree centrality of 20 or higher, BEL167 and BEL 125 (top of Figure 5.13) also further deal with integration and cooperation with the Bilateral Union.

Like KAZ061, which was discussed previously since it has a degree centrality higher than 20, KYR037 (right of Figure 5.13) also addresses military cooperation. This treaty has a degree centrality score higher than 10.

The central bilateral treaties in the CIS treaty network provide the basis for cooperation among all of the CIS member states. It is no accident that so many of the treaties are omnibus Friendship and Cooperation treaties, which provide the broad parameters of both bilateral and multilateral cooperation.

If I were to further lower the degree centrality score, more treaties would become central to the CIS treaty network. However, the importance to this discussion is the fact that all of these treaties all build upon one another to create the treaty network. The treaties belong to three basic categories: Western legal treaties, regional multilateral treaties, and bilateral treaties. However, these treaties are all interrelated and build off of each other to create the treaty network (see Table 5.8).

Table 5.8. CIS Treaty Network Central Treaties (1991–2005)

Degree Centrality	Lodestone Global Order Treaties	Lodestone Regional Order Treaties	Lodestone Bilateral Treaties
>20	Helsinki Act Vienna Convention Paris Charter	CIS Charter Customs Union Economic Union CIS Coop in Production	KAZ017 KYR012 UZB005 KAZ061 ARM136 TUR007 BEL127
>10	Decl. of Human Rights Intl Political Rights Non-Proliferation of Nuclear Weapons	CIS USSR Inheritance CIS USSR Debt Collective Security Treaty CIS Right of Property	TAJ022 BEL083 KAZ152 BEL167 BEL125 KYR037

What is apparent in the CIS treaty network is the deliberate building of a relationship to create an effective regional institution which can create a predictable region where cooperation is beneficial to all of the member states. This deliberate creation of the organization grounded in Western legal structures and liberal ideology. It made clear to member states precisely the type of organization that the CIS was striving to be. However, the deliberate building of an institutional structure is not unique to the CIS.

Each regional organization's institutional structure examined in this chapter was constructed in exactly the same fashion. All of the organizations were grounded within the Western legal framework, and combined regional multilateral treaties and bilateral treaties to create cooperative treaty networks.

These treaty networks effectively illustrate several important facts about regional governance. First of all, looking at the institutional design features is not sufficient to determine the effectiveness of a regional organization. For example, scholars have determined the CIS a failure at regional governance due to the fact that it was established using flexible design features and could not effectively constrain member states' behaviors. Yet the CIS has been effective at creating regional governance and combining a multilateral and bilateral approach to regional governance.

Having examined each of these organizations separately, it has been possible to see how each of the organizations fits the same pattern. Each of the organizations is nested within the Western legal framework and deliberately constructed in exactly the same fashion. In fact, by examining all of the organizations together, we can see the same treaties used as the central lodestone treaties throughout all of the regional organizations (see Table 5.9).

Table 5.9 illustrates the fact that all of the regional organizations have certain central treaties which are central to all of the regional organizations. If Russia deliberately created each regional organization through careful treaty negotiation and institutional design, then the fact that all of these treaties are central across all of the regional organizations indicates that these are the most important treaties of regional governance. However, it

Table 5.9.   Central Treaties in all of the Treaty Networks (1991–2005)

Lodestone Global Order Treaties	Lodestone Regional Order Treaties	Lodestone Bilateral Treaties
Helsinki Act	Customs Union	N/A
Vienna Convention	Economic Union	
International Declaration of Human Rights	CIS Charter	
Treaty of Non-Proliferation of Nuclear Weapons		

should be noted that Table 5.9 includes data from GUAM, which was a regional organization explicitly established to limit Russia's regional influence. That is why there are no bilateral lodestone treaties in Table 5.9. The member states of GUAM have not fully accepted Russia's regional order. I will first analyze the treaties in Table 5.9, which includes GUAM member states, and then will examine the treaties that are common across all of the regional IGOs and then examine those treaties that are common across all of the regional IGOs except GUAM.

It should be noted that by far the majority of the central treaties that are central to all of the regional IGO treaty networks are those that are from the Western legal framework. Of these, the Helsinki Act is the most important. The Helsinki Act not only places the regional governance system developed by Russia into the Western legal framework, but it also places Russian regional governance into a decidedly European context. Further, the Helsinki Act brought together the Soviet Union, the United States, and much of Europe. It was a real turning point in relations between the West and the Soviet Union, where the two sides began a thawing in the Cold War. By tying regional institutions to the Helsinki Act, Russia is not only indicating that its regional order is a cooperative one with the West that emphasizes state sovereignty and the inviolability of state borders.

Interestingly, not all of the treaties that tie the treaty networks to the Western legal framework are shared across all of the treaty networks. Specifically, the Eurasian Union has less of the Western legal treaties as central treaties than all of the other treaty networks. The Paris Charter and the International Declaration of Human Rights are not as central to the Eurasian Union as the other shared Western legal treaties. One of the reasons for this is that right now there are few members of the Eurasian Union. As more members join, Russia and the other member states will need to tie the Eurasian Union more to the Western legal framework. Another reason for this is that the current member states have a very effective cooperative relationship both bilaterally and multilaterally. The Eurasian Union therefore does not need to be as closely tied to the Western legal framework as the other regional IGOs examined in this chapter.

One of the side effects of not tying the Eurasian Union as closely to the Western legal framework is the fact that the Eurasian Union begins to look like a purely Russian construct that could be threatening to the West. Its goals of resembling the European Union in terms of integration yet not being closely tied to the Western legal framework has led to many Western political observers declaring that the true intent of the Eurasian Union is to reestablish the Soviet Union. It remains to be seen how effective the Eurasian Union will be in integrating some of the former Soviet states as well as how closely tied it will become to the Western legal framework.

While the Eurasian Union treaty network is not as closely tied to the Western legal framework, it is very closely tied to the regional multilateral and bilateral lodestone treaties. However, the GUAM treaty network is not closely tied to either the regional multilateral or the bilateral lodestone treaties. When considering only those central treaties that are central to all of the regional IGO treaty network, including the GUAM treaty network, several important regional treaties are central. First of all, the Customs Union Treaty and the Economic Union Treaty are two important central treaties. They set the base of economic cooperation for all of the FSU states. The Customs Union Treaty works to establish a free trade zone while getting rid of barriers to trade. The Customs Union Treaty is the precedent for the Eurasian Union. On the other hand, the Economic Union Treaty worked to increase trade between the states and to increase economic cooperation.

Additionally, the CIS TNC Agreement is central to all of the treaty networks of the regional IGOs . This agreement dealt with corporations that operate in other FSU states such as Gazprom, the Russian natural gas company. This agreement was extremely important to allow these companies to operate in the FSU states and to be able to compete with other large transnational corporations especially in the energy sector.

Finally, the CIS Charter is central to all of the regional IGO treaty networks. This should not be surprising, since the CIS was the first regional IGO created to manage the dissolution of the Soviet Union. The CIS Charter lay the fundamental aspects of regional cooperation among all of the FSU states. It was the fundamental multilateral treaty of cooperation for the FSU.

Having included the GUAM treaty network in this analysis, no bilateral treaties are central to all of the treaty networks examined in this chapter. However, this is not surprising. GUAM member states cautiously engaged Russia, and really focused on the Western legal framework for cooperating with Russia. Thus, while they accepted Russia's role as the regional hegemon, they really tried to limit Russia's influence by ensuring that their agreements would be closely tied with Western Europe and the United States. However, it is possible to examine the central treaties for all of the IGOs not including the GUAM treaty network (see Table 5.10).

Interestingly, the only bilateral treaties that are central to all of the regional IGO treaty networks (not including the GUAM treaty network) were between Belarus and Russia and Kazakhstan and Russia. This is not surprising since according to the ranking of cooperative bilateral relationships in the post-Soviet space by Slobodchikoff (2013), the bilateral relationships between

Table 5.10. Central Treaties of all Regional IGO Treaty Networks (Not including GUAM Treaty Network)

Lodestone Global Order Treaties	Lodestone Regional Order Treaties	Lodestone Bilateral Treaties
Helsinki Act	Customs Union	BEL125
Vienna Convention	Economic Union	BEL127
International Declaration of Human Rights	CIS Charter	BEL167
	Collective Security Treaty	KAZ017
Treaty of Non-Proliferation of Nuclear Weapons		KAZ061

Russia and Kazakhstan and Russia and Belarus are the top three most cooperative in the post-Soviet space (see Table 5.11).

In this chapter, I began by examining how bilateral and multilateral approaches to international relations are not mutually exclusive categories. Bilateral and multilateral treaties build off each other to create an institution. This institution is responsible for regional governance.

In the post-Soviet space, there are several multilateral institutions responsible for regional governance in the post-Soviet space. In this chapter, I examined each of these multilateral institutions and carefully examined their most central lodestone treaties, which were those treaties that were the most important to those organizations. These treaties are the architectural basis for each organization, meaning that the organization resembles its lodestone treaties. Since the organization is built out of these lodestone treaties, these treaties indicate not only the emphasis of each organization, but also help to create predictable behavior among their member states according to the issue areas addressed by the lodestone treaties.

Table 5.11. Level of Cooperative Bilateral Relationships in the FSU

Bilateral Relationship	Cooperative Relationship
Russia-Kazakhstan	2.07
Russia-Armenia	1.84
Russia-Belarus	1.80
Russia-Kyrgyzstan	1.72
Russia-Ukraine	1.53
Russia-Uzbekistan	1.47
Russia-Turkmenistan	1.43
Russia-Tajikistan	1.31
Russia-Georgia	.60
Russia-Azerbaijan	.56
Russia-Moldova	.41

It is important to note that the effectiveness of a regional IGO cannot only be measured by its institutional design, but more for the cooperation that it facilitates. Examining the treaty structure of these organizations allows scholars to better determine how these IGOs facilitate cooperation and in what issue areas. Together, these treaties indicate an effective level of regional governance.

In the case of Russia, Russia used each of these IGO's to pursue its own goals. By examining all of the regional IGOs and their architecture together, it is possible to see the commonality between them and determine a more regional security architecture. In the next chapter I will examine precisely how to determine the regional security architecture, how Russia created this regional security architecture, and why this is extremely important to ongoing geopolitical struggles between the West and Russia.

NOTE

1. The degree centrality in the CIS treaty network ranges from 0, where treaties are not nested within any other treaties, to a degree centrality score of 62 being the most central treaty to the treaty network.

Chapter Six

Building a Regional Order

An individual treaty is the fundamental building block of international relations. It is the basic unit of international law. States enter into treaties with one another, usually trying to achieve mutual benefit. One of the problems of individual treaties is that there is really no enforcement mechanism to enforce the treaty. Realist scholars have been quick to point out that since states can violate treaties, they are not important. Yet scholars have long noted states' propensities for not only signing treaties, but also adhering to treaties even when the individual treaties are not beneficial to one of the states (Downs, Rocke, and Barsoom 1996; Kelley 2007; Koremenos 2005; Leeds 2003).

This seeming contradiction is confusing until one thinks of treaties as being more than a solitary static individual agreement. Treaties are dynamic agreements which build upon other agreements to build a relationship, predictable behavior, and create an order. States are concerned that breaking a single treaty can lead to conflict in addition to the loss of predictable behavior among states. Since trade and a state's economy relies on stable rules, it is in the best interest of states to have a stable relationship with other states to ensure reliable trading partners.

The important question becomes how an individual treaty can lead to building a strong and cooperative relationship which can create a relationship based on predictable behavior. The answer to that question is that not all treaties are created equal. Some treaties are simple agreements which are used to cooperate on a small or even important issue, but are designed merely to cooperate on an individual issue and not build a cooperative relationship and stability. At a very basic level, these treaties are an ad hoc method of cooperation. The reason for this is that individual issues may be resolved, but there is no effort to build a larger cooperative relationship.

153

Examples of such an approach to treaty building can be found in Russia's relationships with many of the GUAM member states. Those states are extremely wary of Russia's regional influence. While those states still needed to cooperate with Russia in certain specific areas, they were extremely wary of building a cooperative relationship with Russia. Thus, while the GUAM member states signed individual treaties with Russia, they did not try to build a cooperative relationship with Russia.

The next question that logically follows is how to determine a cooperative relationship versus one in which treaties are signed in an ad hoc manner. The key to determining this lies within the treaty itself. An individual treaty which specifically mentions another treaty is building upon a previous treaty. The two treaties become tied together, making both treaties stronger. The second treaty is therefore nested within the first treaty.

Nesting treaties within previous treaties is not done by accident. Nesting treaties within previous treaties accomplishes a couple of important tasks for states. First of all, by tying the treaties together, the states are reaffirming their commitment to cooperation in a specific area addressed by both treaties. This is extremely important because it begins to build up trust between states where there might have been a lack of trust to begin with. In the case of the FSU, there is a general lack of trust between the FSU and Russia. The other FSU states are wary of Russia's power, and consider Russia to be a neighborhood bully that might not respect their sovereignty.

The second important achievement of nesting treaties within other treaties is that it strengthens both treaties. If a treaty is violated that is tied to another treaty, the state that violated that treaty has in effect violated both treaties (Slobodchikoff 2013b). This is extremely important because it allows cooperation even when the resource of trust is not present. Specifically since there is a lack of trust of the regional hegemon, tying treaties together to strengthen them effectively serve to constrain the behavior of the hegemon since the cost of violating the nested treaty is significantly higher than merely violating an individual treaty.

By examining treaties in a contextual relationship, we can then begin to see how these treaties combine to form a treaty network. This is the importance of using social network analysis. Social network analysis allows scholars to track the relationships between treaties, determine the treaty networks, and to see which treaties are the most central to any given treaty network.

The central treaties are the foundations of any relationship. They are the lodestone treaties upon which a relationship is built. The lodestone treaties are in turn nested within the treaty network. The relationship is like a Russian nested doll or matryoshka, where each doll fits into another doll. The individual treaty is the smallest doll, which is nested within the lodestone treaty, which is in turn nested within the treaty network.

Each treaty network can have several lodestone treaties nested within the network. Each lodestone treaty can have several treaties nested within it. It should be noted that treaties can be nested within multiple lodestone treaties. Further, a treaty can be nested within another treaty, which in turn is nested within a lodestone treaty. In other words, there is a very complicated relationship among these treaties and the networks that they combine to create.

Ultimately, it is insufficient to examine an individual treaty without examining how that treaty is related to other treaties in the treaty network. To understand a relationship, one has to examine the treaty network and the relationship between individual treaties. Not all treaties are the same. Some treaties are lodestone treaties which may not look important when scholars examine the text of the treaty, yet in the context of the treaty network become central lodestone treaties.

At the most basic level, treaties are the most fundamental means of cooperation between states. The most basic level of interstate cooperation is bilateral, meaning between two states. Treaties are the fundamental instrument used in bilateral cooperation. Therefore, a bilateral relationship can be examined using the same analysis described above. Specifically a bilateral treaty is signed. It can be nested within lodestone treaties, which in turn are nested within the treaty network, in this case the bilateral relationship.

Prior studies have examined bilateral relationships in terms of treaty networks. For example, Slobodchikoff (2013b) examined all of the bilateral relationships between the FSU and Russia. He found that treaty networks were extremely important for the quality of the relationship. Specifically, the denser the treaty network (defined as the number of treaty ties divided by the number of bilateral treaties), the more cooperative the bilateral relationship. More specifically, he found that the denser the bilateral treaty network, the less likely a militarized interstate dispute (MID) would be to occur. In other words, the denser a treaty network, the less likely violent conflict would be to occur between the two states.

There could be several different reasons for this. First of all, a treaty network increases the cost of violating treaties, which is a leading cause of interstate conflict. The treaty network increases the cost of violating treaties to the point that states are not willing to violate the treaties.

The second reason that a dense treaty network prevents violent conflict is that a treaty network is a constraint on the behavior of each state. Since states don't necessarily trust each other at the time that they begin their relationship, as they begin to tie together these treaties into denser treaty networks, they are beginning to build not only a cooperative relationship between the states, but also they are beginning to build trust.

Whatever the ultimate reason, denser treaty networks lead to less violent conflict between states. That is not to say that there are no disagreements or no conflict between the states. Merely that the two states can generally resolve their conflicts in a peaceful manner through cooperation. There is a large caveat to this argument. Specifically, the assumption that this argument is based on is that there is no regime change that takes place, and that the regime cares about the cost of violating treaties. If there is a coup d'état or a sudden regime change, the new regime might not choose to be bound by the agreements of the previous regime, which might mean that they are more willing to violate a treaty network, which in turn could lead to violent conflict between the states.

In Chapter 2 of this book, I examine bilateral relations between each of the FSU states and Russia. Using network analysis provides interesting insight into how bilateral relationships are constructed between Russia and the other FSU states. Moreover, it is possible to examine Russia's bilateral strategy to reassert its regional hegemonic position vis-à-vis the other states in the region. However, to do so, Russia needed cooperation from the other FSU states. Not all of the states in the FSU were as open to cooperating with Russia. For example, two of the states in the Southern Caucasus region were not open to cooperating with Russia (Georgia and Azerbaijan).

In building its regional order and reasserting its regional hegemonic status, Russia did not utilize a single bilateral approach. In other words, its regional order does not consist of merely a bilateral approach to creating this regional order. The bilateral relationships were certainly important to the creation of its regional order, yet not the only strategy that it used.

In Chapter 3, I describe Russia's multilateral approach to regional governance in the former Soviet space. In fact one of the puzzles facing scholars of international relations who study the post-Soviet space is that there are more multilateral organizations in the post-Soviet space than there are in any other region of the world. This fact alone would be logical if Russia was successful at building multilateral institutions. However, according to most scholars of the post-Soviet space, Russia's multilateral institutions are relatively weak and flexible organizations which are not able to provide much regional governance. In fact, many have argued that despite the fact that these organizations exist, Russia really pursues its hegemonic interests through a bilateral strategy instead of a multilateral strategy.

Certainly, the main multilateral organization in the post-Soviet space, the Commonwealth of Independent States (CIS), was designed to ease the dissolution of the Soviet Union. It was not designed as a regional governance organization, but rather to facilitate the effective dissolution of the Soviet empire. While many of the FSU states initially viewed it as an organization with limited usefulness beyond the initial split of the former empire, Russia began to see the possibility of using the organization to increase Russian regional hegemony and its regional leadership role in the FSU.

With the increasing role of Russian hegemonic power, FSU states initially looked to the CIS as a means of constraining Russia's regional power. They believed that they could work together multilaterally to limit Russian influence in the FSU. Some of the FSU states realized that the CIS would facilitate cooperation among the FSU states, while other states wanted to try to further limit Russia's regional influence.

Whether states liked the CIS or saw it as a vehicle for Russia to increase its hegemonic influence, the CIS became the umbrella organization under which all of the other multilateral organizations in the post-Soviet space operated. Those states that were mistrustful of Russian hegemonic power utilized the CIS in a very limited fashion to cooperate on issues that would benefit them while not cooperating with the CIS on issues in which they didn't trust Russia.

Those states that were really mistrustful of Russia's hegemonic status formed their own multilateral institution which was specifically designed to limit Russia's influence. Their stated intent was to try to maintain closer relations with the West, specifically the EU and NATO, to try to contain Russia's influence. Despite GUAM's aims, GUAM has not been very successful as an organization, and is not an effective counter organization to the CIS.

All of the other multilateral organizations in the post-Soviet space grew out of the CIS. In fact, even GUAM grew out of the CIS structure, except it was designed to specifically counter the CIS. It is interesting to note that almost all of the multilateral organizations in the post-Soviet space have a similar institutional design, and are either interventionist or structured organizations according to the classification of IGOs.

The multilateral organizations in the post-Soviet space can be compared to treaties in and of themselves. Specifically, each of the multilateral organizations examined in this book is nested within the CIS. The CIS is the overarching organization among all of the multilateral organizations in the post-Soviet space.

Much like individual treaties are nested within other treaties, so too are multilateral organizations nested within other multilateral organizations. For example, the Eurasian Union is nested within both the Russia-Belarus Bilateral Union as well as the Eurasian Economic Community. Further, the Eurasian Union and the Eurasian Economic Community are nested within the CIS structure.

To make matters even more complicated, multilateral treaties are fundamental aspects of these organizations. Thus, multilateral treaties are nested

Chapter Six

within their respective multilateral organization, which are in turn nested within other multilateral organizations. In the case of the post-Soviet space, multilateral treaties become lodestone treaties within their respective organization, which in turn is nested within an organization such as the CIS.

BILATERAL AND MULTILATERAL STRATEGIES: SEPARATE BUT EQUAL?

When examining treaty networks, it is possible to see how bilateral treaties are nested within other bilateral treaties, which become lodestone treaties within bilateral treaty networks. Similarly, multilateral treaties are nested within other multilateral treaties, which are nested in multilateral organizations, which are nested within a multilateral treaty network (see Figure 6.1). As Figure 6.1 shows, the two theoretical approaches to the bilateral and multilateral treaty networks are separate. Thus, in the post-Soviet space, there would be an individual bilateral treaty network for each bilateral relationship between an FSU state and Russia, and there would be an individual multilateral treaty network for each multilateral organization in the post-Soviet space.

Figure 6.1 is a simplified approach to both bilateral and multilateral treaty networks. Specifically, there can be many different bilateral treaties nested

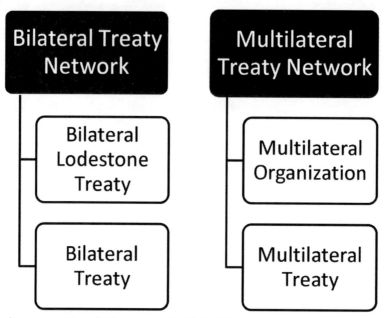

Figure 6.1.   Nested Bilateral and Multilateral Institutions

within many different lodestone treaties. Similarly, there can be many multilateral treaties nested within different multilateral organizations and even different multilateral treaty networks. What Figure 6.1 specifically does not allow is an examination of treaty networks that examines both bilateral and multilateral treaty networks in the same examination. For example, Figure 6.1 says that Russia can have a bilateral strategy in its foreign policy. It can also have a multilateral strategy in its foreign policy, however, Figure 6.1 precludes there being a joint strategy which combines a bilateral and multilateral approach in Russia's foreign policy towards the FSU.

In Chapter 4, I test whether it is really appropriate to study the bilateral and multilateral foreign policy strategies as different approaches. If each was truly a separate approach, bilateral treaties would be merely nested within other bilateral treaties, and there would be no cross nesting where a bilateral treaty would be nested within a multilateral treaty. To test this premise, I examined a sample of bilateral security treaties between Russia and some of the FSU states. I specifically examined the relationships of two European FSU states and two Central Asian FSU states with Russia. Further, I chose one large FSU state in each of these regions to discover whether there was any evidence of cross nesting among the bilateral treaties.

To test this premise I coded all of the bilateral security treaties between these states and Russia looking for evidence of treaty nesting. I specifically looked for evidence of bilateral treaties being nested within multilateral treaties. I found that there was indeed evidence of cross nesting. Specifically, many bilateral treaties were often nested in both bilateral and multilateral treaties. Thus, the approach to Russian foreign policy toward the FSU is much more complex than that portrayed in Figure 6.1.

In Chapter 4, I find that bilateral treaties could be nested in both bilateral and multilateral treaties. This means that bilateral and multilateral treaties are the basic unit of cooperation, which are often nested within other bilateral and multilateral treaties, which are in turn nested within a multilateral treaty network (see Figure 6.2).

As Figure 6.2 shows, it is possible to have both lodestone multilateral and lodestone bilateral treaties nested within a multilateral treaty network. This means that when examining a hegemon's foreign policy strategy, both bilateral and multilateral strategies must be examined. Further, not only should they not be examined as separate strategies, but rather they should be examined in conjunction with one another paying special attention to how the bilateral strategy interacts with the multilateral strategy.

Ultimately, what Figure 6.2 shows is that the hegemonic foreign policy strategy employed is more of a regional strategy. Indeed, Figure 6.2 clearly indicates that there is a coordinated effort by the regional hegemon to tie to-

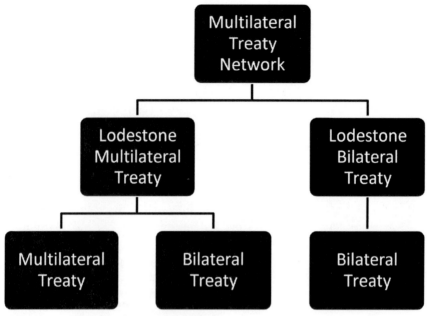

Figure 6.2. More Complex Treaty Networks

gether the various treaties into a cohesive approach of relations between the states in the region.

The fact that the regional hegemon uses a distinct and coordinated foreign policy strategy raises the question as to why the regional hegemon would develop such a strategy. I now turn to a discussion of why the hegemon creates such a strategy toward its regional foreign policy.

BUILDING A REGIONAL ORDER

While it is interesting that a regional hegemon would carefully construct relations with other regional states, this is merely a strategy toward a greater goal. The ultimate goal of such a foreign policy is to create a stable and predictable region. This increases trade opportunities for the regional hegemon as well as the weaker states and ensures the dominance of the regional hegemon. It is important to note that it is in the interest of the regional hegemon to prevent outside influence from spreading into the hegemon's region, as that limits the authority of the hegemon as well as limits the economic and security benefits that a regional hegemon possesses.

In this chapter, I have discussed how the regional hegemon creates a regional centered foreign policy. Figure 6.3 clearly shows how a regional order is built. In this case, figure 6.3 shows each FSU state as being a regional actor. Russia, as the regional hegemon cooperates with them using bilateral treaties to initially create a relationship with the state. The initial bilateral treaties become the lodestone treaties for the bilateral relationships. The hegemon then works to create multilateral organizations which provide a direction and clear set of rules for regional cooperation.

As explained previously, bilateral and multilateral treaties are nested within lodestone bilateral and multilateral treaties. These treaties are really very important, as they are not only the building blocks of the regional treaty networks, but they specify the rules, principles, and institutions illustrated in Figure 6.3. Figure 6.3 also shows how the regional order must follow the rules, principles and, institutions within the global order prescribed by the global hegemon.

The lodestone treaties (both multilateral and bilateral) specify the rules, principles, and the institutions of the regional order. Interestingly, each multilateral organization within the regional order has slightly different lodestone treaties which establish its rules for interaction among its member states. Therefore, while the lodestone treaties establish the rules for interaction, it is not immediately apparent how to define the regional order.

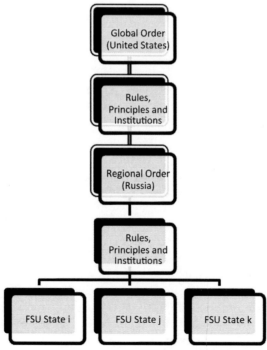

Figure 6.3. Russia's Regional Order Nested in the Global Order

In Chapter 5 I identify lodestone treaties which were consistent to all of the multilateral treaty networks across the post-Soviet space. These lodestone treaties are the most important of all of the lodestone treaties since they are the treaties that make up the regional order. In other words, the regional order is specifically illustrated by those lodestone treaties that are shared across all of the multilateral treaty networks in the post-Soviet space.

These important lodestone treaties serve as a type of mission statement to all of the states within the regional order as to what rules are most important to follow in its interactions with other states in the region, especially with the hegemonic state. The important lodestone treaties also serve as a signal to other states outside of the regional order that help define the specific regional order and its rules and institutions.

Specifically defining the regional order is extremely important. Yet, of even more importance is determining the place of the regional order within the hierarchy of the global order. Much like the important regional bilateral and multilateral lodestone treaties that are constant across all of the regional institutions in the post-Soviet space define the regional order, those lodestone treaties are nested within certain important global treaties.

The important global treaties help to define the global order. Most specifically, in the case of a regional order, the regional order is specifying how it is specifically nested within the global order. Again, in Chapter 5, I examine the global lodestone treaties that were extremely important within the regional order. The global lodestone treaties that are constant across all of the regional multilateral treaty networks are important for several reasons. First, the regional hegemon is specifying that the regional order is part of the global order. The hegemon is not dissatisfied with the global order, and wants the weaker states within the regional order to understand the global context within which the regional order operates.

The second important reason that the global lodestone treaties are so important to the regional order is that they signal to the global hegemon that the regional order is in compliance with the global order. The global hegemon is constantly looking for threats to the global order, and if the regional hegemon specifically signals compliance with the global order, then the global hegemon has no need to be concerned. Instead, the global hegemon can actually work to facilitate trade and cooperation among the states within the regional order that is nested within the global order.

Finally, the global lodestone treaties are important in that they signal to the global order which parts of the global order a specific regional order understand to be the most important. For example, in the case of the post-Soviet space, one of the most important global lodestone treaties was the Helsinki Act. The Helsinki Act was extremely important not only because it addressed security in Europe, but it also stressed the inviolability of a state's borders and its sovereignty. Further, it stressed the fact that all conflicts should be resolved peacefully whenever possible. This is the global order that the United States as the global hegemon has established. By making the Helsinki Act one of the most important global lodestone treaties in the regional order, Russia was stating its understanding of the global order following the collapse of the Soviet Union, and signaled its willingness to not only join the global order, but also help maintain the global order.

Much like the regional hegemon provides the regional order, which is the set of rules of interaction and cooperation for the states that are located within a specific region, the global order also provides rules for interaction and cooperation among all of the regional orders in the world. If a regional order does not signal its intent to cooperate with the global order, then this could be the first sign of dissatisfaction of a regional hegemon with the global order, which is one of the prerequisites to conflict according to power transition theorists.

HEGEMONIC STABILITY THEORY, POWER TRANSITION THEORY, AND REGIONAL ORDER

Hegemonic stability theory predicts that the world is the most stable when there is a clear global hegemon that can create a global order that all of the other states in the global system must follow (Keohane 1980; Volgy and Imwalle 1995; Webb and Krasner 1989). The global hegemon can create a global order that is beneficial for all of the states involved. An example often given by proponents of hegemonic stability theory is the period of Pax Britannia, where the British Empire created a global order which focused on trade. States prospered under British global hegemony. However, not all of the states in the global system were satisfied with the global order established by the British.

Hegemonic stability theory predicts peace and prosperity at the global level providing that all of the great powers in the global system are satisfied with the global order. However, hegemonic stability theory does not predict conflict. Thus, power transition theorists modified hegemonic stability theory to predict conflict between great powers. Specifically, power transition theorists argued that two factors had to be present for there to be interstate conflict between a great power and the global hegemon. First, a great power had to be dissatisfied with the global order. Second, a great power had to increase its power to be able to challenge the power of the global hegemon. When the great power reached power equity with the hegemonic power, as long as the great power was dissatisfied with the world order, power transition theorists would predict violent conflict to occur between the two states (DiCicco and Levy 1999; Kim 2002; Lemke and Werner 1996).

While power transition theory is an incredibly powerful theory, power transition only happens very rarely, so it was very difficult to test on a large scale. However, certain scholars have shown that power transition theory applies not only to the global order, but also at the regional level (Lemke 2002). Specifically, Lemke (2002) argues that regional hierarchies mirror the global hierarchy. Basically, a regional hierarchy will be nested within a global hierarchy, and that the regional hegemon will resemble a global hegemon, merely on the regional level. Lemke (2002) argues that power transition occurs at the regional level as well as on the global level.

Other scholars have adapted power transition theory even further to show that a hegemon's global reach is finite, and the ability to establish a global order decreases over geographical distance (Rhamey Jr, Slobodchikoff, and Volgy 2014, 2013; Rhamey and Slobodchikoff 2010). Specifically, the importance of this research showed that a global hegemon did not have enough power and reach to cover the whole global system. In the geographical areas where there was power parity between the hegemon's power and the power of other great powers, there was an increased likelihood of conflict occurring either between the hegemonic power and the great power or between more minor powers who recognized that the hegemon didn't have the reach in that geographical area to ensure that its global order was adhered to by all of the states.

Following the collapse of the Soviet Union, the United States reasserted itself as the preeminent global hegemon. No other state could even closely challenge the United States. Thus, it should be no surprise that Russia was very eager not only to engage the West when rebuilding its relations with the world, but also creating a regional order that was nested within the Western legal system and the global order.

The West has not fully accepted Russia within the global order. On the one hand, the United States began to engage with Russia especially in programs like destroying nuclear weapons and security issues. However, the United States has continued to be wary of Russia and its latent power. One of the ways in which it tried to distance Russia from the global order was the enlargement of NATO. NATO first enlarged to Eastern Europe and the Baltic States. Then NATO further began discussing enlarging NATO by offering membership to some of the states in the FSU.

Russia genuinely felt threatened by NATO enlargement, and began protesting US actions and requested that NATO not expand beyond Eastern Europe. Russia stated that it did not find Western influence to be acceptable in the FSU, where it had already established its regional order. Russia essentially established the Russian version of the Monroe Doctrine, warning the United States and Western Europe that it was really willing to go to war to prevent the FSU states from joining NATO (Slobodchikoff 2013a).

The United States further antagonized Russia by withdrawing from the Anti-Ballistic Missile Treaty, which had been a fundamental deterrent to nuclear war during the Cold War since neither side would have been able to prevent a nuclear attack. With the number of nuclear weapons that both sides had during the Cold War, a first launch attack of a nuclear weapon would mean that the other side would respond by using nuclear weapons as well. This would lead to mutually assured destruction, which neither side wanted.

However, the United States not only withdrew from the Anti-Ballistic Missile Treaty, but also avidly worked on creating a missile defense system which would be capable of destroying ballistic missiles which would mean that the United States could launch a first strike nuclear attack against another nuclear state and not fear mutually assured destruction.

The official justification for developing the missile defense system was that the United States feared an attack from a rogue state such as North Korea or Iran. However, the United States was working closely with Poland to place necessary military equipment in Eastern Europe. Russia argued that the missile defense system was a relic of the Cold War, and that the United States was in reality trying to develop a missile defense system that would be capable of preventing Russia from bombing the United States, while opening up Russia to the possibility of a first strike nuclear attack from the United States.

In February, 2014, relations between Russia and the United States soured further over events in Ukraine, where Russia argued that the West was beginning to play geopolitical games and try to destabilize Russia's regional order. It is too early to tell whether or not these events and the hostility between Russia and the United States will lead to Russia recreating a regional order that is not so nested in the global order. Russia may yet become a dissatisfied state within the global order and could begin to recreate its regional order in a way that could have far reaching repercussions for the global order. The most logical way of doing this would be to begin to create the Eurasian Union in a way that it would not be nested within the global order. This would be merely a first step in challenging the global order.

Ultimately, Russia is not a global power the way the Soviet Union was during the Cold War. However, with declining US capabilities over geographical space, Russia can certainly challenge the global order at the regional level. 2014 is an important year, in that it decides whether Russia will continue to operate its regional order nested within the global order or whether Russia will decide to begin to challenge the global order by recreating its regional order. Events in Ukraine in 2013 and 2014 have led to a strategic decision by Russia. It must choose whether the current regional order that was established following the collapse of the Soviet should be continued or whether Russia needs to create a new regional order.

Whether Russia decides to continue to follow the current regional order or establish a new regional order, the process is the same. In this book, I have tried to closely examine how a regional hegemon creates a regional order, what tools it uses, and how those tools are carefully utilized to ultimately build a regional order. Every regional hegemon must create a regional order using these same tools.

Traditional studies in international relations examine the power states have and discuss both global and regional order in the abstract. However, this study has attempted to delve into the actual process of creating a regional order as well as defining a regional order. The lodestone treaty approach to identifying the most important building blocks of a regional order have important implications for other regions as well as identifying future regions where there might be dissatisfaction with the global order. This might in turn be able to predict certain regions in which conflict is more likely, as the states in the region or the hegemon are dissatisfied with the global order. It should be noted, however, that according to power transition theory, dissatisfaction is only one part of predicting conflict. A regional hegemon would have to develop the capabilities to challenge the global hegemon.

While it may be extremely difficult for a regional hegemon such as Russia to challenge the global hegemon and the global order, nevertheless, Russia can certainly challenge the global order by developing a new regional order. However, creating a new regional order is not easy. Only through careful and deliberate negotiations with weaker states as well as the use of multilateral organizations, is a state able to create a new regional order. Thus, it is logical that regional orders are only created after very rare events.

The collapse of the Soviet Union provided a rare opportunity to examine the creation of a new regional order. However, it is not a unique event. Much of Africa is still in turmoil, and there is still political unrest in many regions of the world. By examining how Russia was able to create its regional order, scholars can better understand the process as well as the structure of a regional order. Future research will need to expand beyond the FSU to examine regional orders in other regions to see how other hegemons are able to create their regional orders nested within the global order.

References

Acharya, Amitav. 2007. "The Emerging Regional Architecture of World Politics." *World Politics* 59(04): 629–52.

Aggarwal, Vinod K. 1998. *Institutional Designs for a Complex World: Bargaining, Linkages, and Nesting.* Cornell University Press.

Alexandrov, Mikhail. 1999. *Uneasy Alliance: Relations between Russia and Kazakhstan in the Post-Soviet Era, 1992–1997.* Greenwood Publishing Group.

Allison, Roy, S. White, and M. Light. 2005. "Belarus between East and West." *Journal of Communist Studies and Transition Politics* 21(4): 487.

Allison, Roy. 2004. "Regionalism, Regional Structures and Security Management in Central Asia." *International Affairs* 80(3): 463–83.

Ambrosio, Thomas. 2008. "Catching the 'Shanghai Spirit': How the Shanghai Cooperation Organization Promotes Authoritarian Norms in Central Asia." *Europe-Asia Studies* 60(8): 1321–44.

Åslund, Anders, and Andrew Kuchins. 2009. *The Russia Balance Sheet.* Peterson Institute.

Åslund, Anders, and Martha Brill Olcott. 1999. *Russia after Communism.* Carnegie Endowment for International Peace.

Bahgat, Gawdat. 2002. "Pipeline Diplomacy: The Geopolitics of the Caspian Sea Region." *International Studies Perspectives* 3(3): 310–27.

Balmaceda, Margarita Mercedes. 1998. "Gas, Oil and the Linkages between Domestic and Foreign Policies: The Case of Ukraine." *Europe-Asia Studies* 50(2): 257–86.

Barabanov, Mikhail. 2008. "Nagorno-Karabakh: Shift in the Military Balance." *Moscow Defense Brief (Centre for Analysis of Strategies and Technologies)* 12(2): 9–12.

Black Sea Economic Cooperation. 1998. "Charter of the Organization of the Black Sea Economic Cooperation."

Blockmans, Steven. 2008. *The European Union and Crisis Management: Policy and Legal Aspects.* Cambridge University Press.

Boehmer, Charles., Erik. Gartzke, and Timothy. Nordstrom. 2004. "Do Intergovernmental Organizations Promote Peace?" *World Politics* 57(1): 1–38.

Boulding, Kenneth Ewart. 1962. *Conflict and Defense: A General Theory*. Harper.

Bremmer, Ian. 1994. "The Politics of Ethnicity: Russians in the New Ukraine." *Europe-Asia Studies* 46(2): 261–83.

Bueno de Mesquita, Bruce. 1981. *The War Trap*. Yale University Press.

Bull, Hedley. 2002. *The Anarchical Society: A Study of Order in World Politics*. Columbia University Press.

Burant, Stephen R. 1995. "Foreign Policy and National Identity: A Comparison of Ukraine and Belarus." *Europe-Asia Studies* 47(7): 1125–44.

Cameron, F., and J. M Domański. 2005. *Russian Foreign Policy with Special Reference to Its Western Neighbours*. Brussels, Belgium: European Policy Centre.

Capoccia, Giovanni, and R. Daniel Kelemen. 2007. "The Study of Critical Junctures: Theory, Narrative, and Counterfactuals in Historical Institutionalism." *World Politics* 59(03): 341–69.

Carbone, Roberta. 2013. *The Eurasian Economic Union Paper May2013*. Centro Eistein di Studi Internazionali.

Carter, Barry E., Phillip R. Trimble, and Allen S. Weiner. 2007. *International Law*. Aspen Publishers.

Chinn, Jeff, and Steven D. Roper. 1995. "Ethnic Mobilization and Reactive Nationalism: The Case of Moldova." *Nationalities Papers* 23(2): 291.

Chung, Chien. 2006. "China and the Institutionalization of the Shanghai Cooperation Organization." *Problems of Post-Communism* 53(5): 3–14.

Cohen, Ariel. 2006. *The Dragon Looks West: China and the Shanghai Cooperation Organization*. Heritage Foundation.

Dahl Martinsen, Kaare. 2002. "The Russian Takeover of Belarus." *Comparative Strategy* 21(5): 401–16.

DiCicco, Jonathan M., and Jack S. Levy. 1999. "Power Shifts and Problem Shifts: The Evolution of the Power Transition Research Program." *The Journal of Conflict Resolution* 43(6): 675–704.

Downs, George W., David M. Rocke, and Peter N. Barsoom. 1996. "Is the Good News about Compliance Good News about Cooperation?" *International Organization* 50(3): 379–406.

Dwan, Renata, and Oleksandr Pavliuk. 2000. *Building Security in the New States of Eurasia: Subregional Cooperation in the Former Soviet Space*. M.E. Sharpe.

Everett, M. G., and S. P. Borgatti. 1999. "The Centrality of Groups and Classes." *The Journal of Mathematical Sociology* 23(3): 181–201.

Fearon, James D. 1995. "Rationalist Explanations for War." *International Organization* 49(3): 379–414.

Garnett, S., and D. Trenin. 1999. "Russia and Its Nearest Neighbors." In *Russia After Communism*, eds. Anders Åslund and Martha Brill Olcott. Washington D.C.: Carnegie Endowment for International Peace.

Gayoso, Carmen A. 2009. "Russian Hegemonies: Historical Snapshots, Regional Security and Changing Forms of Russia's Role in the Post-Soviet Region." *Communist and Post-Communist Studies* 42(2): 233–52.

Germanovich, Gene. 2008. "The Shanghai Cooperation Organization: A Threat to American Interests in Central Asia?" In *China & Eurasia Forum Quarterly*.

Gilpin, Robert. 1983. *War and Change in World Politics*. Cambridge University Press.

Goldman, Marshall I. 2010. *Petrostate: Putin, Power, and the New Russia*. Oxford University Press US.

Grieco, Joseph M. 1988. "Anarchy and the Limits of Cooperation: A Realist Critique of the Newest Liberal Institutionalism." *International Organization* 42(3): 485–507.

Grieco, Joseph, Robert Powell, and Duncan Snidal. 1993. "The Relative-Gains Problem for International Cooperation." *The American Political Science Review* 87(3): 727–43.

Guang, Pan. 2009. "The SCO's Success in Security Architecture." In *The Architecture of Security in the Asia-Pacific*, ed. Ronald Huisken. ANU E Press.

Guneev, Sergei. 2014. "Eurasian Economic Union Treaty to Be Signed in May— Russian Official." *RIA Novosti*. http://en.ria.ru/russia/20140410/189145317/Eurasian -Economic-Union-Treaty-to-Be-Signed-in-May--Russian.html (April 12, 2014).

Hansen, Flemming Splidsboel. 2013. "Integration in the Post-Soviet Space." *International Area Studies Review* 16(2): 142–59.

Hansen, Holley E., Sara McLaughlin Mitchell, and Stephen C. Nemeth. 2008. "IO Mediation of Interstate Conflicts." *Journal of Conflict Resolution* 52(2): 295 –325.

Hemmer, C, and P. J. Katzenstein. 2002. "Why Is There No NATO in Asia? Collective Identity, Regionalism, and the Origins of Multilateralism." *International Organization* 56: 575–608.

Henley, Jon. 2014. "A Brief Primer on Vladimir Putin's Eurasian Dream." *The Guardian*.

Hewett, Edward. 1988. *Reforming the Soviet Economy: Equality versus Efficiency*. Washington D.C.: Brookings Institution.

Hill, William. 2002. "Making Istanbul a Reality: Moldova, Russia, and Withdrawal from Transdniestria." *Helsinki Monitor* 13: 129.

Huasheng, Zhao. 2004. "Security Building in Central Asia and the Shanghai Cooperation Organization."

Huntington, S. P. 1968. *Political Order in Changing Societies*. New Haven: Yale University Press.

Ikenberry, G. John. 2001. *After Victory*. Princeton University Press.

Ingram, Paul, Jeffrey Robinson, and Marc L. Busch. 2005. "The Intergovernmental Network of World Trade: IGO Connectedness, Governance, and Embeddedness." *American Journal of Sociology* 111(3): 824–58.

Jackson, Nicole J. 2003. *Russian Foreign Policy and the CIS: Theories, Debates and Actions*. Psychology Press.

Jervis, Robert. 1978. "Cooperation Under the Security Dilemma." *World Politics* 30(2): 167–214.

Jones, Seth G. 2007. *The Rise of European Security Cooperation*. Cambridge University Press.

Kalicki, Jan H. 2001. "Caspian Energy at the Crossroads." *Foreign Affairs* 80(5): 120–34.

Kanet, Roger E., Deborah Nutter Miner, and Tamara J. Resler. 1992. *Soviet Foreign Policy in Transition*. Cambridge University Press.

Kaufman, Stuart J. 1996. "Spiraling to Ethnic War: Elites, Masses, and Moscow in Moldova's Civil War." *International Security* 21(2): 108–38.

Kaufman, Stuart J., and Stephen R. Bowers. 1998. "Transnational Dimensions of the Transnistrian Conflict." *Nationalities Papers* 26(1): 129.

Kelley, Judith. 2007. "Who Keeps International Commitments and Why? The International Criminal Court and Bilateral Nonsurrender Agreements." *American Political Science Review* 101(03): 573–89.

Keohane, R. O. 1980. "The Theory of Hegemonic Stability and Changes in International Economic Regimes, 1967–1977." In *Change in the International System*, eds. Ole R. Holsti, Randolph M. Siverson, and Alexander L. George. Westview Press, 131–62.

Keohane, Robert O. 1989. "Multilateralism: An Agenda for Research." *International Journal* 45: 731.

Keohane, Robert O. 2005. *After Hegemony: Cooperation and Discord in the World Political Economy*. Princeton University Press.

Kim, Woosang. 2002. "Power Parity, Alliance, Dissatisfaction, and Wars in East Asia, 1860–1993." *Journal of Conflict Resolution* 46(5): 654 –671.

King, Charles. 1994a. "Eurasia Letter: Moldova with a Russian Face." *Foreign Policy* (97): 106–20.

———. 1994b. "Eurasia Letter: Moldova with a Russian Face." *Foreign Policy* (97): 106–20.

———. 1998. "Ethnicity and Institutional Reform: The Dynamics of 'indigenization' in the Moldovan ASSR - PB - Routledge." *Nationalities Papers* 26(1): 57.

———. 1999. *The Moldovans*. Hoover Press.

Kjaernet, Heidi. 2010. "Azerbaijani-Russian Relations and the Economization of Foreign Policy." In *Caspian Energy Politics: Azerbaijan, Kazakhstan and Turkmenistan*, eds. Indra Overland, Andrea Kendall-Taylor, and Heidi Kjaernet. Routledge.

Klein, Margerete. 2009. *Russia's Military Capabilities: "Great Power" Ambitions and Reality*. German Institute for International and Security Affairs. Technical Report.

Kolossov, Vladimir, and John O'Loughlin. 1998. "Pseudo-States as Harbingers of a New Geopolitics: The Example of the Trans-Dniester Moldovan Republic (TMR)." *Geopolitics* 3(1): 151.

Kolstø, Pål, and Andrei Malgin. 1998. "The Transnistrian Republic: A Case of Politicized Regionalism." *Nationalities Papers* 26(1): 103.

Koremenos, B. 2009. *International Institutions as Solutions to Underlying Games of Cooperation*. Barcelona, Spain: IBEI Working Papers. IBEI Working Papers.

Koremenos, Barbara. 2002. "Can Cooperation Survive Changes in Bargaining Power? The Case of Coffee." *The Journal of Legal Studies* 31(s1): S259–S283.

Koremenos, Barbara. 2005. "Contracting Around International Uncertainty." *American Political Science Review* 99(04): 549–65.

Koremenos, Barbara, Charles Lipson, and Duncan Snidal. 2001. "The Rational Design of International Institutions." *International Organization* 55(04): 761–99.

Korhonen, Keijo. 1973. "Treaty of Friendship, Cooperation and Mutual Assistance between the Soviet Union and Finland: Some Aspects of International Politics." *Cooperation and Conflict* 8(4): 183 –188.

———. 2010. Interviewed by Michael O. Slobodchikoff. Tucson, AZ.

Kramer, Mark. 2008. "Russian Policy Toward the Commonwealth of Independent States: Recent Trends and Future Prospects." *Problems of Post-Communism* 55(6): 3–19.

Kubicek, Paul. 1999. "End of the Line for the Commonwealth of Independent States." *Problems of Post-Communism* 46(2): 15–24.

———. 2009. "The Commonwealth of Independent States: An Example of Failed Regionalism?" *Review of International Studies* 35(Supplement S1): 237–56.

Kydd, Andrew. 2000. "Trust, Reassurance, and Cooperation." *International Organization* 54(02): 325–57.

———. 2001. "Trust Building, Trust Breaking: The Dilemma of NATO Enlargement." *International Organization* 55(04): 801–28.

———. 2005. *Trust and Mistrust in International Relations*. Princeton University Press.

Laruelle, Marline, and Sébastien Peyrouse. 2009. "Shanghai Cooperation Organization." *Journal of Central Asian Studies* 18(1).

Latora, V., and M. Marchiori. 2007. "A Measure of Centrality Based on Network Efficiency." *New Journal of Physics* 9(6): 188.

Lemke, Douglas. 2002. *Regions of War and Peace*. Cambridge University Press.

Lemke, Douglas, and Suzanne Werner. 1996. "Power Parity, Commitment to Change, and War." *International Studies Quarterly* 40(2): 235–60.

Linn, Johannes F., and David Tiomkin. 2006. "The New Impetus towards Economic Integration between Europe and Asia." *Asia Europe Journal* 4(1): 31–41.

Lipson, Charles. 1984. "International Cooperation in Economic and Security Affairs." *World Politics* 37(01): 1–23.

Löwenhardt, John, Ronald J. Hill, and Margot Light. 2001. "A Wider Europe: The View from Minsk and Chisinau." *International Affairs (Royal Institute of International Affairs 1944–)* 77(3): 605–20.

Lynch, Dov. 2002. "Separatist States and Post-Soviet Conflicts." *International Affairs (Royal Institute of International Affairs 1944–)* 78(4): 831–48.

Macfarlane, S. Neil. 2004. "The United States and Regionalism in Central Asia." *International Affairs* 80(3): 447–61.

Mahoney, James, and Kathleen Thelen. 2010. *Explaining Institutional Change: Ambiguity, Agency, and Power*. Cambridge University Press.

Malashenko, Alexey and Dmitry Trenin. 2002. *Vremya Yuga: Rossiya v Chechne, Chechnya v Rossij (Time of the South: Russia in Chechnya, Chechnya in Russia)*. Moscow: Carnegie Center for International Peace.

Marks, Edward. 1996. *The CIS and the Caucasus*. National Defense University, Institute for National Strategic Studies. Report No. ADA394193

Martin, Lisa L., and Beth A. Simmons. 1998. "Theories and Empirical Studies of International Institutions." *International Organization* 52(04): 729–57.

Melikova, Natalya. 2003. "Kozak Ne Stal Vinit' Zapad." *Nezavisimaya Gazeta*.

Miller, Eric A, and Arkady Toritsyn. 2005a. "Bringing the Leader Back In: Internal Threats and Alignment Theory in the Commonwealth of Independent States." *Security Studies* 14(2): 325 – 363.

Miller, Eric A., and Arkady Toritsyn. 2005b. "Bringing the Leader Back In: Internal Threats and Alignment Theory in the Commonwealth of Independent States." *Security Studies* 14(2): 325 – 363.

Morgenthau, Hans Joachim. 1948. *Politics Among Nations*. A. A. Knopf.

Mroz, John Edwin, and Oleksandr Pavliuk. 1996. "Ukraine: Europe's Linchpin." *Foreign Affairs* 75(3): 52–62.

Okawara, Nobuo, and Peter J. Katzenstein. 2001. "Japan and Asian-Pacific Security: Regionalization, Entrenched Bilateralism and Incipient Multilateralism." *Pacific Review* 14(2): 165–94.

Olcott, Martha, Anders Aslund, and Sherman W. Garnett. 1999. *Getting It Wrong: Regional Cooperation and the Commonwealth of Independent States*. Washington DC: Carnegie Endowment for International Peace.

Olcott, Martha Brill. 1991. "Central Asia's Catapult to Independence." *Foreign Affairs* 71: 108.

———. 2009. *Kazakhstan: Unfulfilled Promise?* Carnegie Endowment.

Oldberg, Ingmar. 1997. "Sunset over the Swamp – the Independence and Dependence of Belarus." *European Security* 6(3): 110–30.

Opsahl, Tore, Filip Agneessens, and John Skvoretz. 2010. "Node Centrality in Weighted Networks: Generalizing Degree and Shortest Paths." *Social Networks* 32(3): 245–51.

Ozer, Ercan. 2002. "The Black Sea Economic Cooperation and Regional Security." In *New Trends in Turkish Foreign Affairs: Bridges and Boundaries*, ed. Salomon Ruysdael. iUniverse.

Pardo Sierra, Oscar B. 2011. "Shaping the Neighbourhood? The EU's Impact on Georgia." *Europe-Asia Studies* 63(8): 1377–98.

Ponsard, Lionel. 2006. *Russia, NATO and Cooperative Security: Bridging the Gap*. Routledge.

Rhamey Jr, J. Patrick, Michael O. Slobodchikoff, and Thomas J. Volgy. 2014. "Order and Disorder across Geopolitical Space: The Effect of Declining Dominance on Interstate Conflict." *Journal of International Relations and Development*.

———. 2013. "Order and Disorder across Geopolitical Space The Effect of Declining Dominance on Interstate Conflict." *Presented at the European International Studies Association Conference.* Warsaw, Poland.

Rhamey, J. Patrick, and Michael O. Slobodchikoff. 2010. "MIDS at the Margins." *Presented at Peace Science Association Meeting*, Dallas, TX.

Riasanovsky, Nicholas Valentine. 2000. *A History of Russia*. Oxford University Press.

Rowe, Elana Wilson, and Stina Torjesen, eds. 2008. *The Multilateral Dimension in Russian Foreign Policy*. Routledge.

Ruggie, John. 1993. *Multilateralism Matters : The Theory and Praxis of an Institutional Form*. New York: Columbia University Press.

Ruggie, John Gerard. 1994. "Third Try at World Order? America and Multilateralism after the Cold War." *Political Science Quarterly* 109(4): 553.

Rumer, Eugene B. 1994. "Eurasia Letter: Will Ukraine Return to Russia?" *Foreign Policy* (96): 129–44.

Scheineson, Andrew. 2009. *The Shanghai Cooperation Organization*. Council on Foreign Relations.

Schweller, R. L. 1996. "Neorealism's Status-Quo Bias: What Security Dilemma?" *Security Studies* 5(3): 90–121.

Shadikhodjaev, Sherzod. 2008. *Eurasian Economic Community (EurAsEC): Legal Aspects of Regional Trade Integration*. East Asian Bureau of Economic Research. Trade Working Paper.

Sinclair, Sir Ian McTaggart. 1984. *The Vienna Convention on the Law of Treaties*. Manchester University Press ND.

Slobodchikoff, Michael O. 2013a. "Russia's Monroe Doctrine Just Worked in Ukraine." *Russia Direct*.

———. 2013b. *Strategic Cooperation: Overcoming the Barriers of Global Anarchy*. Lexington Books.

Snidal, Duncan. 1991. "Relative Gains and the Pattern of International Cooperation." *The American Political Science Review* 85(3): 701–26.

Stewart-Ingersoll, Robert, and Derrick Frazier. 2012. *Regional Powers and Security Orders: A Theoretical Framework*. Routledge.

Stribis, Ioannis. 2003. "The Evolving Security Concern in the Black Sea Economic Cooperation." *Southeast European and Black Sea Studies* 3(3): 130–62.

Tarr, David G. 2012. *The Eurasian Customs Union among Russia, Belarus and Kazakhstan: Can It Succeed Where Its Predecessor Failed?* Rochester, NY: Social Science Research Network. SSRN Scholarly Paper.

Tokluoglu, Ceylan. 2011. "The Political Discourse of the Azerbaijani Elite on the Nagorno-Karabakh Conflict (1991–2009)." *Europe-Asia Studies* 63(7): 1223–52.

Tolkacheva, Anna. 2006. "Evropejskij Vybor Moldavii." *Pro et Contra Post Soviet Conflicts* 10(5–6): 53–64.

Torjesen, Stina. 2008. "Russia, the CIS and the EEC: Finally Getting It Right?" In *The Multilateral Dimension in Russian Foreign Policy*, eds. Elana Wilson Rowe and Stina Torjesen. Routledge, 153–62.

Trenin, Dmitri. 2007. "Russia Redefines Itself and Its Relations with the West." *The Washington Quarterly* 30(2): 95–105.

Triska, Jan F., and Robert M. Slusser. 1962. *The Theory, Law, and Policy of Soviet Treaties*. Stanford University Press.

Volgy, Thomas J., Elizabeth Fausett, Keith A. Grant, and Stuart Rodgers. 2008. "Identifying Formal Intergovernmental Organizations." *Journal of Peace Research* 45(6): 837–50.

Volgy, Thomas J., and Lawrence E. Imwalle. 1995. "Hegemonic and Bipolar Perspectives on the New World Order." *American Journal of Political Science* 39(4): 819–34.

De Waal, Thomas de. 2010. *The Caucasus: An Introduction*. Oxford University Press.

Wallander, Celeste A. 2007. "Russian Transimperialism and Its Implications." *The Washington Quarterly* 30(2): 107–22.

Walt, Stephen M. 1985. "Alliance Formation and the Balance of World Power." *International Security* 9(4): 3–43.

———. 2002. "The Enduring Relevance of the Realist Tradition." In *Political Science: The State of the Discipline*, eds. Ira Katznelson and Helen V. Milner. W. W. Norton & Company, 197–230.

Waltz, Kenneth Neal. 1979. *Theory of International Politics*. McGraw-Hill.

Wasserman, Stanley, and Katherine Faust. 1994. *Social Network Analysis: Methods and Applications*. Cambridge University Press.

Webb, Michael C., and Stephen D. Krasner. 1989. "Hegemonic Stability Theory: An Empirical Assessment." *Review of International Studies* 15(2): 183–98.

Weber, Steve. 1991. *Multilateralism in NATO: Shaping the Postwar Balance of Power, 1945–1961*. [Berkeley]: International and Area Studies University of California at Berkeley.

Welt, Cory. 2010. "The Thawing of a Frozen Conflict: The Internal Security Dilemma and the 2004 Prelude to the Russo-Georgian War." *Europe-Asia Studies* 62(1): 63–97.

Willerton, J. P. 1992. *Patronage and Politics in the USSR*. Cambridge University Press.

Willerton, John P, Michael O Slobodchikoff, and Gary Goertz. 2012a. "Treaty Networks, Nesting, and Interstate Cooperation: Russia, the FSU, and the CIS." *International Area Studies Review* 15(1): 59 –82.

Willerton, John P, Gary Goertz, and Michael O. Slobodchikoff. 2012b. "Mistrust and Hegemony: Regional Institutional Design, the CIS, and Russia." *Presented at the Political Economy of International Organizations Annual Conference*. Philadelphia, PA.

Willerton, John P. et al. 2006. "Complex Security Institutions: Nested Bilateralism in the Commonwealth of Independent States." In *Shambaugh/ITRAG Conference. Building Synergies: Institutions and Cooperation in World Politics. University of Iowa*, Iowa City, IA, 12–14.

Wolchik, Sharon L., and Jane Leftwich Curry. 2011. "Democracy, the Market, and the Return to Europe: From Communism to the European Union and NATO." In *Central and East European Politics: From Communism to Democracy*, Rowman & Littlefield, 418.

Yuan, Jing-Dong. 2010. "China's Role in Establishing and Building the Shanghai Cooperation Organization (SCO)." *Journal of Contemporary China* 19(67): 855–69.

Zhalimbetova, Roza, and Gregory Gleason. 2001a. "Bridges and Fences: The Eurasian Economic Community and Policy Harmonization in Eurasia." *Central Asian Monitor*: 18–24.

———. 2001b. "Eurasian Economic Community (EEC) Comes Into Being." *Central Asia Caucasus* Analist.

Zverev, Alexei. 1996. "Ethnic Conflicts in the Caucasus 1988–1994." *Contested borders in the Caucasus*: 13–71.

Index

About the Author

Michael O. Slobodchikoff has published two books on Russian relations with post-Soviet states. His first book is *Strategic Cooperation: Overcoming the Barriers of Global Anarchy* (2013). He has also published peer reviewed articles in the *Journal of International Relations and Development*, the *International Area Studies Review*, the *Journal on Ethnopolitics and Minority Issues in Europe*, and *Studies of Changing Societies*. He is also the editor of the Russian, Eurasian, and Eastern European Book Series through Lexington Books. Dr. Slobodchikoff specializes in relations between Russia and the former Soviet states, international conflict and peace, and comparative politics. He is a regular contributor to Russia Direct, the Russian International Affairs Council, and has often served as an analyst on Russian relations with Ukraine for BBC World News. He has also served as an analyst on Russian relations with the United States for Voice of Russia Radio. Dr. Slobodchikoff has a Ph.D. and M.A. in Political Science from the University of Arizona, an MBA in International Management from Thunderbird, The American Graduate School of International Management, and a Bachelor's Degree from Georgetown University.